Presented To:

_____

From:

_____

Date:

_____

God's Divine Design for

DATING

and

MARRIAGE

God's Divine Design for

DATING
and
MARRIAGE

A Perfect Love for Imperfect People

CHRYSTAL ARMSTRONG

DESTINY IMAGE₀ PUBLISHERS, INC.

P.O. Box 310, Shippensburg, PA 17257-0310

"Promoting Inspired Lives."

This book and all other Destiny Image, Revival Press, MercyPlace, Fresh Bread, Destiny Image Fiction, and Treasure House books are available at Christian bookstores and distributors worldwide.

For a U.S. bookstore nearest you, call 1-800-722-6774.

For more information on foreign distributors, call 717-532-3040.

Reach us on the Internet: www.destinyimage.com.

ISBN 13 TP: 978-0-7684-3915-1

ISBN 13 Ebook: 978-0-7684-8952-1

For Worldwide Distribution, Printed in the U.S.A.

1 2 3 4 5 6 7 / 15 14 13 12

ACKNOWLEDGMENTS

A great debt of gratitude is owed to the many, many people who have provided encouragement, prayer, counsel, and their time to help the vision for this book become a reality. To my parents, William and Jeanetta Robertson, grandmother Ella M. Jenkins, sister Frederica Robertson, and aunts, uncles, and cousins, I could not have been born into a better family. Everything I aspire to be I dedicate to you. Thank you for being there.

To Pastor Daryl Arnold and the Overcoming Believers Church bloodlines and New Life COGIC, for your support and the opportunity to serve, I am eternally grateful for you all.

To my brothers and sisters and second moms, including Lions Den, Damien Jolivette, Christopher Otuonye, Kimberly Shun and Willie Watkins, Kenneth and Denetria Moore, Betty Conley, Alysha Miller and Vesta Henry, Emory Quince, Leah Walker, Ty Fisher, Quinton Rayford, Aneisha Davis, Eric and Theresa Cash, Christopher Martin, Shavondra Davis, and Nicole Chandler for listening to my ideas, for reading my drafts, and for your incessant questions about the book that reminded me that I could not give up in the process. To Sean Welch for praying for me and for being my friend. I love you all.

To Dr. Johnnie and Sandra Cannon, Rhea and Marcus Carmon, Chris and Andrea Poynter, and to Aleathea and David Dupree, for the inspiration. To Bishop Roderick and Lady Erika Johnson, and to Pastor Byron and Lady Marcella Murray, for seeing and investing in the God in me. To my favorite professor and mentor, Dr. Heather Hirschfeld, for helping me believe that someone would be willing to read the words I write.

To Destiny Image Publishers for providing this opportunity.

And last but certainly not least, to God…my relationship with You is the greatest gift I could ever be given. Thank You for showing me what it means to love, and to be loved.

CONTENTS

INTRODUCTION

When God gave me the title and plan for this book, I felt unprepared, confused, and yes, a little angry. On one hand, I accepted that I was a writer. After all, I spent four years (okay, five) in college studying rhetoric and writing, but I had no experience and no idea what would it would take to get published. I had recently accepted a call to ministry, and I enjoyed serving and ministering to youth and other young adults. On the other hand, I was single (recently brokenhearted) with no immediate prospects and no idea of how to find or maintain a successful long-term relationship while pursuing a career and ministry. I believed in love and wanted it, but had no idea how to find it. Every Christian relationship book I'd ever heard about was based on a man/woman/couple testifying about how God blessed them in marriage and what process they went through, throwing in a Scripture every now and then along the way. Truth be told, I avoided relationship books. I was convinced that the authors' lives (and consequently, their advice) had no relevance to my life or to my relationships. I had friends who have read every relationship book ever written, only to find themselves even more lonely after building their Christian love-book libraries. I didn't believe that I knew enough, or had enough of a testimony, or knew enough people to be able to write a book, especially on this topic. Skeptical at best and rebellious at worse, I told God that I would write a book on relationships after He blessed me in finding my mate and obtaining success, after we had built the perfect marriage and ministry, and after I had some more connections. That's when it would make sense to me!

Over the next five years, I committed and over-committed myself to anything and everything—to school, to church, to my employers, to my friends and family, and to relationship after relationship. I thought that it was up to me to create the life that God had promised me, in my own strength and with my own strategies. Before I knew it, I was absolutely miserable. I felt like my life was falling apart, like God had allowed the enemy to attack every area. I had no transportation and no place to live, I'd left school, I was unhappy and stressed at my full-time job, and I was burnt out and becoming unproductive in ministry. My family was also suffering— in addition to struggling financially, several family members were on the verge of painful divorces, and one by one, members of my family began to suffer with serious illnesses. I threw a temper tantrum with God, stomping around my apartment and trying to move Him with my tears. I threatened to give up on the idea of true love, to give up my virginity, to walk away from ministry, to end my life, crying out, "God, I'm doing everything in my power to live for You. I'm trying my best, giving my all. I feel like You're setting me up." I told God that He'd let me down and left me to struggle alone. God, seemingly amused, responded calmly, "I need you to know the fullness of My love toward you. I need you to trust Me." He asked me if I was finally tired enough to place everything in His hands and to do things His way. I was.

I had to hit rock bottom in order to get fed up with the habits of religion, failure, compromise, bad self-image, and people-pleasing in my life. God challenged me to spend time with Him and to learn

Him intimately as my friend, my Father, and the lover of my soul. I needed to trust Him in order to allow Him to truly order my steps and lead me through the process to the promise and purpose that He had established for my life. After failure and frustration, disappointing myself and others, I quickly realized that I had no other choice. I decided to pursue God with my whole heart, to live life His way, to trust His timing, and to invest in and stir up the gifts that God had given me. I fell asleep every night in conversation with Him, and began each day the same way. I sang Him love songs and wrote love letters to Him and to a husband who I've yet to meet, and I allowed Him to love me, to speak the words of affection, admiration, acceptance, and affirmation that I'd been waiting and working to hear. I regained my confidence, my anticipation for marriage, my passion for life, and my passion for serving God's people. He challenged me, as I now challenge you, to build a life based on His divine design—ordered by the wisdom of His Word and motivated by His love.

In that difficult season, God spoke to me and reminded me that He gave me a vision, a dream, and instructions concerning a book that I was supposed to write. I couldn't wait on marriage to write about marriage; in fact, the only way for me to obtain a God-centered, God-directed relationship was to discover God's purpose and plan. In order to move into the next stage of my life, I had to complete what God had instructed me to do. In the month following that revelation, my spiritual father preached a New Year's Eve sermon based on the parable of the unproductive fig tree in Luke 13. For three consecutive years, the owner of the vineyard in Jesus' parable came to the fig tree that he planted seeking fruit, and found none. The owner told the dresser of the vineyard to cut the tree down. If the tree could not or would not produce the fruit it was planted to produce, it had no purpose. The dresser promised to prune the tree, to get rid of the dirt around it, and to fertilize it so that it could grow. He asked for one more opportunity, one more year, for the tree to produce its fruit. As he preached that sermon, I knew that the Holy Spirit was speaking directly to me. I purposed in my heart to remain wherever God placed me, to submit to the pruning and purging process, and to complete the book God was trying to birth through me by the end of the year.

God revealed to me that His purpose for the believer and for the Body of Christ has been the same since the beginning of mankind's existence—for us to be objects of His affection, who reign in the Earth and reflect back His love through lives of obedience and worship. His purpose is to redeem, restore, and establish a people in the Earth who generate His glory, walk in royal dominion, and reproduce generations who will do the same. According to John 3:16, *"God so loved the world, that He gave His only begotten Son, that whosoever believeth in Him should not perish, but have everlasting life"* (KJV). The whole Kingdom of God is built on the pattern of relationship! In fact, it is Christ who argued that the whole of the law can be summed up in two commandments, both based on love and the establishment of covenant relationship, that you *"Love the Lord your God with all of your heart and with all your soul and with all your mind,"* and that you *"Love your neighbor as yourself"* (Matt. 22:37,39). In His Word, God has laid out His plan to establish relationship with mankind, and He has also given us human relationships as a method of providing a reflection of His love in the earth.

God gives us a vision, a dream, a desire, a destination. But He doesn't stop there. If we trust in Him, He also charts the course for us to arrive at that which He has purposed for us. If you are anything like me, God has placed His love in your heart and a vision for relationship inside of your spirit. You crave intimacy, you desire to please God, you want the love that people write about in R&B/Pop songs and celebrate in the movies. You have an image of the love and the life you want to create, but you aren't sure how to get there. I have good news for you. Through His Word and the gift of the Holy Spirit, God equips every believer with a navigation system. We focus in on the sound of His voice, and all we have to do is listen to the step-by-step directions He provides, which ensure that we reach our destination. His promise to lead us, to navigate our paths, is found throughout the Scriptures:

The steps of a good man are ordered by the Lord, and He delighteth in His way (Psalm 37:23 KJV).

A man's heart deviseth his way: but the Lord directeth his steps (Proverbs 16:9 KJV).

A man's steps are directed by the Lord. How then can anyone understand his own way? (Proverbs 20:24)

I know, O Lord, that a man's life is not his own; it is not for man to direct his steps (Jeremiah 10:23).

The truth is that though we know God wants to order our steps, we fail to recognize that He has already done so. We look at and apply the wisdom offered by the world, and we fall short of investigating and embracing the wisdom that God has already outlined through instructions and patterns in His Word. Taking the advice of well-meaning advisers, we "wait on the Lord," or "wait on our mate," often failing to recognize that "wait" is an action word and that there is an exact process of preparation for entering covenant relationship. Instead of passively waiting on "our change to come," we should be passionately pursuing His presence and walking in obedience to His Word and His voice.

According to Hosea 4:6a, we, God's people, are destroyed for a lack of knowledge because we reject knowledge. Our refusal to pursue relationship with God and to allow Him to teach us through the example of His love leaves us open to trying to fulfill voids in our lives through other means. Hosea calls this choice idolatry (false relationship with false gods) and warns us about falling victim to the *"spirit of prostitution"* discussed in that same chapter. Tired of waiting, we find ourselves clinging to whatever crosses our paths, content to have something, anything, to occupy our time, and someone, anyone, to talk to.

A prostitute is one who goes through all the motions of intimacy, pleasing a customer without experiencing any of the satisfaction that those motions were designed to bring. No longer even desiring the pleasure that accompanies an intimate act, the prostitute is content with a few pieces of green paper as a token of the time spent. How does the spirit of prostitution operate in our lives? Bored with life, you may find yourself in clubs or bars, pouring yourself into your children or into work, or dating people just to have something to do, and crying yourself to sleep at the end of the night more frustrated and lonely than when the night began. You may scroll through the contact lists on your cell phone, just wanting to hear another voice besides your own, and realize that you keep offering yourself in conversation, friendship, and intimacy in search of some type of connection without finding what you seek in return. You may say "yes" to everything that is asked of you, keeping busy and waiting on someone to validate your importance and significance, and becoming frustrated when your efforts are unsuccessful or are overlooked. You may engage with your spouse out of obligation without desire, or you may find yourself with partner after partner, seeking love and acceptance, or perhaps some sense of validation or accomplishment, rushing to take a shower and wash off the sin that you're immediately convicted by. Perhaps you've developed an addiction to drugs, or alcohol, or smoking, or shopping, or food, or pornography, seeking some orgasmic release from stress or built-up frustration, while spiraling out of control trying to regain fleeting highs. In Hosea 4, God tells the prophet that the people *"will eat but not have enough; they **will engage in prostitution but not increase**, because they have deserted the Lord..."* (v. 10).

Is this where you find yourself, going through the motions of life and relationships without ever climaxing? When is the last time you were truly intimate with God alone? When is the last time you allowed His presence to consume and fulfill you? The truth is, we are not satisfied in our lives, in going through all the motions, because we have left our first love. We have become so distant from Him that we have begun to think, and live, and love like the rest of the world. Because we are so far from His heart, we struggle to know the plans He has for us, to receive the provision He already made to fulfill those plans, or to trust the directions and promises He has given us through His Word and through His Spirit.

My testimony to you is that compromise *never* produces climax. Running into the arms of the world and pursuing relationships on your own terms will only produce anger, hurt, disappointment, and frustration in your life. In trying to do things your way, have you also walked away from God? Are you ready to learn about and return to the love, protection, provision, and fulfillment He has reserved for you?

Here's the good news: God has always had a plan to reconcile His people back to Himself and to unite man and woman in holy matrimony. God challenges the believer in Romans 12:2, to no longer conform to the patterns of this world, but to be transformed by the renewing of our minds. It is only then that we will be able to test and approve the good, pleasing, and perfect will of the Lord for our lives. When we change our minds, seeking the truth and the love of God, and change our patterns, so that our lives and relationships are purpose-driven and God-centered, we can experience the pleasure and satisfaction that accompanies covenant love built God's way.

Any afternoon of television channel-surfing will reveal the problematic pattern of relationships reflected in our culture and in the world. The popularity of dating and relationship reality programming; the recent shifts in cohabitation, marriage, and divorce rates; the increase in the number of teenage parents and single-parent households; the enormous memberships to matchmaking and networking websites; and the recent battles over same-sex marriage legislation all reflect our society's fascination—and sometimes frustration and/or confusion—in regard to dating, courtship, love, sexuality, and marriage. As we prepare for a radical revision of the way we approach relationships, it is critical that we renew our minds, to refuse compromise, comparison, or conformity. We must dare to be different in our decision to base our relationships on the Word and will of God and not on what we see around us. This book reintroduces God's plan and God's order for covenant relationship, examining God's divine design for matrimony and providing the believer with a step-by-step guide to developing an individual lifestyle, and then, in God's timing, a marriage that reflects the glory of God. God outlines His systematic plan for relationship in the blueprint of the Old Testament tabernacle.

The tabernacle was an immaculate, sacred, beautiful space designed by God and built by God's chosen people, birthed out of His love and desire to simply be with them. There was an exact process of preparation for redemption and intimacy contained in the layout and pattern of the tabernacle. In following God's design, Moses and the children of Israel built a structure in which God could dwell among mankind in His full glory. Likewise, there is a process of preparation through which a bride and a groom are united in order to create a marriage structure that is a dwelling place for God and that is crowned by His presence and blessing. In the chapters that follow, we will trace the problematic state of modern relationships, and we will explore God's eternal plan to restore them. As we walk through the tabernacle—its function, its furnishings, its fulfillment—we will also see, very practically, the steps we should take in pursuing God and pursuing God-centered relationship.

Writing this book has required a renewing of my mind, and it has truly been a transforming experience. I began writing because

I needed to believe in true love again, because I had to rebuild my faith in God and in His plan for my life. I was ready to trust God, and I finally realized that the only way I would experience true happiness and realize the dreams and vision He had given me, was to chase after Him and live life His way. I started researching this book with the desire to find true love in a man, and instead, the search for love led me directly to God, my Creator, my Father, my Friend, the author and finisher of my faith. The book that you now hold in your hands is the proof of the power of returning to your first love, and of allowing Him to show you what love is supposed to be. His promise to me is that by walking in surrender and submission, that in understanding and decreeing His systematic plan for love and marriage, I am establishing that pattern in my life and reclaiming it for this generation. He has promised me that at the end of this process, I will find a love that looks like Him. His promise to you is the same.

God wants a radical relationship revolution for His people. As we turn our hearts towards Him, He has promised to turn around our relationships. *God's Divine Design for Dating and Marriage* establishes a new standard: redefining love as divine, marriage as beautiful, and sex as sacred. Refuting the patterns found in this world, this book provides a new blueprint and incites change in the way we live and love. Whether you're single, engaged, married, divorced, or separated, God has a plan for you. You are about to enter the greatest love relationship that you've ever known, and you will never be the same.

Let the journey begin.

SECTION 1

*(Dis)Agreement: The Fall of Mankind and
the Decline of the Marriage Model*

Chapter 1

A CRISIS OF LOVE: DIAGNOSING THE COURTSHIP COMPLEX

"Perception is reality." —Lee Atwater[1]

As I began writing this book, I sat down for coffee with a friend of mine, a co-laborer in the gospel, who had recently ended a 15-year marriage. As I introduced the topic of this study and began a dialogue about relationships and the process of divorce, he answered the question that I hadn't found the words to ask and began to explain the dissolution of his union. "*Television love* ruined my marriage," he stated simply, quietly, plainly. Upon further prompting, he explained that both he and his ex-wife, teenagers at the time of their union, entered marriage with unrealistic expectations of themselves and of their partners. Television taught him that a wife should be an ego-builder, kitchen expert, and sex goddess! Similarly, she said "I do" to the expectation that her husband would be a flower-wielding, wealth-building, feet-sweeping, superman kind of fellow. Neither had any idea of what marriage was intended to be, pressured into their union in an effort to legitimize the child they had on the way. Like so many other couples, they entered into a lifelong covenant based on the picture and pattern of love and relationships that they witnessed and wanted, and found themselves disillusioned and disappointed when the reality of marriage failed to meet their expectations. Having been built upon media-generated ideals and a lack of understanding of the purpose and plan for marriage, their union was doomed from the start.

Understanding Television Love

"Television love" is a fluid term, one whose meaning has changed with each generation. During the 1950s and 1960s, the example of television love belonged to couples like Lucy and Ricky and Fred and Ethel (*I Love Lucy*), Ralph and Alice and Ed and Trixie (*The Honeymooners*), Ozzie and Harriet (*The Adventures of Ozzie and Harriet*), and June and Ward Cleaver (*Leave It to Beaver*). For these couples, conflict always included comedic banter and was resolved by the end of each episode. Physical affection was non-existent, as television programmers prohibited sleeping in the same bed, and even the word *pregnant* was forbidden, especially during prime-time viewing. For this generation, love was laughter, sexuality was submerged by suburbia, and marriage was a moral construct.

By the 1970s and 1980s, significant changes in television programming occurred that mirrored changes in society at large. These decades witnessed the decline of family sitcoms in exchange for shows with socially contemporary focuses. Television love presented the opportunity for the exploration of contemporary issues, as the relationships featured on the sitcoms opened up discussions to much larger debates and transitions in families, communities, and attitudes. The conversations, struggles, and triumphs of couples during this period both reflected and influenced their real-life counterparts.

All in the Family's Edith and Archie Bunker exchanged traditional love ideals for weekly revelations of back-door attitudes toward race, class, and gender. The connection of sitcom love and social ills was expanded and expounded upon by television couples like George and Weezie Jefferson and James and Florida Evans in *Good Times*. For more traditional family discussions and values, a viewer could turn to *The Brady Bunch* or *The Cosby Show*, though both shows broke barriers in regard to family structure (two divorcees form a blended family) and race and success (an African-American doctor and lawyer raise their children successfully and happily, which earned *The Cosby Show* record-breaking ratings). Physical attraction and sexuality began to emerge as a theme, though underlying, and the focus on the family in prime time was replaced by an interest in the lives and careers of the alluring single characters on *Charlie's Angels* and *Three's Company*.

In the past two decades, the fictional representation of relationships in the media has changed as much as the morals and values of the audience. The most popular comedic couples of the 1990s include The Bundys of *Married with Children,* Homer and Marge from *The Simpsons*, and Dan and Roseanne Barr of *Roseanne*. As these couples emerged, the concept of dysfunction became less and less dysfunctional—normalized and laughed at on television sitcoms and talk shows. Audiences began to anticipate and cheer for "hook-ups," but only maintained interest in certain shows because of the subsequent "break-ups." The relationships of characters on shows like *Dallas, Saved by the Bell, Beverly Hills 90210,* and daily daytime soap operas kept audiences on the edges of their seats, waiting to see who fought, who got jealous, who married and divorced and remarried, who had sex and who found out. After 20 years, my grandmother is still watching *The Young and the Restless*, waiting on Victor and Nikki to marry *again* and live their happily ever after....

Within the past few years, there has been increasing demand from audiences to make television more like "real" life.

Within the past few years, there has been increasing demand from audiences to make television more like "real" life, and to have representative examples of individuals with all types of lifestyles. The focus of the most popular shows within the past ten years has transitioned away from marriage and showing positive love relationships, to highlight the difficulty in finding and in keeping love. Television love has become the lack thereof. It has evolved (or dilapidated) into television friendship, or plain old television sex.

The portraits of love on shows like *Sex and the City, Will and Grace, Desperate Housewives,* and *Friends,* are both entertaining and profitable. Unfortunately, they are also educational and representative. Today, conflict no longer concludes at the end of the episode—it lasts for seasons, or for an entire series. "Love" leads to more Prozac and Zoloft, depression and anxiety, and restraining orders, not laughter. Sexuality is no longer submerged and physical affection is no longer hidden; in fact, physical attraction is the priority and in the absence of real love, sex and alcohol seem to be the only sources of pleasure. Marriage has nothing to do with morality—at its best, it is a woman's triumph over loneliness, and at its worst it is an unnecessary source of unneeded drama and anger. This survey of the history and contemporary status of television love reflects what we already know about real-life relationships. They are in trouble.

 Television marriage has nothing to do with morality—at its best, it is a woman's triumph over loneliness, and at its worst it is an unnecessary source of unneeded drama and anger.

The Need for a Relationship Revolution

According to the 2006–2008 National Survey of Family Growth, 84.9 percent of American women and 91.3 percent of American men have engaged in premarital sex.[2] A poll conducted by *Time* magazine suggested that 61 percent of frequent church attenders do not even believe that it's wrong for an adult to have sex outside of marriage. A recent Barna study confirmed this statistical range, also citing that over 60 percent of born-again adults believe that cohabitation before marriage is also acceptable.[3] Because individuals wait longer to marry (the current average age is 28), they are sexually active as singles for a longer interval of time, and, consequently, have increasing numbers of sexual partners. In 2007, 19 million new cases of sexually transmitted disease were reported to the Center for Disease Control.[4]

Though 90 percent of Americans believe that adultery is morally wrong, a 2002 article in *The Journal of Couple and Relationship Therapy* reports that 45-55 percent of married women and 50-60 percent of married men engage in extramarital sex at some time or another during their relationship.[5] When you account for the possibility that both spouses are not counted in those engaged in affairs, popular estimates report that approximately 80 percent of marriages in America will be impacted by adultery.[6]

According to the American Academy of Matrimonial Lawyers, several reasons are consistently given by divorcing couples: failed expectations and unmet needs; poor communication; financial problems; a dramatic change in priorities; infidelity; addictions and substance abuse; physical, sexual, or emotional abuse; a lack of conflict resolution skills; and last, but not least, Facebook. The academy reports, however, that the number one reason given for divorce in this country is "a lack of commitment" to the concept, and then the reality, of marriage.[7]

The most oft-quoted divorce statistic places the rate at about 50 percent. In truth, the divorce rate has decreased steadily each year, and the most recent studies suggest that the rate is closer to 40 percent.[8] Over the past ten years, all the statistics reveal that fewer people are getting divorced, which would be great news, except that over the same period, statistics also reveal that more people are having sex at younger ages and with more partners, and that fewer people are also getting married. For the first half of 2007, there were 7.3 marriages and 3.4 divorces for every 1,000 persons. Compare this to ten years earlier when there were 9.0 marriages and 4.3 divorces per 1,000 persons.[9] The truth is that fewer people are getting divorced because more people are giving up on the concept of marriage before they ever meet at an altar.

 What the statistics reveal is the need for a radical new way to look at love, sex, and marriage.

On an episode of the Dr. Phil Show entitled "Marriage Hungry," it was reported that approximately 88 percent of Americans believe that they have a "soul mate" waiting for them.[10] I, like many of you, count myself a part of that number. If we were to look at the statistics listed above alone, the evidence that our relationships are doomed for failure would be overwhelming. Fortunately, the statistics do not show that we have any reason to fear loneliness, or infidelity, or divorce, or that we should give in to pressures (or our own feelings) to have sex outside of covenant. What the statistics reveal is the need for a radical new way to look at love, sex, and marriage.

If God created us and our mates, doesn't it just make sense that our success in those relationships is dependent upon our willingness to come together God's way? God never intended for us to feel our way through relationships, or to enter or build them the way that the world does. When we approach relationships like those in the world, with the same attitudes and behaviors, we sentence ourselves to the same disastrous results just described. God calls us to present our bodies to Him as living sacrifices, *"holy and pleasing to God"* as our *"spiritual act of worship"* and to no longer conform to the patterns of this world, but to be transformed by the renewing of our mind (see Rom. 12:1-2). In order to prepare for transformation—first of ourselves, then of our relationships—let's further explore the world's pattern in regard to love and sex.

What's Television Love Got to Do With It?

The calling to work with youth and young adults has always kept me humble, busy, youthful, and *current*. I have discovered that it is impossible to relate to and reach those to whom I minister without understanding the things that are important to them, without listening when they speak, and without earning the right to be heard. Consequently, I spend my Saturday mornings watching Power Rangers and the complete "Disney Channel on ABC" lineup. I mentor and disciple teenagers and college students through text messages and Facebook postings. And I've become pretty well versed in the latest dance crazes from YouTube, learning to do the "Dougie" and to "Swag Surf" while teaching my youth the importance of critically analyzing, and not subscribing to, the influence of the world through music.

In working with these young people, and in my own academic study, it has been extremely interesting over the years to take up the question of media influence on popular attitudes and behavior. I have listened to debates and read academic research studies addressing the relationship of movies, books, television, video games, and music to the behavioral patterns of the individuals who consume them. Though many people believe that cultural and media outlets influence behavior and patterns in the public, others may argue that trends in the media only reflect the larger trends in society and in consumer tastes.

 My lifelong experiences and observations have provided enough evidence to conclude that there is a definite correlation between what we see, what we hear, what we believe, what we accept, and what we do.

Though I have not studied the subject enough to take a position on either side of this controversial issue, my lifelong experiences and observations have provided enough evidence to conclude that there is a definite correlation between what we see, what we hear, what we believe, what we accept, and what we do. The relationship is clear when the typical attire for the teenage boys in our urban ministry shifts from white T-shirts and baggy Dickies to tight graphic T-shirts, boot-cut jeans, and chain belts based on the most popular rapper of the day. It is obvious, when the children I work with and teach know every word to every song in every part of the *High School Musical* trilogy, but struggle to memorize multiplication charts and Bible verses. It is apparent, when students in our collegiate fellowship skip Bible study because its timing coincides with *American Idol* or an NBA play-off game.

What's true for those young people is true for us all—ultimately, what we consume reflects our tastes and influences our attitudes, and possibly, our behaviors. In the last decade, the question of influence—whether television, movies, music, and video games can lead to certain behavior—has become extremely controversial. The logic behind the debate of the media's influence on the public versus the public's influence on the media is about as circular, and as pointless, as the "What came first, the chicken or the egg?" debate. The truth is lost in the question itself, which never acknowledges or emphasizes the power of the reciprocal relationship: that neither would be possible without the other, and that both reflect on the nature and potential of the other.

In other words, the dysfunction that has evolved in television relationships would not be possible or popular if it was not also present in our society, *and* the dysfunction that has evolved in real relationships and families would not be perpetuated if it were not a part of the culture so influenced by the media. Any failure to recognize or acknowledge these facts ignores the deeper concern that they point to: that there is something dysfunctional, disheartening, and damaging in our society's approach to love and relationships, directly related to our sources of information regarding love and relationships. Whether it is the cause or the effect, television love reveals that our understanding and practice of love, of affection, of respect, of commitment, of devotion, and of marriage is fundamentally failing.

 There is something dysfunctional, disheartening, and damaging in our society's approach to love and relationships.

After an hour-long dose of *Divorce Court, The Maury Povich, The Oprah Winfrey,* or *The Dr. Phil* shows, there is no room for doubt that our relationships and marriages are in danger. Nowhere is this more apparent than in reality television. The most popular types of reality television in recent years have been "reality competitions" or "reality game shows." Replacing many sitcoms in prime-time programming, these shows film participants who compete week after week to win a prize. On most shows, participants are eliminated one at a time, and the individual or team that survives the longest is declared the winner. Dating-based competition programming, in which one contestant is able to choose a mate from among a group of suitors, dominates the airwaves. The participants compete, over an episode or over a series, to earn the attention and affection of the object of their desire, and are eliminated if their appearance, their efforts, or their exploits fail to satisfy the contestant. On these shows, the search for television love is practiced and performed, but never truly perfected.

A brief overview of these shows will provide a window of understanding into this generation's modern understanding of how love is performed. The search for love is a competition...and for this generation, love itself is a game.

 The search for love is a competition...and for this generation, love itself is a game.

When Keeping It Real Goes Wrong

The appeal of programming in the dating-based competition genre extends across boundaries of age, race, and socio-economic background. Examples include *Love Connection, The Dating Game, The Bachelor,* and its spin-off, *The Bachelorette, I Love New York, A Real Chance at Love, For the Love of Ray-J, Rock of Love, A Shot of Love, Who Wants to Marry a Millionaire, The Cougar, Temptation Island, Next,* and *Parental Control.* For this exploration of how love is performed, however, I would like to focus on the show that I consider the most outrageous of them all, *Flavor of Love.*

Flavor Flav is the onstage persona of William Drayton Jr., born in 1959, who gained his fame during the 1980s and 1990s as a founding member of the hip-hop group, Public Enemy. By 2006, his tumultuous journey through the music industry—past a crack cocaine addiction, into prison for burglary, drugs, domestic violence, and attempted murder charges, and toward seven children—landed him the starring role on his own dating reality show. Though Flav proved himself to be a less-than-ideal candidate for marriage, women from across the country lined up to be named "the one" for Flavor Flav. It was clear from the first episode that this game show was far more about competition among women than the search to find true love.

Prior to the taping of the series, each young woman left her home, her job, and her priorities to move into the Flavor of Love mansion in order to take her chance at earning the choice and affection of the famous rapper. At the beginning of each season, each of the female participants parades (often scantily clad) in front of the star of the show, and she is stripped of her real identity and assigned a "nickname" based on the most striking aspect of her personality or anatomy, by which she is known for the remainder of the season. From the very first episode, the participants express their "love" for Flav. This affection seems to be based on the ladies' affinities to his fame, his wealth, or to the opportunity they have on the show to gain exposure for their own career explorations, as opposed to his personality, his commitment and stability, his physical attractiveness (or in Flav's case, the lack of all of those things). They love him before they know him!

On the show, intimacy is earned through competition. During the duration of the season, the women participate in ridiculous contests—cooking fried chicken, playing babysitters to small children, dressing up and acting like nurses, strip teases, etc.—in hopes of earning private time with Flav. When they aren't competing against one another, they're drinking alcohol compulsively, arguing and fighting with one another in jealous rages, or strategizing new methods of seducing him. Each week, contestants are eliminated from consideration based on their failure to impress or hold the attention of Flav—sent home in tears with confessions of disappointment and anger when their love (or lust) is unrequited. In the final episode of each season, he chooses his "queen," the final contestant standing, who is rewarded with a set of gold teeth instead of an engagement ring. After three seasons, Flav decided to marry none of the 60 women who had competed for his affection.

The fascination with *Flavor of Love* and its counterparts was contagious, as ratings soared and the conversations with the young people in our youth groups, with my college-educated colleagues, and with older relatives and mentors all turned to which participants were the most entertaining and who was most likely to be eliminated each week. I received text messages before and after each episode, reminding me to tune in at the appointed time and soliciting my response to the shocking behavior that we witnessed each time we watched. Although most of the national audience watched out of curiosity or for the scandal, I viewed with a critical gaze, amazed at just how much art imitates life.

Although many viewers were outraged by the behavior of the participants, I was consistently horrified by the corresponding behavior of everyday people. Consistently, young women and young men (and old women and old men) displace their priorities and forfeit their identities in the search for love and affection. They find infatuation—based on a potential mate's smooth words, charisma, looks, influence, or income—settling for lust after a person they barely know instead of commitment to a person they understand and trust.

All too often, men and women find themselves competing to earn the time and the attention of an individual who just isn't that into them, only to discover that others are doing the same thing with that person. Jealous rages and rituals of seduction are far less entertaining when they lead to real-life broken hearts. All too many of the singles I know find themselves trapped in an elimination game, waiting on the man or women of their dreams to change, to grow up, to stop cheating, and to finally choose them. And all too many of them find themselves disappointed season after season. If love is a game, and all its partakers merely players, certainly there is no way to win, no way to have a happily ever after when the credits begin to roll.

Crisis of Love, A Crisis of Culture

According to the Merriam-Webster dictionary, *culture* can be defined as "the integrated pattern of human knowledge, belief, and behavior that depends upon the capacity for learning and transmitting knowledge to succeeding generations." It is "the set of shared attitudes, values, goals, and practices"[11] that influence perception and behavior. It is our mental blueprint, the pattern on which our behavior is built—a body of learned behaviors heavily influenced, but not controlled by, the mass media. Popular (pop) culture represents the informal voice of the mainstream in our country, and it is primarily manifested in the language, clothing, and entertainment (sports, music, film, literature) of a group of people. In order to understand the culture of relationships in this country, one cannot look only at the patterns of attitude and behavior suggested by our definition of television love, but we must begin to examine all of the influences offered to an individual within this society and within his or her social groups. Where do we learn about love? About sex? About marriage? What truly influences the decisions that we make?

 Popular (pop) culture represents the informal voice of the mainstream in our country.

The "MTV generation," a term coined to encompass members of both Generation X and Generation Y, refers to individuals born between the 1970s and 1990s. Its members are proficient in the uses of technology, as they came of age during the technology era. Email, cell phones, and social networking are the lifelines of this group. Members of this group grew up memorizing the dance steps to their favorite music video. They are often described as socially liberal, sexually liberated, and fiscally driven. This generation has witnessed the rise of the Internet, the takeover of hip-hop culture, Playstation 2, the birth of MP3, the AIDS epidemic, and 9/11. What do the cultural markers of this generation suggest about its attitudes toward sex, relationships, and marriage? I'm glad that you asked...

Online News Reports

A June 2009 web-based inquiry using Google produced some very interesting results when searching for "marriage and news." There were several news reports on the legalization of same-sex marriages, as New Hampshire recently became the sixth state to pass legislation to recognize it. The vast majority (almost 70 percent) of the top 100 results were reports on gay marriage legislation, as the focus on marriage shifts away from the church and to LGBT rallies and forums. Related articles included reports of the battles in California around the passage and repeal of Proposition 8, the recent announcement of Chastity Bono (the transgendered daughter of Sonny and Cher) that "she" had begun the process to become a "he," and the ongoing debate between gay rights activists and African-American politicians about whether or not gay rights is the modern civil rights issue and if, consequently, blacks should be sympathetic and supportive of their cause.

The other news reports were even more shocking. Thomas Beatie, featured on *The Oprah Winfrey Show* and other daytime talk shows, is the man who changed his gender externally but kept his female organs. He gained notoriety as the first man to give birth when he decided to carry the couple's baby produced through artificial insemination. He recently gave birth to a second child.

Mia, a 20-year-old single mother, recently gave birth to a set of twin boys. A paternity test revealed a devastating result: she had slept with two men in a small enough time frame that the twins had different fathers. She appeared on several morning news broadcasts with her other children and her boyfriend, visibly pregnant again.[12] A 68-year-old Indiana woman now holds the record for marriages. She has been married 23 times, with the shortest lasting only 36 hours. She can't remember the order of her husbands, though she has gained fame for her many marriage exploits and the talk show appearances and news articles that it has produced. Her last marriage has been reported to be a complete publicity stunt, as she wed the man who also holds the record for the most marriages (28). At the time of the writing of this book, she was residing in an assisted living facility with a reported $1.33 in her banking account.[13] A 29-year-old man in Knoxville, Tennessee, is setting records of his own, recently gaining national news attention for fathering 20 (possibly 21) children by 11 mothers over 10 years. He was quoted in an interview, recorded after a child support hearing, revealing, "I had four kids in the same year—twice."[14] If these reports are not enough to convince you that there is a crisis of love, carried through the vehicle of our culture, perhaps these other markers will help make the case.

Language

The online slang dictionary listed 147 terms, posted by bloggers, to refer to sexual acts. Here is a sampling of the list in alphabetical order (excluding the four-letter words): *bang, beat, boink, bone, break off, bump uglies, chop, cut, dig, do the nasty, frequenting, get laid, get mounted, give (one) the business, hit that, horizontal refreshment, kicking it, kill it, knock boots, lay pipe, poke, put out, quickie, rail, ram, raw dog, ride, run a train, score, screw, shag, slap and tickle, slay, swerve, tap, tax, and wax.*[15] What happened to terms of endearment? Similar searches on the slang dictionary for the terms "love" and "marriage" produced no generational translations. Feel free to draw your own conclusions here.

Gaming

Grand Theft Auto (GTA) is reportedly the most controversial and most commercially successful action series in gaming history. With nine different games released almost yearly since 1997, GTA has sold over 70 million units. The game combines elements of action, adventure, role playing, and driving/racing. The individual playing the game has complete control of the direction of the game as he or she takes on the role of a criminal who completes illegal missions (assassinations, drug dealing, and pimping) to ascend the ranks of organized crime.

In the games, the protagonist is encouraged to pick up prostitutes to relieve stress, and gains extra points for robbing or assaulting them. In Grand Theft Auto: San Andreas, the main character is able to carry out "date missions" with up to six girlfriends. Successful missions lead to improved relationships with each girl, who then offers the protagonist gifts including cars, wardrobes, and free services. In its controversial mini-game modification, the main character is actually able to enter a girlfriend's bedroom, and the player controls the characters actions during sexual intercourse. Though this game was re-rated "Adult Only," the top demographic group of consumers of the game series is teenage males, who are learning that sex and the exploitation of females is all about self-gratification, connected in theme to both violence and power.

Music

This generation has been fueled by the drive to find its own soundtrack. From the inception of MTV and the music video to the release of Apple's iPod, most of the best-selling recording artists of all time (across several genres) released their most popular albums between the 1960s and 1990s. The best-selling album of all time is Michael Jackson's *Thriller,* which sold 28 million copies domestically. Shania Twain sold 18 million copies of *Come On Over,* earning her the titles of top female and top country artist. The top-selling pop group was The Backstreet Boys with their self-titled album, and the top-selling rap solo artist was Kid Rock with *Devil Without a Cause.* The top-selling R & B Group of all time is Boyz II Men, selling 12 million copies of *II,* and Outkast's *Speakerboxx/Love Below* was the top album by a hip-hop group. Though all of these albums carry relationships as a major lyrical theme, discussing and describing love and sex ad nauseam, not a single song on any of these albums mentions marriage or covenant.

At a recent gospel skating event sponsored by our ministry, I encountered a young man from the community who had been invited by some of our teens. Though Kirk Franklin and TobyMac's music blared from the rink's speakers, this young man preferred the music streaming through his headphones from his iPod. In an attempt to open a conversation with the young man, I asked him his name, his age, and what he was listening to. The artist's name was Plies, a rapper with best-selling albums entitled *The Real Testament* (2007), *Definition of Real* (2008) and *Da REAList* (2008). The young man was singing along to the artist's "Please Excuse My Hands," featuring the lyrics: "Before I kiss ya and make love to ya I wanna touch/ Can you please face the wall you bout to get strip searched/ My hands talkin to me they want now whats under ya skirt/ let me be da one to help ya wit ya shirt."

The song's chorus, featuring the melodic harmonies of Jamie Foxx, repeats: "Please excuse my hands, I apologize/ they have a one track mind to squeeze on your behind/ Baby, just excuse my hands." Many of our young people are ill-equipped to deal with their own hormones and emotions, and song lyrics on albums that describe themselves as "the real" teach them that sex has no consequences and requires no commitment. I was not surprised when, later in the evening, a deacon in our ministry caught the same young man kissing a young lady in a dark corner of the skating rink, touching her inappropriately with Kirk Franklin playing in the background.

Relationships as Reactions to Our Realities

Though individuals are influenced by the cultures in which they participate, our first learning environments are inside, not outside, our homes. Culture is learned behavior, and the blueprints on which our behavior is based are most often drafted by the relationships we participate in and witness very early in our lives. Our relationship decisions are as much an outgrowth of our environmental conditions as our individual choices. The culture of our families provides a foundation on which our other relationships are built, and most of our foundations are cracked.

 Though individuals are influenced by the cultures in which they participate, our first learning environments are inside, not outside, our homes.

Research suggests that our relationship patterns are birthed out of generational influence. A recent article on this topic in the

Journal of Marriage and the Family, reveals that the children of divorce have a higher risk of divorce when they marry, and an even higher risk if the person they marry comes from a divorced home. The study found that when the wife alone had experienced a parental divorce, her odds of divorce increased to 59 percent. When both spouses experienced parental divorce, the odds of divorce nearly tripled.[16]

According to a 2009 CNN report, births to unwed mothers reached an all-time high in 2007 at 1.7 million, or almost 40 percent. The article quoted LaShonda Henry, 28, a single mother, who reported that not only was she unmarried, but that her mother never married, and her grandmother didn't walk down the aisle until she was in her 60s. LaShonda said that "culturally speaking" marriage was not an expectation or a priority for her. The article states that the stigma attached to sex outside of marriage has all but disappeared.[17]

In fact, 28 percent percent of white children, 51 percent of Hispanic children, and 72 percent of black children will grow up in a single-parent household, without a model of commitment, and the numbers for the next generation will increase as their children grow up without models of commitment.[18] For individuals from single-parent or divorced households, a decision to commit or to wait for marriage becomes more difficult because it is outside their cultural and the household norm. It is evidenced when a mother allows her teenage daughter's boyfriend to spend the night in her home, with a justification that "at least she knows where they are." Or when a father gives his preteen son a box of condoms and teaches him that sex is the determining factor in manhood.

Studies indicate that sexual abuse is a reality in many households. Reported cases of child sexual abuse continues to reach epidemic proportions, with a reported 322 percent increase in a single decade.

Statistics reveal that 1 in 4 girls and 1 in 6 boys will be sexually abused before the age of 18. For those individuals, their first physical encounter is overshadowed by violence, by powerlessness, by secrecy. Subsequent relationships can manifest as extensions on the same continuum or as reactions against the original trauma. The long-term effects of child abuse include fear, anxiety, depression, anger, hostility, inappropriate sexual behavior, poor self-esteem, feelings of guilt and/or shame, tendency toward substance abuse, and difficulty with trust and forming close attachments.[19] Many adults enter relationships having never come to terms with or experienced healing from these childhood traumas. Most of those relationships are doomed from the beginning.

U.S. Census Bureau data reports that poverty and the stresses associated with financial need are the major factors contributing to the breakup of American families. The greatest factor in childhood poverty is family structure, and the greatest factor in family structure is poverty. These facts suggest a dangerous cycle, impacting generation after generation who continue patterns of poverty directly related to dysfunctional relationships. As the structure of the nuclear family in our society disintegrates, the future opportunities for our children diminish and produce new generational curses. Other factors associated with the ability to build and maintain stable relationships based in family upbringing and environmental influences include the following: a lack of mentorship, substance abuse, an abusive environment, bad communication styles and ineffective methods of conflict resolution (bickering, arguing, nagging), lack of attention or affection toward the children, and witnessed patterns of infidelity.

 There is a crisis in courtship, a crisis of love, and a demonic attack on the institution of marriage and on the family.

How can we expect healthy relationships when so many of our influences, public and private, are unhealthy? There is a crisis in courtship, a crisis of love, and a demonic attack on the institution of marriage and on the family. In one way or another, all of us are affected. For many of us, the statistics and examples discussed in this chapter are more than facts; they are descriptors of our experiences, of our pains. Perhaps you, like me and so many others, find yourself in more than one of the above categories, impacted by cultural influence and norms, affected by generational curses and things that have happened to you in your past, and haunted by your own mistakes in relationships. Maybe you had no model of marriage and commitment, have had to overcome sexual abuse, or grew up under the stresses of poverty. Perhaps you've been influenced by the world, defining sex and looking for love based on a recipe from a *Cosmo* article, your favorite romantic movie, or an Internet porn site. If, by chance, you've fallen in the past—into sexual sin, into love with the wrong person, into a cycle of hurt, or abuse, or frustration, or manipulation—you are not alone. It may have been your reality, but it does not have to be your truth.

At the end of statistical facts and society's fictions, there lies a future ahead. Christ is the mediating factor, the atmosphere changer, the curse breaker. If we are compelled by Christ's love to choose to live for Him, He promises to create in us a clean heart, to renew in us a right mind, and to give us hope and an expected end (see Ps. 51:10; Jer. 29:11). In order to claim and reclaim the type of holy, fulfilling relationships we desire, we must be willing to flee from the ways of this world and the devices of the devil, and find ourselves and that love in the arms of our God.

 In Him we find healing and a model of what love is intended to be.

In Him we find healing and a model of what love is intended to be. We have a promise in Second Corinthians 5:17, where the apostle Paul writes, *"Therefore, if any* [one] *be in Christ, he is a new creature: old things are passed away; behold, all things are become new"* (KJV). That means you! That means your relationships! The enemy had a plan to destroy us and to prevent us from experiencing the love God ordained for us…but guess what? God's plan and God's purposes are so much greater.

Endnotes

1. Lee Atwater, conservative political mastermind, has been largely credited with coining this phrase. The biographical film about his life and this quote can be accessed at "The Lee Atwater Story: Introduction." FRONTLINE Online. http://www.pbs.org/wgbh/pages/frontline/atwater/etc/synopsis.html/.

2. "Key Statistics from the National Survey of Family Growth." *Survey of Family Growth.* Centers for Disease Control and Prevention. http://www.cdc.gov/nchs/nsfg/abc_list_p.htm#premarital. 2 July 2010 (accessed 6 March 2011).

3. "Christians are more likely to experience divorce than are non-Christians," *Barna Research Group.* http://www.barna.org/. 21 December 1999 (accessed December 2009). Barna no longer has this report online. However, a review of the report can be found at http://www.adherents.com/.

4. "Trends in Reportable Sexually Transmitted Diseases in the United States, 2007." *Sexually Transmitted Disease Surveillance 2007.* Centers for Disease Control. http://www.cdc.gov/std/stats07/trends.htm. 13 January 2009 (accessed December 2009).

5. From Atwood and Schwartz. *Journal of Couple and Relationship Therapy.* 2002, quoted in Lindsey Richardson, "Percentage of Married Couples who Cheat." *Info Library.* 2007. http://www.catalogs.com/info/relationships/percentage-of-married-couples-who-cheat-on-each-ot.html.

6. Ibid.

7. The American Association for Matrimonial Lawyers is a nonprofit association of attorneys who specialize in family law. An online version of their booklet "Why Marriages Fail" can be accessed through their website. "Making Marriage Last." *American Association for Matrimonial Lawyers.* http://aamlillinois.org/making-marriage-last.cfm (accessed 6 March 2011).

8. The statistics and rates discussed here are based on data from the U.S. Census Bureau and the National Center for Health Statistics (CDC) for 2002. A discussion of the trends in divorce statistics is available online in the online article "Divorce Rates." *Americans for Divorce Reform.* http://www.divorcereform.org/rates.htm (accessed 7 March 2011).

9. Data from the Statistical Abstracts of the 1997 & 2007 U.S. Census, available online for download in .pdf form through www.census.gov.

10. An online article based on this 1999 episode and containing this statistic from University Wire, and other statistics connected to marriage and divorce, can be found in Dr. Phil's online archives at http://www.drphil.com/articles/article/351.

11. "Culture," *Merriam-Webster Dictionary Website*, http://www.merriam-webster.com/dictionary/culture (accessed 15 March 2011).

12. Gerard DeMarco. "Mother Gives Birth to Twins with Different Dads." *Today.com.* http://today.msnbc.msn.com/id/30864533/ns/today-parenting/. 21 May 2009 (accessed 8 March 2011).

13. "Most Married Woman-World Record Set by Linda Wolfe." *World Records Academy.* http://www.worldrecordsacademy.org/society/most_married_woman-world_record_set_by_Linda_Wolfe_90178.htm.

14. Amber Miller. "Father, 29, in Child Support Court Says He Has 21 Kids." *Volunteertelevision.com.* http://www.volunteertelevision.com/home/headlines/45871127.html. 22 May 2009 (accessed 8 March 2011).

15. "Sex." *Urban Dictionary.* http://www.urbandictionary.com/define (accessed December 2009).

16. Amato and Cheadle (2005). "The Long Reach of Divorce: Divorce and Child Well Being Across Three Generations." *Journal of Marriage and Family.* 67(1), 191-206.

17. Jessica Ravitz. "Out-of-Wedlock Births Hit Record High." *CNN.com.* http://articles.cnn.com/2009-04-08/living/out.of.wedlock.births_1_out-of-wedlock-unwed-mothers-wedding-dress?_s=PM:LIVING.

18. Ibid.

19. T. Sorenson and B. Snow (1991). "How Children Tell: The Process of Disclosure in Child Sexual Abuse." *Child Welfare.* 70 (1), 3-15.

Chapter 2

DIVINE DESIGN AND DISOBEDIENCE: TRACING THE ORIGIN OF DATING DEVIANCE

"This can't be life. This can't be love. This can't be right. There's gotta be more. This can't be us." —Jay-Z, "This Can't Be Life"

So shall they fear the name of the Lord from the west, and His glory from the rising of the sun. When the enemy shall come in like a flood, the Spirit of the Lord shall lift up a standard against him (Isaiah 59:19 KJV).

During a recent women's conference, I met a woman named Desiree, with whom I've kept in contact over the past few months. Desiree approached me after a panel discussion in which I shared my testimony of living saved and single while working in ministry. I was transparent, sharing my failures, the frustrations, and my faith in God and His plan for me, and consequently, she felt free to do the same in our conversation. Desiree loved God, but she had become extremely bitter toward men and the idea of marriage after a painful divorce and a recent breakup, both caused by a myriad of issues and culminating in infidelity. She felt betrayed. She was angry at men, at her friends who didn't tell her, at God who she felt should have warned her, and at herself.

I listened to her account of everything that happened, and when she calmed long enough to listen through her sobs, I asked her why she was still holding on to the memory and the pain of everything that occurred. Was she still in love with either of the men she described? Was she afraid of being hurt again? Was she willing to give up her peace of mind to hold on to offense, when it was clear that the other party had moved on? She told me that she felt stuck because she never had "closure." She couldn't move forward because she didn't understand why things had gone so terribly wrong. "I just want him to tell me why!" she exclaimed repeatedly. "I want to know what I did wrong, and why he didn't just talk to me, and why men cheat, and why I keep falling in love with the wrong man, and…."

I told her that closure would never come through being able to ask those questions because the men involved would never be able to provide a satisfying answer. Psychologists and sociologists and experts far more versed in human behavior may provide some insight to the uncertainty of why we do the things we do, but the truth of the matter is that the issues we face in relationships—communication problems, abuse, cheating and adultery, betrayal, fear, and so on—can all be traced to a source and an origin far deeper than anything most of us have a vocabulary to express. When two people are broken, it is impossible for their relationships to be whole. Our relationships have led to brokenness and to breaking up since the Fall of mankind when God's plan for us and for marriage was broken as the reality of sin was introduced in the Garden of Eden.

When two people are broken, it is impossible for their relationships to be whole.

I told her that closure would only come through forgiveness, based on an extension of the grace that we have received from God instead of a request from either man. I told her that she was an overcomer and encouraged her to trust that all things work out for the good of those who love God and are called according to His purpose (see Rom. 8:28), knowing that God could take any situation and transform it for her benefit and His glory. I challenged her toward self-reflection—to truly examine herself and her patterns as the beginning of her own growth and progress. Over time, we studied and she began to see the origin of her failures in relationships, a problem originating with satan, producing results that we still experience today, and concluding the moment we come into the knowledge of God's love and will for us.

Breaking Relationship News

The definition of love and the practice of relationships wasn't written or established in the modern moment! The cultural failures of love and relationships described in the first chapter and experienced by Desiree and others may be today's reality, but it was never intended to be that way. God created and united man and woman on purpose, with purpose, and for purpose. No matter how bad things seem—in our society and in our individual lives—we serve a God who is so much greater. He has a plan for our relationships and for marriage that goes far beyond the modern moment.

In this chapter, we'll explore the origin of the dysfunction we see in modern relationships, tracing the deviance to its source, the serpent known as satan. We'll also find the solution to the dysfunction in the faithfulness and sovereignty of the Lord, looking unto Him as the author and the finisher of our faith, the beginning and the ending, the Alpha and Omega. God has written our love story, and no matter what weapons the enemy forms in our lives and in our culture, they won't prosper against us. From Genesis to Revelation and beyond, God has always known how our love story is going to end.

 God has written our love story.

Breaking Doctrinal News

The creation story didn't begin at Genesis 1:1! According to Ephesians 1:3-5, the saints—the believers who are faithful in Christ Jesus—have been blessed in the heavenly realm with every spiritual blessing; we were chosen in Him *"before the creation of the world to be holy and blameless in His sight,"* and in love, He predestined us to come into relationship with Him according to His pleasure and will through His grace. Before God created anything, He carried us inside of Him! He already knew us, already loved us, already blessed us, already created a plan for us to reunite with and grow with Him through Christ. As a result of that love, God created the entire world with us in mind.

Genesis 1:1-2 tells us that God began to create the heavens and the earth, but the earth was formless, void, empty, and dark. The triune God (the Father, the Son, and the Holy Spirit) came into agreement and decided to contour the conditions of Earth to make it habitable for mankind. I submit to you that it is by no coincidence that Earth is the only planet where the conditions are absolutely perfect to sustain life. The Bible teaches us that Earth, too, was uninhabitable until He decided that it would be home for us. For five days, God spoke, the Word (Christ) performed what was spoken, and the Spirit sustained what the Word produced. God renovated Earth to produce a setting in which mankind could live—establishing the lighting, the temperature, the landscape, markers of time, the food source, and a little entertainment—in order to manifest the perfect environment for the life He would produce in us.

God is strategic in His creation, placing potential into what He creates for what will later come into being. His strategy, since the beginning, is *to create and separate, then to operate and celebrate!* God pulls the light out of darkness and separates them, and then He forms it into the day and night. Evening and morning were the contrasts that formed a complete day. God pulls the firmament out of the water and separates them, and then He forms the land and the seas. Land and sea were the contrasts that formed a complete Earth. God pulls the vegetation from the ground and animals out of the seas, the sky, and the land. He is careful to specify that the plants be seed-bearing, and He commands the animals to multiply. When He creates them, He places within them what they will need to reproduce more of themselves. He separates the animals according to their kind, ensuring that they can only produce by coming into union with a partner of its own species. God formed man, pulled woman out of him, and reunited them to multiply and form mankind. He steps back from the whole of His creation, and knowing that His heavenly pattern was established in the Earth, He saw that it was good. Finally, the atmosphere was set for God to manifest His love, to create mankind, the object of His eternal love.

Back to Eden: Understanding God's Sovereignty and Strategy

In prayer and meditation some time ago, the Spirit of God began to challenge me. He asked me what I believed was God's final creation. I answered man/Adam, and He said I was only partially correct. I answered woman, who was pulled out of man, and once again, I was only partially correct. God told me that His final creation was *marriage*, the power contained in the union of man and woman. Why is this so significant? On the sixth day, God is completing His creative work by formulating a reflection of Himself.

 God told me that His final creation was marriage, the power contained in the union of man and woman.

Then God said, "Let Us make man in Our image, in Our likeness, and let them rule over the fish of the sea and the birds of the air, over the livestock, over all the earth...." So God created man in His own image, in the image of God He created him; male and female He created them (Genesis 1:26-27).

God's ultimate creation is marriage, which is designed to reflect the nature of God and His relationship to His people. In the making of mankind—of marriage—God continues the same pattern for creation that He had already established in the Earth. *He creates, He separates, He operates, then He celebrates!*

Creation

We learned from Ephesians 1 that man was chosen *in Him* before the foundation of the world. Once the world was established, however, God created a way to orchestrate His divine plan by illustrating His love and His sovereign choice. In Genesis 2:7, we learn that *"the Lord God formed the man from the dust of the ground and breathed into his nostrils the breath of life, and the man became a living being."* God is a Spirit, and through the Spirit—the breath of

God—man was born. God poured life for mankind out of Himself, into a container made from the dust of the ground. Mankind was born from above—in the image of God—and our bodies were created to only contain the breath of God within us. God refers to Himself as plural, and likewise, mankind has a plural nature—the body, the soul (will, intellect, and emotions), and spirit. Man is created out of God, and God placed within man the potential to reflect His nature and reproduce that reflection in the earth.

Before we go any further, you need to understand that God created you exactly as He intended for you to be. You are fearfully and wonderfully made—your skin tone, your eye color, your hair texture, your talents, short or tall, personality and all! Though you are unique, God did not create you alone. He always ordered His creation "according to its kind," but you'll never be able to unite with people like you until you start acting like yourself. You should not feel the need to change who you are in order to please anyone—parents, friends, mates, haters, supervisors, pastors, or yourself. When God created you, He created a place for you. He made you on purpose, with purpose, for purpose, and the same is true for the person He created to walk with you. Trust me when I say that your entire life will change, and you will feel so much better, the moment you discover who He created you to be and just how much power He has placed inside of you.

Separation

God takes man and places him in the Garden of Eden. He imparts, empowers, and instructs Adam, giving him dominion over the Earth and charging him with its care. In His description of Adam, God reveals two things about Himself when He says, *"It is not good for the man to be alone"* and *"no suitable helper was found"* for him (Gen. 2:18,20). Adam is made in the image, the reflection, of God, so if it is not good for man to be alone, God is also revealing He did not desire to remain alone. Just as no suitable helper for Adam could be found, God had to create a helper for Himself, a people who could display His glory and share the joy of His presence, who could extend His dominion within the Earth. God desired to be with us, just as Adam desired a suitable (tailor-made!) helpmate. Just as God poured us out of Himself, God pulled woman out of man. He created man as "seed-bearing," then removed the part of Adam that would receive and nourish the seed. According to our pattern, God is revealing Himself as "seed-bearing." Consequently, mankind becomes an extension of Him with the potential to receive the seed of the Word, of Christ, and to reproduce fruit of the Spirit through intimacy with Him.

 Adam is made in the image, the reflection, of God, so if it is not good for man to be alone, God is also revealing He did not desire to remain alone.

So the Lord God caused the man to fall into a deep sleep; and while he was sleeping, He took one of the man's ribs and closed up the place with flesh. The the Lord God made a woman from the rib He had taken out of the man, and He brought her to the man (Genesis 2:21-22).

God pulls a rib from Adam, the part of his anatomy designed to cover and protect his vital organs. Woman was separated from Adam for a time in order to be shaped into the helpmate he needed. God was foreshadowing that man would be separated from Him in order to be shaped into what He needs us to be. For us, the season of singleness is our period of preparation. Though separation can be painful, lonely, and frustrating, we must begin to view our separation from our mates as the time that God has given us to undergo the process that will prepare us to walk in His purpose. It is not designed to be permanent, but you prolong the season if you continue to try to unite with "seed-bearers" or ribs that do not belong to you. The season of separation is your time to be with you. It only becomes difficult when you refuse to trust that God knows what is best.

 The season of separation is your time to be with you.

Operation

Both man and woman are subject to divine operations. Adam falls *"into a deep sleep,"* and while he is sedated, God removes his rib. *Before* he can be reunited with that rib, with his helpmate, the torn place in his body must be healed—"closed up with flesh." The same is true for God's relationship with mankind, and for the relationship of man and woman. The breach between God and man had to be filled with flesh, with Christ. The breach within man must be filled with Christ.

A man must take the time to heal, from issues in his past, from societal ills, and from his own mistakes, before he is free to even recognize woman. He has to wake up! Men of God, receiving your wife will require you to change your posture, to get in position, and to open your eyes. Stop sleeping—don't be deceived by beauty or by charm. Allow God to show you what a helpmate is supposed to look like, and what it is He has prepared for you to do. Woman was made from the bone of Adam, from the structure of man, and was created in the image of God. As bone, woman had the potential to be rough around the edges, or to be easily broken. *Before* she can be reunited with Adam, God has to shape her, and the same is true for the Body of Christ. Before God could bring us back to Himself, there has to be a process of development.

Women, before you can be reunited with your Adam, you must allow God to truly mold you—to work out the things in your attitude, your expectations, and your habits that may need to be adjusted. God's desire is to soften you and to carve out and consecrate a place in your life for Himself and for the seed of your mate (his hopes, his dreams, his potential) so that they can grow and be produced in the earth. God has to spend time with you, to establish in you an expectation for how you are to be treated, and to train for partnership in the fulfillment of family and your Kingdom assignment.

Celebration

After their operations, God brings woman to the man, and they are reunited. The man exclaims, *"This is now bone of my bones and flesh of my flesh; she shall be called 'woman,' for she was taken out of man"* (Gen. 2:23). Adam looks at his scars, then at woman, and he immediately recognizes that she is everything that he has been missing. He knows that she was pulled out of him because she is made of all the same substance as he is. He knows that he needs her because she is everything that he is not. How do you know when you have found the right person? How long does it take to know that a person is your spouse? I submit to you that your confirmation comes when you can honestly testify that you have found "bone of bone" and "flesh of flesh."

Adam has experienced the frustration of looking and trying and being unable to find a suitable helpmate, and it is only after relinquishing control of the process to God that he is able to walk into the process through which she is presented. They can only know after they have completely and separately submitted themselves to

God. He knows and is walking in his assignment; she has been formed and shaped to assist him. It only becomes clear after their surgeries. You can only know that you have found your mate when you realize that you share everything that it will take in order for your futures, your journeys, and your Kingdom assignments to merge into one. They are equals, they are partners, and they are a perfect union.

Whenever you find that gift, and it grows through the bond of love, you have something to celebrate, and so does God. The Bible says in Genesis 1:28 that, when God put man and woman back together, He blessed them. The Hebrew word for "bless" in that passage is *ba'rak*.[1] Its root meaning is to kneel; its implication is to confer upon one an act of adoration and to bestow a benefit. He bestowed fruitfulness and increase, dominion and influence. The final thing God did in creation was to establish a pattern for His relationship with us, and anytime we walk in that pattern and accurately reflect His love for mankind, God blesses us. God entered the Sabbath and now He waits for us, knowing that in marriage, He foreshadowed the process of redemption and reconciliation that was to come. Like Adam, He entered rest, looking forward to enjoying the object of His adoration.

Divine Reflection: The Design for Relationship and Marriage

According to the strategy outlined above, marriage is best understood as a creation of God that should follow His plan. In other words, it should not be based upon biological clocks, built upon superficial or sexual feelings, or influenced by unplanned pregnancy or financial arrangements! Humanity was created to reflect God's divine nature in the Earth, and marriage was established as the mechanism to house and reflect His divine love in the earth. God created a mirror image of Himself in man. He then repeats the process, pulling woman out of man and making her the mirror image of him. The union of man and woman was designed to be a mirror image of the relationship of God to the object of His affection, humanity. Marriage is how God creates a picture of His love to the world.

 Humanity was created to reflect God's divine nature in the Earth.

God blessed them and said to them, "Be fruitful and increase in number; fill the earth and subdue it. Rule over the fish of the sea and the birds of the air and over every living creature that moves on the ground" (Genesis 1:28).

The only way to attain a relationship ordained by God, blessed by God, and producing the type of increase, productivity, power, and dominion that God has established for you, is for you to walk in complete agreement and submission to the plan that God put in place. Marriage was ordained to paint a picture of God's love, and you must allow God to produce that in you and out of you as you rest in His sovereignty. From the very beginning of time, God outlined His blueprint for relationship in the earth, providing us with a pattern and a promise—a divine outline of what to expect in our process toward a God-designed, God-centered, God-glorifying relationship. Here is His divine design.

The Pattern

A perfect union must contain three elements: an understanding of divine purpose, submission to divine timing, and a commitment to divine mission.

God chose marriage as a portrait of reconciliation and redemption in the earth. How radical would it be to make dating and marriage decisions based on the fulfillment of a divine call to serve in relationship as a ministry unto the Lord? If both individuals are driven by this purpose, it will eliminate selfish purposes for and within the marriage. The relationship emerges as God-centered, as both partners aspire to please the highest authority in order to gain His continued blessing upon themselves and the generations they will produce. If they recognize that their individual lives, and consequently their relationship, should reflect and reproduce God's image, they will remain focused on God, and His glory will be produced through His relationship with them. If you are single, it's time for you to get focused. If you are married, it may be time for you to refocus.

The timing of the relationship must also be reflective of God. *Divine timing is order!* God cannot unite the two individuals He has ordained to walk together until they are both in order. Too many people get together when they are out of the will of God or when their lives are in disarray, and when they unite, they reproduce this disorder and create chaos and confusion! Just as God established complete order and filled the earth before uniting man and woman, so God's desire is to create order in every area of your life before uniting you and your mate: order in your mind, order in your emotions, order in your work habits, order in your finances and your spending, order in your time management, order in your health. So many marriages suffer because the couples hooked up when one or both partners were out of order! Let's begin to reflect God—don't introduce your disorder into someone else's life, and don't allow him to introduce his disorder into yours. Take the time to get yourself together—your marriage will be blessed because of it.

 Don't introduce your disorder into someone else's life, and don't allow him to introduce his disorder into yours.

The final element in a godly union is a commitment to divine mission. Without goals, a target, and a destination, a relationship is destined to stop progressing or to keep running in circles as the individuals chase after one another. Individuals waste far too much time in relationships because they have nothing to work toward, so they just keep working on each other—working on each other's faults and working on each other's nerves! A divine directive should drive a godly couple. Man and woman were commanded to fill the earth and subdue it—to reproduce and to reign. A couple should be committed to building their family, building the Kingdom, and building a legacy. There is nothing more rewarding than the fulfillment that comes from achieving goals and watching vision fulfilled, particularly when it is the result of unity, agreement, and true partnership.

The Promise

I told you earlier in this chapter that real love—accompanied by commitment, purity, comfort, acceptance, support, and understanding—is God's promise to those of us who desire it and are willing to achieve it God's way. The Bible teaches us that at the completion of their process, man and woman were united and began to walk together. Just as there are three elements in the pattern, there are three portions of the promise, all contained in Genesis 2:24-25. Man and woman were *"one flesh," "both naked,"* and *"felt no shame."*

When the Bible speaks of man and woman becoming one flesh, it is referring to much more than their physical bodies. The Hebrew word for "flesh" in this passage is *basar.*[2] It translates "body," "person," or "self," and its root word speaks of "freshness" and "fullness." The promise contained here is the opportunity for a new beginning. In marriage, two truly become one—with one goal, one plan, one vision, one direction—joined in spirit, joined in soul, joined in mind, and joined in body. The union maximizes the potential within each individual. The intimacy produced in that type of connection makes a godly union inseparable, and the power contained in marital agreement is absolutely unstoppable.

We also learn in the text that Adam and Eve were naked. They were completely open, bare, free—both physically and metaphorically. The promise for us is that in godly marriage, we find someone with whom we can be completely naked. That means you can be your full self without fear of judgment or rejection from your spouse—no standards to uphold, nothing to hide. In God's divine design, both partners are able to operate in complete liberty, equality, and supernatural attraction. When we walk in uprightness toward God, we have access to and the ability to appreciate the best parts of our mates, and we allow our mates to see the best parts of ourselves.

The final portion of the promise that we see in the relationship of man and woman is that they are without shame. They felt no need to cover up or to hide—they didn't have to hide their relationship with other people, and they had nothing to feel guilty about with God. The promise is that when we handle relationships God's way, we are able to walk completely upright—no embarrassment, dishonor, disgrace, humiliation, or inadequacy. No secret clinic visits, no rumors or ruined reputations, no tear-filled apologies to God for messing up (again). Godly men and women are free to hold hands and embrace in public, to post their permanent statuses and family pictures on Facebook, and to express their love to one another in an undefiled bed. And speaking of that undefiled bed, the Hebrew translation of *"no shame"* also means *not disappointed or delayed*.[3] In other words, you don't have to try out the goods when God created the goods just for you! Our promise is that if we serve God and dedicate our relationships to Him, He will ensure that we get exactly what we need, exactly when we need it—mentally, emotionally, and physically!

God is always there, pursuing us and desiring true intimacy with us.

Not only did God make these promises a part of the relationship of man and woman, but He also established the same components within our relationship with Him. In fact, you must experience them with Him before it is possible for them to be introduced to your relationship with another human being. God is always there, pursuing us and desiring true intimacy with us. If you seek Him, I promise that you will find the love I just described. After many years of searching for it in all the wrong places, I found it in God. And I look forward to sharing that love with a man who has experienced God's love for himself.

The Perversion Plan: Rebellion, Demonic Influence, and Disobedience

Love is the manifestation of the supernatural essence of God, the principle thing for mankind, the cord that binds heart to heart and spirit to spirit. It should come as no surprise that it has come under the most severe attack. The enemy has been forced to watch and to bear witness to God pouring out and replicating His love for us since the beginning of time, and the enemy, in his envy and bitterness, hates nothing more than the power produced by unity and love. Since the Garden, he has been infiltrating relationships and perverting love, sex, and marriage in an effort to separate us from one another and from God. He was given no power to destroy us, or to destroy love or the pattern that God created, so he formulated a plan to convince us to forfeit the divine design of love and marriage and the blessing that accompanies our obedience to God's plan. Fortunately for us, the love of God, and the love we are called to have for one another, is inextinguishable, and as we learn the devil's schemes, we will be more prepared to resist his deceptions. In this section, we will expose satan's plan: to infiltrate relationships, separating man from woman and humankind from God, in an effort to gain his own glory.

Remember the creation narrative, the Garden of Eden, the wonderful story of Adam and Eve? We learn in Genesis that by the seventh day of creation, God had begun His rest. He had set everything in order. He had married man and woman. God had given Adam instructions and the couple complete authority in the earth to replicate the pattern that He had established. All that God required from man and woman in order for them to remain in the place of supernatural provision, uninhibited dominion, and His glorious attendance was that they maintain His order and walk in obedience to His Word. Access to everything they could ever want or need was at their grasp, with only one condition.

God spoke to Adam and commanded him,

*You are free to eat from any tree in the garden; but you must not eat from the tree of the **knowledge of good and evil**, for when you eat of it you will surely die* (Genesis 2:16b-17).

God required order and obedience, and He was careful to warn Adam of the consequences of consuming the wrong type of seed. There were many types of trees in the garden, with all types of fruit, but the trees that were placed at the center of the garden were the tree of life and the tree of the knowledge of good and evil. The tree of life produced fruit leading to life, and the tree of knowledge produced two kinds of fruit—good and evil—*both* of which lead to death.

According to Genesis 3:1, the serpent, who was also a created being, was more cunning than any other animal. The serpent, satan, plotted to undo God's handiwork as he watched and waited until creation was finished. With no authority in the earth, satan was powerless to destroy what God had established, so he was forced to attempt to gain power through the strategy of influence. He knew that relationship was God's final creation, and he was smart enough to know that if he could duplicate relationship, he could influence Adam and Eve enough to gain humanity's authority and power.

Satan's strategy was to *counterfeit relationship*—to copy what God did in order to steal what God gave to mankind. His goal was to make sure that death was introduced. He wanted mankind to be permanently separated from God, and he also devised a plan to separate man from woman. Marriage was the final creation, and marriage was the first thing satan attacked. Satan knew that he could not challenge God, so he set out to destroy God's reflection. If he could get humankind to listen to him, he could plant the seeds that would eventually produce death, division, and destruction. Satan's strategy was to penetrate the mind of Adam and Eve in order to reproduce actions and attitudes that would take glory from God and bring worship to himself.

 Marriage was the final creation, and marriage was the first thing satan attacked.

The Hebrew root word for serpent is *nachash*. It means "to hiss, i.e. whisper a spell; generally, to prognosticate, to enchant, to learn by experience and to diligently observe."[4] His form in the Garden reveals his methodology—he operates in a hiss, in a whisper, in a suggestion or a prediction. His propositions are enchanting, as he convinces an individual that he or she must explore and experiment in order to have an understanding of what the world has to offer. His strategy has not changed today. He is still whispering and suggesting, whether through media influence, generational curses, thoughts of seduction, or peer pressure—convincing individuals to experiment with things that God never intended for us to experience.

How do you know when it's a satanic suggestion? You know because it will be cloaked in secrecy, forced by false urgency (gotta do it now!), motivated by a drive or excitement toward temporary "pleasure." It's the pressure to use drugs to escape problems; it's the drive for premarital sex or extra-marital affairs—the more illicit, the better—it's the temptation to lie, to steal, to cheat, to gossip—all activities that lead to division, to death, to destruction. According to Revelation 12:9a, *"The great dragon was hurled down—that ancient serpent called the devil, or Satan, who leads the whole world astray"* was thrown down to the earth, and he's been wreaking havoc ever since. Verses 12-17 of the same passage tell us that he is filled with fury, knowing that his time is short, and that he is actively pursuing and waging war against the Church (the woman) and its offspring (those who obey God and hold on to Jesus).

The Conspiracy

According to Ezekial 28:11-19 and Isaiah 14:12-15, the job of lucifer (the king of Tyre/satan), in fact his very nature in the highest heavenly realm, was to reflect God and to give Him glory in worship. He was the model of perfection and beauty, covered in reflective stones and anointed and ordained as a guardian. When he began to absorb the worship instead of reflecting it—corrupted by pride and his own wisdom—he was expelled from the heavens and fell to the earth. Satan doesn't appear in the Garden until Adam and Eve are brought together. He knows that mankind has been chosen, ordained, and created to extend the dominion of God from the heavens into the earthly realm. Mankind is God's new reflection, created in God's image and His likeness. Satan quickly ascertained that the key to the Kingdom was relationship because it was the mechanism God chose to use reflect Himself and to reproduce His love on the earth. He started implementing the same strategy he used in the heavens, a strategy so effective that he was able to divide the heavenly hosts and convince a third of the angels to follow him out of the presence of God. He had no authority to destroy what God had created, but he could corrupt it if mankind allowed him to undermine the authority God had delegated to them. He set out to distort and destroy God's plan for relationship, creeping into the minds and the unions of men and women and inspiring rebellion. Satan wanted the people of God to reflect his essence, so he inspired them to paint a picture of rebellion in the earth by counterfeiting the relationship pattern that God had already instituted. Satan observed that the key to increase and multiplication in the earth was through sowing seed, so he set out to sow some seeds of his own: disorder, doubt, deception, and disobedience.

 Satan wanted the people of God to reflect his essence.

The first strategy of the serpent in the Garden was to attack the order that God had instituted by planting *seeds of disorder*. God gave instruction and dominion to Adam, and in Genesis 3, satan inverted that order by giving instruction and offering dominion to woman. After speaking with satan, woman was empowered to usurp the authority of Adam and gave him instructions, and their submission to the advice offered by the serpent led to their downfall.

Many people have tried to place the blame for the Fall of mankind on Eve and/or on Adam, playing into satan's device to divide and separate people by gender. Instead, I place the blame where it belongs, with satan. He is still working to invert God's order—we see it anytime a man "shuts down" or refuses to speak up, stand up, and walk in authority within his home, the community, and the Church. When women step into the roles of pursuer, instructor, caretaker, or manipulator within romantic relationships, or when authority is usurped in congregations, satan has succeeded in inverting God's order. Both men and women are culpable and compliant when order is inverted.

Satan opened his conversation with woman by planting a *seed of doubt*. He slyly asked her, *"Did God **really** say 'You must no eat from any tree in the garden?'"* (Gen. 3:1). His strategy was to cause her to question God's instructions, and later, he caused her to question God's warning about the outcome. Seeds of doubt are planted by an assault on the truth of God's Word and God's character. It happens when satan influences an individual (or an entire culture) into believing that pornography, promiscuity, and homosexuality might be okay after all. It's when we find reasons to continue dating people God has told us are not right for us. Or when satan starts working to convince a man or woman that it is fine to stray outside of your marriage if your needs aren't being met at home. Satan works in a whisper, a thought, or a question in your mind, and he begins to twist and turn God's Word until a person is confused or content to violate it or to tolerate satan's violation of it.

The devil has been a murderer from the very beginning. His goal is to steal, kill, and destroy: to steal authority, to kill relationships, and to destroy our connection to God. According to John 8:44, *"… there is no truth in him. When he lies, he speaks his native language, for he is a liar and the father of lies."* It is in the Garden that the enemy began spreading his *seed of deception*, giving birth to lies. He deceitfully told Eve that if she ate the fruit that God forbade, she would surely not die, and he promised her that, *"[her] eyes will be opened, and [she] will be like God, knowing good and evil"* (Gen. 3:5).

 Eve was already like God, made in His image and likeness.

He promised her one thing that she already possessed and another thing that God never intended for her to acquire. She was already like God, made in His image and likeness, and God never wanted man and woman to distinguish between good and evil. They were only supposed to be exposed to *life!* The enemy deceives us the same way, convincing us that we are missing out on something by choosing to live in obedience to God. God has already promised us everything we need, and if we trust Him, the only thing we'll miss is the knowledge and consequences of sin.

The Bible says that *"when the woman **saw** that the fruit of the tree was good for food and pleasing to the eye, and also desirable for gaining wisdom, she **took** some and **ate** it. She also gave some to her husband, who was with her, and he ate it"* (Gen. 3:6). The enemy had been talking to Eve, and by verse 6, what she had been hearing about was then in her line of sight, and what she had been looking at was then within her grasp, and what was within her grasp was then within her body. The enemy always plants the *seeds of disobedience*, hiding the penalties of sin and making it seem exciting, harmless, fun, and beneficial. When satan is enticing or seducing you, he often fails to mention that the pleasure is fleeting. It can be all too easy to ignore the cost of disobedience to God and rebellion against His Word and His order. You can't wait until sin is within your grasp; you have to learn to cut off temptation when it approaches your ears and your eyes.

 When I speak of sin, I am referring to everything that demonstrates that we have missed the mark that God has for us.

When I speak of sin, I am referring to everything that demonstrates that we have missed the mark that God has for us— sexual immorality, gossip, pride, selfishness, fear, anxiety, depression, anger, unforgiveness, and so on. You must become aware of how the enemy slithers into your life. He has no new tricks—what weapon is he forming against you? When you recognize the enemy's devices and how he attacks your life, you can resist his advances. When you walk in your dominion and take authority—over your mind, your emotions, your body, and your household—the Bible promises that the enemy will flee from you. If we, the children of God, can come into agreement and take a stand in this generation to truly reflect the image of God and to refuse compromise, the enemy may come at us in one direction, but the strength of God's relationship and love toward us will send him running seven different ways.

The Consequences

The seeds planted by the serpent produced an immediate harvest of dysfunction that is still growing and expanding today. Adam and Eve's compromise produced a curse upon the serpent and upon the land, and it generated consequences for the human race. God kept His word, reminding Adam and Eve that disobedience and the consumption of the fruit from the tree of the knowledge of good and evil would lead to death. Though they continued to breathe, the things that made life worth living were immediately subtracted. As soon as they consumed the fruit,

> *Then the eyes of both of them were opened, and they realized they were naked; so they sewed fig leaves together and made coverings for themselves. ...and they hid from the Lord God among the trees... (Genesis 3:7-8).*

Immediately, they lost their innocence and their intimacy with God and with one another by exchanging the sanctity of their union for an affair with the enemy. They *knew* both good and evil. They were able to reproduce good and evil in their relationships with God and one another, but they were disconnected from their access to the source of life.

There was an instantaneous reversal of the promise of God in operation in their lives, as they exchanged the blessing that rests on a godly relationship for the curse that rests on one that distorts His reflection. As made evident in the verdicts read to Adam and Eve, compromise creates distorted, dysfunctional relationships:

1) It introduced difficulty and pain in the process of having and raising children.

2) It reversed and misplaced the direction of desire, causing woman to chase man.

3) It replaced submission with subordination, laying a foundation for inequality and abuse.

4) It cursed the ground, making it difficult for a man to provide for himself and his household and to make any progress or get ahead (see Gen. 3:16-18).

I have been charged by God to let you know that there is immediate fallout for disconnecting from God. Sin has consequences.

 Sin habits and lifestyles do not create the atmosphere necessary for healthy, productive relationships or for spiritual increase or abundance.

Just because your HIV or pregnancy test comes back negative, or no one knows what you're doing, does not mean that you get away with it. Sin habits and lifestyles do not create the atmosphere necessary for healthy, productive relationships or for spiritual increase or abundance. In fact, sin is the instant cause of division and disagreement, and it always leads to exposure and to shame. Satan is still trying to influence your thoughts and behavior, attempting to trick you into disobedience and doubt so that you'll forfeit the promises of God in exchange for stuff that looks good and tastes good but produces death. Don't forfeit the blessing God has in store for you, in exchange for the curses the enemy wants you to live under.

Dysfunctional Relationship: A Biblical Concept, a Modern Reality

The seeds satan planted in the Garden produced curses that manifested in relationships all the way through the Bible, and that continue even today. Every problem that we see in modern relationships, everything discussed in the previous chapter, can be traced to a biblical origin.

For baby-mama drama, look no further than Abram and Sarai. They received a promise from God but produced their own solution when it didn't manifest in the timing they wanted. Sarai gave Abram permission to sleep with her servant Hagar, and then she got jealous and forced him to get rid of Hagar and the child (see Gen. 16 and 21). The fruit of satan's seeds of disorder and doubt is clearly evidenced in this account, although it is overshadowed by God's commitment to His covenant with Abram.

For homosexuality, sexual immorality, and "gang bangs" look at Genesis 19. The Bible says that two angels were sent to destroy the cities Sodom and Gomorrah because of the people's great sin. Abraham begged that the city be spared if any righteousness could be found there. The angels fellowshipped and lodged with the family of Abraham's nephew, Lot. When the men of the city heard about the angels at Lot's home, *all* of them gathered and demanded to have access to the angels to have intercourse with them. Jude describes the scene in those cities and the behavior of their inhabitants, *"Even as Sodom and Gomorrha, and the cities about them in like manner,*

*giving themselves over to **fornication**, and going after **strange flesh**...*"
(Jude 7 KJV). In this text, we know that the citizens of Sodom were completely driven by their own lustful desires, even if they were contrary to God's laws and ordinances.

When Lot offers his daughters to satisfy their lusts, the men refuse, absolutely driven toward their unnatural desires. *"Fornication"* in the passage speaks of sexual perversion, and the *"strange flesh"* in the passage refers to them seeking sexual fulfillment outside of God's design. Today, a "Sodomite" is an individual who participates in a sexual act that is not vaginal, that does not include physical parts of humankind designed for reproduction. Satan's seeds of disobedience and disorder are still at work, convincing millions of people that fulfillment of their unnatural desire and consuming something forbidden is a part of their identity or their "rights," instead of it being a complete violation and mockery of God's design.

For the desperate women dealing with a lack of available men, continue in the same chapter in Genesis to the story of Lot's daughters. According to the text, Lot and his family fled from Sodom, and when Lot's wife turned to look back at what God delivered her from, she was turned into a pillar of salt. Lot and his daughters settled into a cave, and the oldest daughter began to convince the youngest daughter that they needed to continue their family line. They determined that there were no available men in their proximity, so they seduced the only man in their presence. They got their father drunk, slept with him, and conceived Moab and Ammon, whose descendents continued to reproduce dysfunction and evil throughout the Old Testament. In this story, doubt led to disorder, which produced deception and disobedience. Satan's seeds are still producing fruit today. Just like Lot's daughters, women still perceive a lack of available men and respond in desperation, often scheming and seducing in hopes of self-preservation.

Satan's seeds are still producing fruit today.

For a twisted love triangle, you don't have to watch *The Maury Povich* or *Jerry Springer Show*. Just check out the story of Rachel, Leah, and Abraham's grandson Jacob in Genesis 29. Jacob is caught in the middle of his two wives, who are sisters, and he seems to love every minute of it! The Bible says that Rachel was beautiful and lovely in form, and that Jacob loved her more than Leah, who was *"tender eyed"* (see Gen. 29:16-17,30 KJV). Rachel had beauty and a body, but she was infertile; on the other hand, Leah was not as attractive, but she was extremely productive. Leah was insecure, felt rejected, and jealous of Rachel, and Rachel was insecure and felt jealous of Leah, and Jacob played them both. Each competed against her sister and used her body to give birth in an attempt to gain and keep the attention of one man. Sound familiar?

The first instance of the "pull-out method" involved Jacob's grandson, Onan. Onan was espoused to Tamar, his former sister-in-law, in order to help her produce a child. He had access to her body for the purpose of helping her reproduce. Onan helped himself to Tamar but with no desire to help her produce anything. The Bible says that, *"...whenever he lay with his brother's wife, he spilled his semen on the ground to keep from producing offspring..."* (Gen. 38:9). Onan was comfortable experiencing the pleasure of Tamar's body, but he took advantage of her and refused to commit or contribute anything to her.

Instead of painting a picture of Christ as a kinsman redeemer, Onan got his pleasure and then refused to continue the process. He ruined the portrait and the principle, and God saw his act as evil and Onan died immediately. Tamar reproduced Onan's unrighteousness by dressing as a prostitute and manipulating her father-in-law, Judah, in order to ensure her social standing and her financial future. Out of her hurt and anger, Tamar was willing to trade her reputation and respect for stability and a son, Perez. There is a definite danger in climax without commitment, and there is no benefit in using a woman for her body and spilling seed upon the ground. Such acts, then and now, are evil derivatives of satan's plan to distort God's reflection in relationships.

 There is a definite danger in climax without commitment, and there is no benefit in using a woman for her body and spilling seed upon the ground.

For more fruit of satan's seeds, read no further than two of the greatest men whose lives are recorded in Scripture—the father-son duo of David and Solomon. David's relationship with Bathsheba is a portrait of the abuse of and the attraction to power. Bathsheba, apparently discontent with her husband Uriah who was away at war, decided to bathe on the roof. Her decision doesn't make much sense, unless you know that she lived within view of the palace.

According to Second Samuel 11:2-4, she had *"purified herself from her uncleanness,"* setting the scene for seduction and intimacy. When David sent for her, Bathsheba did not pass up the opportunity to sleep with the king, and she later sent word to David that she was pregnant after she had returned home. David, who was described as a man after God's own heart, was attracted to her flesh and to the excitement of the illicit affair. He was out of order and abused his position, and the seed produced out of their lust could not survive. Instead of leading his men in war, David found himself caught in adultery, lying and murdering to cover his tracks.

Instead of walking in modesty and service to her husband and her own household, Bathsheba acted as a seductress who baited a king with her beauty, her booty, and after he returned to his own household, a baby. Satan is still up to his old schemes. How many men of influence and authority—anointed and elected—have misused their positions and power instead of walking in integrity and leadership. And how many women have made that easier to do by overlooking a decent, hardworking man in exchange for the opportunity to get close to the palace?

 Bathsheba acted as a seductress who baited a king with her beauty, her booty, and after he returned to his own household, a baby.

David and Bathsheba lost a son, the fruit of their illicit affair. Their second son Solomon was destined to become heir to David's throne, and unfortunately, his indiscretions. In Solomon, those indiscretions were multiplied. David couldn't resist one woman; Solomon couldn't resist any of them. In order to continue the reign of David's descendents on the throne, Solomon was instructed to *"…be strong, show yourself a man, and observe what the Lord your God requires: Walk in His ways, and keep His decrees and commands, His laws and requirements…"* (1 Kings 2:2-3). Solomon possessed more wisdom and more wealth than any man on earth, he completed the temple his father could not, and his kingdom was united and blessed above measure. All that God required was that he walk in integrity and refuse to worship other gods.

In First Kings 11:1, we learn that *"King Solomon, however, loved **many** foreign women"*—Pharoah's daughter, Moabites, Ammonites, Edomites, Sidonians, and Hittites, all the enemies of God. Solomon ignored God's command to reject intermarriage and unequal yoking. He was willing to forfeit both the well-being of the kingdom and his son's inheritance of the throne because he was unwilling to reject the sexual relationships that were leading him away from God. Satan still perverts sex and entices individuals away from their inheritance today. Solomon's "love" for his 700 wives and 300 concubines eventually led to the rebellion of his sons and the kingdom, centuries of compromise against God and broken covenant, generations of bondage and slavery for the Israelites, and the eventual destruction of 11 out of 12 of the tribes of Israel. Wisdom, wealth, and the favor of God did not prevent satan's seeds of disobedience and disorder from producing fruit through Solomon. When individuals choose sex over God, entire nations are affected.

 When individuals choose sex over God, entire nations are affected.

The patterns of dysfunction continue throughout the Old and New Testaments, as evidenced in the relationships of Samson and Delilah in Judges, Ammon and Tamar in Second Samuel 13, Ahab and Jezebel in Second Kings, Hosea and his promiscuous wife throughout the Book of Hosea, and in cities like Rome and Ephesus in the New Testament. The examples just discussed at length are unique only because they are all connected to the genealogy of Jesus. That's right—the Messiah was born out of the bloodline of Abraham, Jacob, Judah, David, and Solomon. And you thought your family was dysfunctional!

Satan planted a seed to destroy God's plans for relationships. The joke was on him—the very thing he tried to corrupt produced Christ and ensured his own defeat. And satan has planned to destroy all of us, as we inherited the dysfunction of our mothers and our fathers and created our own. Guess what? He has ensured his own defeat in our lives and in our relationships, too! As soon as we return to God and to God's way, the power of Christ gives us the ability to reproduce righteousness and to triumph over the enemy every time. What the enemy meant for evil, God intends for good, "*...to accomplish what is now being done, the saving of many lives*" (Gen. 50:20).

Not only do relationship problems have a biblical origin, but they also have a biblical solution. God has always had a plan to fix the pattern, to reconcile the relationships between God and His people and between men and women. Satan's plan was to separate, but he had no idea that separation was already built into the strategy of God. God had already turned His love toward us, and nothing, even the devil's schemes and our disobedience, is strong enough to keep God from loving us. It is still in God's plan to bring together godly men and women to show the world that His love still exists, and that it is the most powerful substance on the earth.

 ## The devil hates godly marriage.

The devil hates godly marriage—not only does it reflect God's love and His dominion, but it also is a reminder to satan of his defeat in the heavens, at the cross, and in the earth. The power of the cross is that it closes breaches. It heals, cleans, delivers, and reestablishes God's pattern in the earth. Not only does God give us the opportunity to escape the influence of this world and return to the purpose and the promise of relationships as He intended, but He also has given us an eternal gift—the opportunity to be reconciled back to Him.

Satan's strategic attacks have not changed since the beginning— he is still working to gain influence and, consequently, to attract worship. All he needs is a listening audience, hence his use of the platforms of media, culture, and word-of-mouth (that's right, you!). When I think of him, I picture King Cobra, the notorious villain opposing Mario and Luigi in the Super Mario Bros. video games. (That's right—from the *original* Nintendo, with the cartridges you had to shake up and blow into!) In the game, King Cobra always showed up at the end of each level, and he was always standing between Mario and his prize, the castle and his princess. King

Cobra had spikes and threw hammers, so hand-to-hand conflict was foolish. The only way to defeat King Cobra was to jump on his head!

I hate the devil (actually, the feeling is mutual). I'm so glad that the seed of woman crushed satan's head 2,000 years ago, and I'm glad that God gives us the opportunity to stomp on it a little more in our praise offerings and by living lives of holiness and worship. This book is my foot-stomp, my attempt to get him back for every relationship that he has destroyed around me and for every attack he has launched against my life. I hope that the knowledge of his strategies empowers you to do the same, to reclaim your relationship with God and with your spouse (current or coming), and to crack the devil's skull one more time, in Jesus' name and to the glory of God.

The prophet Isaiah wrote,

So shall they fear the name of the Lord from the west, and His glory from the rising of the sun. When the enemy shall come in like a flood, the Spirit of the Lord shall lift up a standard against him (Isaiah 59:19 KJV).

Isaiah foresaw a day when nations would repent from their transgression, and their Savior would have vengeance against the enemy that caused their fall. In that day, the prophet says that the people will fear the Lord and, consequently, gain wisdom, and when the enemy attacks, the Spirit of the Lord will drive him away. Today is the day, and that Spirit—the same Spirit that raised Jesus from the dead and that quickens our mortal bodies—lives within us. God has given us so many weapons to use against satan's devices—the blood of the Lamb, the name of Jesus, the sword of the Spirit, the shield of faith, the word of our testimonies, the truth of God's Word. In the next section, we will sharpen our weapons, exploring God's definitions and example of love and covenant. I am confident that the knowledge of God's love and divine plan for us will transform our lives, as we apply God's principles and raise the standard for ourselves, our relationships, and our society. In the words of Pastor T.D. Jakes, "Get ready! Get ready! Get ready!"

Endnotes

1. James Strong, *Strong's Exhaustive Concordance of the Bible* (Nashville, TN: Holman Bible Publishers, n.d.), #H1288. Ibid., #H1320

2. Ibid., #H954.

3. Ibid., #H5175.

4. Ibid., #H5172.

SECTION 2

Here Comes the Bride(Groom): Reunion, Redemption, and Restoration

Chapter 3

THE PURSUIT PATTERN: A PERFECT LOVE FOR IMPERFECT PEOPLE

"Love must be as much a light as it is a flame." —Henry David Thoreau

In the previous section, we explored the crisis of love, establishing a performative definition of love and relationships based on a combination of pop culture influence, recent statistics, and our own experiences. The calamity deepens with our understanding that love has become more game-like than God-like. Based on what we watch and experience, from *Flavor of Love* and *Dr. Phil* and into our own living rooms, courtrooms, and congregations, our definitions and practices of love reveal that modern relationships are defined by brokenness instead of bonding and blessing. They cause more heartbreak than healing and create more grief than glory.

Our culture has trivialized our understanding of love. It has stripped marriage and sexuality of their meanings and has marked them with dysfunction. We have traced the dysfunction we see in our understanding of relationships back to its origin: satan, and his goal to infiltrate, influence, and pervert God's original purpose for love, sexuality, and marriage. We have identified his conspiracy to separate us from God and from one another, and we understand his tactics: disorder, doubt, deception, and disobedience. The consequences of satan's influence are evident in every aspect of our modern society, and the results are disastrous. Despite what our society says, our investigation clearly reveals that love is not, and should never be, a game.

We learned the statistics and the results of the enemy's deceptions about relationships from the previous chapter, but it is so much more important that we acknowledge the truth: Real love exists! And so do the things that are supposed to be woven into the fabric of a relationship: commitment, purity, comfort, acceptance, support, and understanding. Unfortunately, over time, marriages that exhibit these characteristics have become the exception instead of the rule. It was never intended to be that way.

Despite the statistics and news reports, God intended marriage to be the permanent union of man and woman, a perfect reflection of His relationship with mankind. Our human love was designed as an extension of the divine, the essence of everything that God is. And sex was created to be a deliberate, heavenly, holy, awesome worship experience—the physical union of two bodies into one in the presence and with the blessing of God. To find the purpose and the pattern for love, we shouldn't look toward romantic comedies, R & B music, or reality television. To know love, to understand sex, to learn relationship, and to fathom marriage, we must look toward the truth of God's Word.

A Godly Example

When I really started to seek God for a new and better understanding of love, He provided me with a real-life example of the type of love that He purposes for His people. I knew that God loved me, but I also needed to see that it was still possible to have a loving relationship with results that differed from what I had been exposed to. In the midst of an extremely "challenging" work environment, God connected me to a supervisor who offered more than assignments and deadlines. Having been happily married for over 40 years, this woman offered godly advice and encouragement, and her love story and testimony increased my faith by demonstrating that "happily ever after" is more than a possibility. It's God's promise to His children.

 Marriage is God's promise to His children.

Dr. Johnnie and Mrs. Sandra Cannon grew up together in Georgia. They began their courtship as high school students—he was the smart, quiet athlete, while she was the equally intelligent, though more outgoing, beauty. For the young couple, courtship consisted of only conversation and television during hour-long visits on Sunday evenings at her parents' home. Their communication and friendship grew into love and commitment, and they knew that they wanted to spend the rest of their lives together. They attended separate colleges, deciding to marry during Christmas break of their senior year. Their families planned their ceremonies on a shoestring budget, and the couple returned to their respective campuses to complete their education. After graduation, with college degrees and less than $100 in hand, the young couple decided to move to California so that he could pursue his doctoral degree in engineering. They had no idea what to expect, but they believed that as long as God was leading them and they had each other, they could make it.

Today, Dr. Cannon is a head scientist with a federal government lab in Tennessee, and Mrs. Cannon is continuing her 30-year career in education and youth services. With three children and two grandchildren, they are partners in life and in family, in serving their community, and in ministry. I asked Mrs. Cannon if they ever had conflict and inquired how they made it through difficult times. Her reply: "At the end of the day, he is my best friend.... We have shared everything, and no matter what, we know that we love and need each other." In other words, failure is not an option—whatever they face, they face as one.

In those lunch hour conversations, our meetings turned into mentoring moments. I learned a great deal about love from Mrs. Cannon and her example. She taught me that commitment isn't reserved for a certain level of success or achievement. It happens in God's timing, and finding your partner is designed to make the journey toward achievement easier and more rewarding. I learned that your mate is supposed to be the person who holds your secrets, awakens your passions, covers your shortcomings, intercedes in struggle, shares inside jokes, and fuels your dreams. She also taught me that love—like trust, honesty, faithfulness, and dedication—is a choice, maintained by understanding and the ability to laugh together.

 In regard to love, marriage, and sexuality, we need a change of mind and a change of heart.

Right now, I reassert the challenge extended by God and discussed in this book's Introduction. In regard to love, marriage, and sexuality, we need a change of mind and a change of heart. According to Romans 12:1-2, we must reject the world's patterns (and therefore its products) in regard to love and relationships and begin to seek transformation. We can't act like the world. We can't believe like the world. We can't love like the world. We can't marry like the world. Before we can discuss relationships any further, we must renew our minds through reviewing the Scriptures so that we can understand and approach love and relationships the way that God intended. Only then can we experience the real love and godly relationships that await us. Finding that love, creating those relationships, is not easy, but it is worth it. The process is supernatural. Beautiful. Forever.

Reclaiming and Redefining Love as Divine

Any exhaustive attempt to review all of the Scriptures in the Bible that deal with love would lead to an encyclopedic volume. In fact, the word *love* (and its variants by tense and number) appears 697 times in the New International Version. Love is the key to understanding the Old Testament. It is the key to understanding the New Testament. It existed before the beginning of time, and it will extend past time's extinguishing. To God, love is the principal, preeminent thing. God takes love so seriously that He makes it the basis of all the commandments—the foundational principle of His law, His greatest desire for and from us.

Accordingly, He instructs us to love Him with all our hearts, souls, and minds, and to love our neighbors as ourselves (see Deut. 6:5; Matt. 22:37-39). God provides us with verse after verse of description and explanation because His desire is for us to know the fullness of His love—intellectually and intuitively. Listed below are several of the aforementioned verses, with an explication of the text's central message about His love.

- His love leads to blessing, productivity, and healing. See Deuteronomy 7:13-15.

- His love is reciprocal and assured. See Proverbs 8:17.

- His love covers a multitude of sins. See Proverbs 10:12; 1 John 4:8.

- His love is the mark of a disciple. See John 13:34.

- His love is strong enough to cause one to give up his life. See John 15:13.

- His love fulfills the law. It does no harm. It does not hurt. See Romans 13:8-10.

- His love is so righteous it doesn't have to be right. It refuses to offend. See Romans 14:15.

- His love is not self-seeking. It edifies and builds. See 1 Corinthians 8:1.

- His love frees one to serve and to pursue purpose. It doesn't bite. It doesn't devour. See Galatians 5:13-15.

- His love is completely humble, gentle, and patient. It is what makes it possible for us to bear with one another. See Ephesians 4:2.

- His love empowers us to imitate Him, as His children. It demands that we flee immorality and live as His holy people. See Ephesians 5:2.

- His love is not evidenced in words or tongue, but in actions and truth. See 1 John 3:18.

According to First Corinthians 13,

Love is patient, love is kind. It does not envy, it does not boast, it is not proud. It is not rude, it is not self-seeking, it is not easily angered, it keeps no record of wrongs. Love does not delight in evil but rejoices with the truth. It always protects, always trusts, always hopes, always perseveres. Love never fails... (1 Corinthians 13:4-8).

Allow me to translate: Love is willing to wait for fulfillment and doesn't mind suffering. Love is gentle and soft spoken. Love has no reason to check a person's voice mails or text messages. It does not call names, ignore someone, or "catch an attitude." It does not make lists of expectations or demands; it does not bring up the past or have running arguments about the same things. Love does not delight in cheating, deception, manipulation, or taking advantage of a person. Love gets excited about honesty and vulnerability. Love *always* shelters, has confidence, expects the best, and survives. Are these the characteristics of the love that you are pursuing? Is this the love that you have experienced? That you are offering to a mate? Not exactly?

The love that is described in this passage is a supernatural love, far beyond anything that we can offer or hope for without supernatural means. In First John 4:7-21, God gives us the recipe for this supernatural love. It's Him! John admonishes us to *"love one another, for love comes from God. Everyone who loves has been born of God and knows God. ...because God is love"* (1 John 4:7-8). Not only does God live in us, but His love is made complete in us *through the power of the cross and through His Spirit.* Any love detached from Him and distant from the definitions provided is a complete perversion, a cheap imitation, a repulsive counterfeit of what God intended. God's love is 24 karat gold—purified by fire, stronger than any other metal, and incapable of breaking. But the love we most often encounter is gold-plated—fading, staining, and holding no real value.

Examine the Details: Separating Real Love From the Counterfeit

I've always been fascinated by the way things of value are copied for mass consumption. As a child, my parents could not afford the most up-to-date, name-brand $100 sneakers for my sister and myself (and even if we could, my mother would not have purchased them). We wore our multi-color "buddies," and graduated to Fikes (fake nikes) and to the Adidas-like shoes (with only two stripes) from Payless. And yes, I'm still recovering from the jokes I heard about those shoes...

Though the source of scorn and ridicule for children and teens, owning a "replica" as an adult is considered a cost-effective strategy. Whether it's Gucci and Coach bags or Rolex watches, bootleg movies, or downloaded albums and copied/burnt CDs, our culture encourages individuals to invest in counterfeits. Though the counterfeiters may do an excellent job of making their products superficially resemble the originals, there is a distinct difference in their value and in how they hold up over time. As a result, counterfeiting is a crime.

When fakes flood a market, it diminishes the value of the real items they counterfeit. When the fakes break down or tear up, it gives the original a bad reputation. What we describe as "sex," as "love," as "marriage," as "a relationship," is often so far from the real thing and so pervasive in our society that we wouldn't know the real thing if it slapped us in the face. We're using God's terms to describe things that are no longer connected to Him, and it's giving Him a bad name.

 We're using God's terms to describe things that are no longer connected to Him, and it's giving Him a bad name.

Can you spot a fake? The process can be difficult, until you examine the real product and its counterfeit side by side. Let's examine the clues:

Counterfeit Clue #1: Inferior Quality

Fake products are always constructed of synthetic or man-made materials. These materials are not only cheaper, but they are also less durable than natural fibers and materials. The soles on fake Nikes are made of a synthetic rubber. Fake purses are often made of a weaker material than genuine leather. As a result, the products are susceptible to wear and tear, and are not resilient over time. The same is true for relationships: real love, real friendship, and real commitment are not denied or destroyed by the pain of trials or the passage of time because they are God-ordained, God-driven, and God-favored. Man-made relationships are destined to fall apart.

Counterfeit Clue #2: Inconsistent Clarity

Fake products feature details that are not sharp, clear, or in focus. A buyer should beware of blurriness of the logo, on the label, or of the wording or numbers anywhere on the product. Blurriness indicates distortion, a defect not present in the original. On a $100 bill, the portrait, borders, serial numbers, and other details are so clear that they cannot be reproduced in duplication. The easiest way to tell a counterfeit is to look for blurred lines and missing details. Here's the application: real love and genuine relationship are marked by clarity of thought, speech, action, intention, and boundaries—any confusion, inconsistency, or blurriness may indicate a counterfeit counterpart or a counterfeit relationship.

Counterfeit Clue #3: Irregular Pattern

Fake products have patterns that are not consistent with the original. Perhaps the patterns are skewed or twisted, or the proportions are not as they should be. Even when the product seems right on the outside, it is almost impossible to duplicate the original manufacturer's efforts on the inside, and it's rare for the buyer to care enough to look. On a fake Gucci or Louis Vuitton purse, the label and material inside is often missing. The colors and details found in Nike shoes are absent in the interior and insole of the fakes. The intricate details and Swiss movements of the gears of the Rolex watch are non-existent in the interior of the replica. To know if the love or the relationship you have bought into is counterfeit, you just need to look beyond the superficial. All you have to do is look inside.

In a good counterfeit, the differences are subtle—unnoticeable to the untrained eye, the ignorant buyer, or the desperate consumer making a hasty decision. All of the experts agree: the only way to develop the ability to distinguish between an original and a counterfeit, to know the genuine article from the fake, is to *know* the real. It takes time and effort to truly know what is real, and when one knows the characteristics of the real article, it becomes easier to spot a fake. The difference in the details is only apparent in consistent and continuous comparison.

Aren't you tired of counterfeit relationships? Of falling in love only to have that love fade? Of having your excitement become disappointment and your intimate desire become plain old sex? If you feel like God has more for you than what you have been experiencing—than what the examples around you show— you're right! The good news is this: God wants you to experience real love—to know relationships and understand sexuality and embrace marriage *His* way. The bad news (which is good, even though it many not feel like it right now) is that you will have to give up your counterfeits, the fakes, the bad habits, the attitudes, and the sin in your life right now to be able to obtain what God has ordained for you.

 God wants you to experience real love—to know relationships and understand sexuality and embrace marriage His way.

Ain't Nothing Like the Real Thing: Time for a Love Upgrade

So many of us have blamed God for love gone wrong, when He tried to warn us it was counterfeit all along. If we had spent more time understanding real love before we started looking for it, perhaps we may not have been deceived. Before we go any further, you must understand that there are two different types of love. There is *God-love*—perfect and complete—based in the Spirit and manifested in a way that requires initial sacrifice, but ultimately builds and brings life. And there is the counterfeit, *world-love*— imperfect and "lacking something"—based in the flesh and manifested in ways that may feel good initially, but ultimately divide, depress, and lead to death. Both types of love behave and feel real, but they begin in two different ways and produce different results. The only way to distinguish God-love from world-love, the real from the fake, is to examine the details and to stop making excuses when love is all wrong.

Song of Solomon is the book in the Bible traditionally believed to describe the progression of the marriage of Solomon and the Shulammite (or the "Lover" and the "Beloved") from courtship to consummation. At the end of the lover's tale, the Beloved gives an introduction to the biblical, supernatural definition of love:

...for love is as strong as death, its jealousy unyielding as the grave. It burns like blazing fire, like a mighty flame. Many waters cannot quench love; rivers cannot wash it away... (Song of Solomon 8:6-7).

According to the text, love is as invincible and as permanent as death itself. It is an all-consuming fire, unable to be extinguished, denied, or completely satisfied. The text later teaches us that love cannot be manipulated, contrived, or purchased. You don't fall into love, nor can you fall out of it. Instead, you are supposed to grow into it and to grow as a result of it. Love, like a fire, is designed to increase and to spread. The Amplified Bible helps to clarify the origin of this type of love, stating that the fire of love is *"a most vehement flame [the very flame of the Lord]"* (Song of Sol. 8:6 AMP). Love originates in the nature of God Himself. It is a work, a gift, of the Spirit.

 You don't fall into love, nor can you fall out of it. Instead, you are supposed to grow into it and to grow as a result of it.

For too many years, the believer has been living according to a worldly definition of love, influenced by satan's deception and manufactured by individuals who have no idea what true love is, how true love acts, where true love is to be found, or why true love is as powerful as it is. Instead of allowing love to be the fire birthed out of our spirits and consuming the other parts of us, we have minimized it to a fire we feel only in our bodies and in our emotions.

...the tongue is a small part of the body, but it makes great boasts. Consider what a great forest is set on fire by a small

spark. The tongue also is a fire, a world of evil among the parts of the body. It corrupts the whole person, sets the whole course of his life on fire, and is itself set on fire by hell (James 3:5-6).

World-love is uncertain, intense, and dangerously fleeting.

God-love begins with an intimate relationship with the Lord, obedience to His Word, alignment with His purpose, and a bond created through the sharing of time, experiences, interests, and direction. This fire consumes *without burning*—it is Moses' burning bush, or the fire on the mountain witnessed from the Israelite camps. It is the fire of glory—beautiful, illuminating, eternal, life-changing. God-love is holistic—blessing your spirit, your mind and emotions, and your body! No one tries to stop it, and if anyone attempted to do so, he or she would fail. Because it is not based in the natural, it cannot be stopped by natural means—it cannot fail.

World-love, on the other hand, is tongue-based intimacy—both literally and lyrically. Lust connected to the works of the flesh always begins with your tongue—it's a kiss on the ear, on the neck, on your lips, and on "other places." Mental/emotional love is connected to the spoken word, to feelings expressed ignorantly or prematurely, to promises (often broken), to discussed plans and orchestrated futures. The tongue causes a fire, a passionate desire that, when disconnected from the Spirit, is designed to consume and *to destroy*. It is the fire of the dragon. It is the forest fire that destroyed homes in California. World-love is as dangerous as the riots in L.A., in Watts, and in Detroit. It is the type of illicit passion that shows up in news reports, that consumes careers, that ends marriages, that divides ministries, that leads to clinical depression, suicidal thoughts, and double homicides. This love, removed from the context of God and His example, is cloaked in secrecy and is never satisfied. It destroys, then moves on to its next target. Unlike God's love, it is destined for failure, and it stops burning as soon as there is nothing left to burn down.

Love, removed from the context of God and His example, is cloaked in secrecy and is never satisfied.

Do you find yourself being burned or burning others in relationships again and again? Keep your tongue (your actions and your words) in check! According to James 1:26, *"If anyone considers himself religious and yet does not keep a tight rein on his tongue, he deceives himself and his religion is worthless."* The consequences of a promiscuous tongue is self-deception—you may be convincing yourself of a love or a course of actions that God never intended and inviting physical, emotional, and spiritual consequences that you don't want. According to James 3, a person who can control his or her tongue is perfect, able to keep everything else in check.

I submit to you that it is time for you to grow into a different kind of love. Paul teaches us that,

When perfection comes, the imperfect disappears. When I was a child, I talked like a child, I reasoned like a child. When I became a man, I put childish ways behind me (1 Corinthians 13:10-11).

Truth be told, all the statistics reveal that there are too many children playing with fire. Most people begin experimenting with love far too soon and are marked by those experiences. It's time to grow up and stop pretending, and to prepare for and experience what is real. We must grow in our knowledge of God and His love in order to grow into loving relationships, without the hurt, anger, and disappointment that we have experienced and caused for others. If you grow up, the love and relationships you enter and build will begin to grow as well. When you know the perfect love of the Father, the immature, immoral love of this world becomes less and less appealing.

Are you unsure about what type of love you are seeking, or what type of love you are living? This chart clarifies the differences in the eternal love God established in His Kingdom and the love that satan perverted for this world and this age. Evaluate yourself and locate your experiences—identifying the category that most reflects where you are in your relationships will help you discover if you are prepared for or are walking in the love that God reserves for His sons and His daughters, or if you're comfortable with the counterfeit.

GOD-LOVE	WORLD-LOVE
Perfect and upright	Imperfect, flawed, perverted
Supernatural—more than expected	Natural—less than expected, or no expectation
Edifies the spirit, engages the heart/mind, electrifies the body	Satisfies the flesh, but only temporarily, and is followed by guilt and consequences
Produces life	Leads to death or dysfunction
Exhibits grace and forgiveness	Generates anger and the desire for revenge
Balance—both give because they want to give, which means both also receive	Manipulation—both give only to get something back (sex, money, attention, commitment, approval, etc.)
Marked by trust and safety	Marked by fear and insecurity
Consistent unity and agreement	Consistent division and argument
Shared vision	Inability to see eye to eye
Bonding in righteousness	Bondage to sin
Leads to worship—proximity to God	Leads to idolatry—distance from God
Fueled by truth/openness	Fueled by lies/deception
Manifested—God builds the relationship after He builds you individually; then together, you build the Kingdom, a family, and a legacy	Manufactured—requires you to build it, to "work on" the relationship or "work on" your partner or "prove" something
Complete	Partial, feelings that "something is missing"

GOD-LOVE	WORLD-LOVE
Commitment	Cowardice
Order	Confusion
Attraction based on a divine connection, common experience, and shared interests and direction—increases over time	Attraction based on physical attributes, flirtation, and "chemistry"—all the things that fade over time
Led by the Spirit; God is the head	Led by satan, the man, or the woman; the "stronger" (or louder) partner is the head
Mutual respect and adoration	Lack of understanding and appreciation
Sees their love as a blessing and responds in gratitude and a desire to serve	Always looking for the next best thing; afraid of "missing out" on something better, so never content
Full of compliments	Full of complaints
Similarities attract and differences complete	Opposites attract, then differences repel
Birthed out of healing	Leads to a cycle of heartbreak
Temporary sacrifice followed by a lifetime of pleasure	Temporary pleasure followed by a lifetime of sacrifice and/or suffering
Two become one	Two remain two
Actions based on what will please God	Actions based on what may please the other person
Friendship, teamwork, and partnership	Hostility, opposition, and warfare
Accessible to God's people only—spiritually mature, consecrated in lifestyle, separated in mindset and attitude	Accessible to all people—gay/straight, saved/unsaved, mature/immature, working/unemployed
Leads to increase and favor	Leaves you broke and broken

World-Love: A Case Study in Counterfeiting and Chemistry

Chris is the guy who, until I received the revelation in this chapter, held the title of my "first love." He was *fine*: 6 feet, 5 inches tall; athletic build; caramel skin; smooth, deep voice; perfect smile and hairline. The brother was amazing. We met in a club when I was a 20-year-old college student. My friends and I were commanding all the attention on the dance floor, and he was posted up along a wall. Every time our eyes met, sparks began to fly. I was dancing, and he was talking with his homeboys, but our attention was focused completely upon each other the entire night. We kept eye contact and flirted until he found his way over to me. We talked until the club closed down, and then he walked me to the car and asked for my phone number. Our first phone conversation lasted eight hours. In the very early hours of the morning, we confessed our secrets and our fears, discussed our strained relationships with our exes and with family members, and we promised to always be there for one another. We ended our first phone call, professing our love for one another, and the most amazing thing is we meant it.

On our first date, we went to the movies, but we couldn't tell you which movie or what it was about because soon after it started we were all over each other. Our first kiss was magical—romantic music in the background, birds chirping, confetti flying—yes, all that. It lasted about three hours—from the movie theater to the backseat of his SUV. I'd never felt anything like it. That date was followed by a whirlwind summer romance. We lived almost an hour apart, so we spent our nights together on the phone and our weekends on dates that started innocently and progressed intimately. He was smart and talented and driven, a rapper and aspiring urban fashion icon who'd left college to pursue his dreams. Our times together were exciting and adventurous, and being with him made me feel special, beautiful, and important—all the things that I did not feel on my own.

 Our phone calls and visits became more and more intense. We were in love.

When I returned to college that fall, we made all kinds of promises to one another—to make the three-hour drive twice a month to visit, to talk every day and pray together every night, to stay faithful and to pursue our goals until we were able to be together permanently. When he drove me back to campus, we developed a list of our short-term and long-term goals. He took my list back to his home and reminded me daily of what I was working toward, and I placed his list upon my wall, encouraging him to stay focused on his pursuit. Our phone calls and visits became more and more intense. We were in love.

About six months into the relationship, everything began to change. We argued more and talked less. My happiness and excitement became insecurity, irritation, and disappointment. He developed a bitterness that I never understood and reacted in ways that indicated a deep-seated anger that had nothing to do with our relationship. I used to complain that he had changed—then I realized that it had taken that long for me to see him for who he really was. My Prince Charming was really a frog! Okay...so maybe he wasn't a frog. It just became very clear that we were very different people, with very different perspectives, and very different expectations of love and life and relationships.

My focus was on handling responsibility—working, finishing school, ministry, purpose. His focus was on building his career— which included many nights of "networking," hanging out at clubs and with his friends. He didn't even believe in marriage; in fact, he thought that it would ruin a relationship. I, on the other hand, was looking forward to starting a family—already committed to the idea that he was my husband and waiting for marriage before taking the final step of sexual intercourse. I thought that I could teach him what love was and heal his pain, but the more I tried to express my version of love to him (continuing our daily conversations, expressing my devotion to him, pressing him toward prayer, pushing him to go back to school, going broke helping him financially, encouraging his goals, and trying to write his business plans), the more he seemed to resent me.

 I thought that I could teach him what love was and heal his pain.

When we broke up, I cried for a week straight. It felt like someone had died. I should have known that our relationship wouldn't last— though we talked about God, He was not at the forefront of our relationship. God told me that he was not the person for me, that I should be focusing on building my life instead of repairing our relationship, but I was so driven by the "chemistry," the physical attraction and deep, passionate connection we shared, that I wouldn't let go even after things turned sour. My first clue came during a date when he and his best friend took me to see *The Passion of the Christ*. The nice older lady who sat on my right hand shared her tissues with me. We cried hysterically through almost the entire movie, and then testified to one another that the experience really opened our eyes to the depth of the love and the sacrifice that Christ made for us. Chris and his best friend sat on my left side. They made jokes and laughed the entire movie, then complained that it was a waste of money! Laughing at *The Passion* should have given me a clear sign…but no! I was in love and determined to make things work.

For the next six years, I went from relationship to relationship, still seeking the love I had with Chris and finding myself disappointed when other men couldn't compare to the guy on which my understanding of love was built. Every few months, Chris would call out of nowhere, wielding apologies and reigniting the flame that still smoldered between us. We'd visit each other, he'd borrow money and make promises, and we cycled through seasons of attraction and abandonment. Chris did not know how to love me, and in all honesty, I did not know how to love him. Neither of us had fully accepted the love of God.

When I really stopped to completely evaluate the relationships I'd been in and the men I'd dated, I realized that every one of my serious relationships that preceded Chris and then followed him, followed the exact same pattern. I was the common denominator. I couldn't teach Chris or any other man how to love because my understanding of love was completely messed up, too. I had spent my life thinking that love had to be earned—convinced that I was not good enough as I was by a lifetime of rejection from an absent biological father and peers who hated my glasses and my skin tone. I knew God as Lord, but I had yet to understand Him as Father, as Husband, as Friend.

As a result, I went from relationship to relationship, looking for a spark, for "chemistry," then working to create or maintain it. I was trying to earn acceptance, understanding, and a commitment, when God was there pursuing me and waiting on me to pursue Him all along. Before there was a Chris, there was a Christ, who loved me deeply, truly, eternally. I wasted so much time when God was trying to show me how love was really supposed to feel. I didn't have to work for His love, or convince Him of my good qualities, or teach Him what a man was supposed to be. He embraced me unconditionally, provided for me, and showed me the plans He had for my life.

 It is impossible for an individual who has not been consumed by the fiery love of God to understand or to express that love to another human being.

By definition, it becomes impossible for an individual who has not been consumed by the fiery love of God to understand or to express that love to another human being. First John 4:19 teaches that the only reason, the only means, through which we are enabled and empowered to love is to first be loved by God. I am sure that you have your own "Chris" story—a relationship that set up your definition of what love is (or is not) supposed to be. Before you can move forward, it is critical that you consent to God changing your expectations of yourself and of your mate. To change your relationship pattern, God has to become your relationship paradigm.

Have you allowed God to know you completely? To embrace you intimately? To overwhelm you with His love? Until you can answer yes to those questions, you are ill-prepared and ill-equipped to even begin to know what to look for or to offer in a loving relationship. You are delaying the process of God blessing you with your mate, and if you continue to pursue relationships without a healthy paradigm for love, you have sentenced yourself to settling for drama, stress, mediocrity, emptiness, and heartache. You have given up God's best in exchange for just "having someone." God tells us to avoid "unequal yoking" to protect us—to prevent us from sharing His love with someone who will never be able to replicate it because he or she hasn't received or experienced that love from Him. I am so glad that God, in His grace and His mercy, pursued me until I recognized that He is my first love. Because His love is my standard, I am able to resist the temptation to settle or compromise for anything less. Even now, He is also pursuing you. He wants to love you the way you want to be loved. Only then can we offer and receive that love in our relationships with someone else.

From Eden to Gethsemane to Zion: Setting the Stage for Courtship, the Real Love Story

We don't have to look toward romantic comedies, reality television, magazines, the Internet, or to our own bad relationships to learn what love, sex, and marriage is supposed to look like. For the greatest love story ever told, we need only read the Bible. It has all the elements of the perfect story: the exposition (the background story in Genesis and the Old Testament); a central conflict (satan as the villain rebels against God, the hero, and attempts to convince God's people to do the same); a central theme (God's love, His sovereign plan, and His chosen people triumph over all of the enemy's schemes); a climax (the cross, our Christ, and the power of resurrection); and the denouement (the conclusion of the matter, where satan is defeated once and for all and God is reunited with the people He has chosen). In His Word, God gives us a perfect love story and a pedagogical pattern that teaches us what real love is and how relationships are supposed to operate.

In the beginning of Genesis, God created a mirror image of His union with mankind in the relationship of Adam and Eve. Adam was complete, just as the God in whose image He was created is completely self-existent. Interestingly, God said it was not good for Adam to be alone, and consequently, God is revealing to us that He also did not desire to remain alone. God wanted for Adam what He wanted for Himself: an object of love and devotion to reflect His glory. The relationship between Adam and Eve before the Fall (cleaving to one another, equal, naked, without shame, walking in dominion) reflects the perfect state of the relationship between God and mankind. Throughout the Bible, and continuing today with you and me, God is pursuing His people, the object of His love and devotion.

After the attack on the institution of marriage and the Fall of the human race, God ejected Adam and Eve from Eden and all that Eden represents. But God had already developed a plan for restoring humanity, redeeming their sin, and reconciling all people to Himself. God also has a plan for reconciling men and women, as evidenced in His methodological analogy of marriage that we see exemplified and explained in both the Old and New Testaments. God had already turned His love toward His sovereignly chosen people and put His plan in place in the Garden. The plot of our perfect love story is a narrative of *pursuit*: God pursues His people. God calls for His people to respond in love expressed through trust, worship, and submission. Satan also pursues God's people and is defeated. God and His people are intimately and eternally reunited. The End.

The plot of our perfect love story is a narrative of pursuit: God pursues His people.

God, when explaining His relationship to His people, identifies Himself throughout Scripture as our bridegroom and husband. In Isaiah 54:5-6, God tells Israel,

> *For your Maker is your **husband**—the Lord Almighty is His name—the Holy One of Israel is your Redeemer; He is called the God of all the earth. The Lord will call you back as if you were a **wife** deserted and distressed in spirit—a wife who married young, only to be rejected....*

God is persistent in His love and pursuit, even when the people He loves and has committed Himself to look for fulfillment outside of relationship with Him over and over again. He pleads with them through the prophet Jeremiah, *"'Return, faithless people,' declares the Lord, for **I am your husband. I will choose you**...and bring you to Zion'"* (Jer. 3:14).

God promises to continue His pursuit, but entreats the people to respond to that pursuit in love, obedience, and fidelity. He recognizes that His people have been seduced away from Him since the Garden, their attention diverted and their value diluted. He promises in Hosea 2 to expose our sin, but also to draw His people back to Himself and restore them. The prophet wrote:

*"In that day," declares the Lord, "you will call Me 'My husband';
you will no longer call Me 'My master.' I will remove the name
of Baals from her lips....In that day I will make a covenant for
them with the beasts of the field and the birds of the air and
the creatures that move along the ground. Bow and sword and
battle I will abolish from the land, so that all may lie down in
safety.* **I will betroth you to Me forever***; I will betroth you in
righteousness and justice, in love and compassion. I will betroth
you in faithfulness, and you will acknowledge the Lord"* (Hosea
2:16-20).

God engaged Himself to Israel—He proposed marriage and
covenant—to a people who used Him, then rejected Him, over and
over again. But His love is perfect, it is complete, and He has a
plan to restore His people so that they can become the bride He
desires and so that reconciliation will be possible. He knows that
the people cannot become the bride He desires on their own, so He
sends Himself to the earth to provide the way. He sends His Son,
Jesus Christ, as the Lamb who makes substitutionary atonement
and removes the penalty for sin from the people, and as the Lion
who defeats satan and empowers the people to walk in their God-
given authority over the serpent. And He sends the Holy Spirit who
seals, sanctifies, protects, and prepares God's people to be united
with their bridegroom.

 **God uses marriage as the word picture to
express redemption.**

God uses *marriage* as the word picture to express redemption,
the reconciliation of Himself and mankind, and, consequently, the
reconciliation of man to woman. In this love story, God pursues
His bride and calls for her to respond in love to that pursuit, all the

way from Eden in Genesis to Zion in Revelation. Both must make the ultimate sacrifice. It is the apostle Paul who tells us that we are compelled by Christ's love to no longer think from a worldly point of view but to live our lives for God as our husband. God wants us to leave behind the ways of this world and to return to Him wholeheartedly. He is our first love. He desires intimacy with us and created us for that purpose. The Bible says that,

All this is from God, who reconciled us to Himself through Christ and gave us the ministry of reconciliation: that God was reconciling the world to Himself in Christ....And He has committed to us the message of reconciliation (2 Corinthians 5:18-19).

God's desire is for us to stop looking for love in all the wrong places and to find ourselves in His arms and in His perfect, loving will. Once we reconcile with Him, He gives us the opportunity to be ambassadors of that same love by extending ourselves to and receiving from others in a beautiful, supernatural way that points back to the glorious grace of our God.

As Revelation 19 opens, a great multitude begins to shout, exclaiming,

...Hallelujah! Salvation and glory and power belong to our God, for true and just are His judgments. He has condemned the great prostitute [the enemy] *who corrupted the earth by her adulteries...* (Revelation 19:1-2).

The heavens are celebrating the power and glory of God in His triumph over the enemy and his schemes to corrupt the relationship that God established with His people. In verse 6, the multitude begins to shout, announcing the arrival of the bridegroom (Christ) and His bride (the Church), exclaiming,

... "Halleluiah! For our Lord God Almighty reigns. Let us rejoice and be glad and give Him glory! For the wedding of the Lamb has come, and His bride has made herself ready. Fine linen, bright and clean, was given her to wear." (Fine linen stands for the righteous acts of the saints) (Revelation 19:6-8).

The heavenly hosts, who have watched the entire love story unfold, are gloriously celebrating the happy ending and new beginning.

God is revealing the essence of what a wedding should be in the Book of Revelation—it is a triumph over the enemy in both individuals' lives, and it is a divine union that reminds the earth that God's love is real and that He will soon return for His bride. The invitees are individuals who have watched the story of the couple unfold, who have seen their tragedies and their triumphs, their struggles and their successes. They are witnesses of the faithfulness of God and the power of real love. The wedding should occur after a God-ordained and a God-orchestrated process, a step-by-step progression that we refer to as *courtship*. Courtship is more than dating; it is the unfolding of a divine plan to reconcile two people into one purpose for the glory of God. Every aspect of our relationships—the courtship, the wedding, the sexual consummation, the marriage—is designed to be a reflection of God's pursuit and eternal partnership with His people.

 Courtship is more than dating; it is the unfolding of a divine plan to reconcile two people into one purpose for the glory of God.

In the chapters that follow, we will further explore courtship and marriage according to the example and pattern that God has provided in His Word. He outlines every detail, demonstrating the expanse of His love and desire for us to live and love in response to what He offers us.

Nowhere is this process of pursuit better exemplified than in the Song of Solomon, also known as the Song of Songs. Song of Songs is that love story summarized; it is known as an allegorical representation of the relationship of God (the Lover) and Israel/ the Church (the bride). The book is a romantic text of growing desire, as courtship progresses toward consummation. The beloved desires to be summoned into the chamber of the king; the lover calls for her to show her face, to let him hear her voice (see Song of Sol. 1:4; 2:14). They are separated, searching for one another and surviving the passing of several seasons. She has been hidden away, practicing submission, saving herself for her lover, and preparing herself for intimacy.

He approaches, pursuing her, wearing his crown of authority and displaying his ability to provide for her. They meet in the garden (symbolic of Eden/New Jerusalem), a place of promise and productivity, and in their union, we see the reversal of every curse upon relationships instituted within satan's deception and the Fall of mankind. The lover's desire is for the beloved, and she belongs to him (see Song of Sol. 7:10). The consummation of their union—and the spiritual, emotional, and erotic satisfaction that accompanies it—builds into an unquenchable flame. It is a love that will last for all eternity—the love of God for us, the real love God created for us to share.

Love, dating, weddings, marriage, and sex all take on a completely different significance when we understand them from God's point of view. They are beautiful words, with supernatural, eternal, majestic applications. We are so blessed to serve a God who loves us so completely that He gives us the opportunity to share His love with a person that He perfectly designed for us. It is so amazing to know that if we trust Him, we will not only experience the beauty of reconciliation here on Earth, but we also will know the depth of His love for all eternity. The enemy's plan was to separate us—to cause us to sin, to fall, to fail, to be devoid of intimacy with God and to have dysfunctional relationships forever. He didn't anticipate, however, that the longer and harder the separation, the greater the joy we would experience when we are reunited. The same is true for our relationships—he may have deceived, divided, and/or distracted us for a season, but it just increases our expectation and our excitement. It's true that making up, finally achieving and receiving that which you've missed or lost, can actually strengthen the bonds that the enemy attempts to break.

 Before we go any further, I need to let you know that God knows exactly where you are right now.

Before we go any further, I need to let you know that God knows exactly where you are right now. He knows what you're going through. He knows what it is like to be single—to desire intimacy and find yourself alone and wanting and waiting. He knows what it is like to be in a committed relationship with someone who hurts you, who abuses you, who neglects your needs. He knows what it is like to be in a marriage that is not what you expected, to be disappointed by a mate who just won't act right. He knows what it is like to lose the person you loved the most. He experienced frustration, betrayal, loneliness, anger, disappointment, being used, being taken advantage of, being unappreciated....

Guess what? Not only was God able to hold on, to remain faithful, to continue to love and to trust and to hope, but He has also given us the ability, the faith, the strength, and the example to do the same.

For we do not have a high priest who is unable to sympathize with our weaknesses, but we have one who has been tempted [tested] *in every way, just as we are...* (Hebrews 4:15).

God has given us access to His throne and the ability to seek Him for wisdom, for strength, for grace, and for mercy whenever we need it. Whatever season of relationship you're in right now, I can assure you that it feels so good to be in a love relationship with God, to be held in His highest regard, to be accepted unconditionally, to know that He has a plan for us. You can trust Him with your heart, with your life, with your relationships, and with your future. He wants to teach us how to love.

Chapter 4

ENTERING THE COURTS: MARRIAGE, COVENANT, AND THE TYPOLOGY OF THE TABERNACLE

"God has set the type of marriage everywhere throughout the creation. Every creature seeks its perfection in another. The very Heavens and earth picture it to us." —Martin Luther

In her July 2009 article in *Time* magazine entitled, "Is There Hope for the American Marriage," Caitlin Flanigan asks the question so key to this book, a question so many of you have asked again and again.[1] She eloquently describes the paradox of relationship expectation: individuals cherish marriage but hold it to an impossible standard and, as a result, stop seeking it or never find it. People like drama—following love stories like Brad and Angelina or Jay-Z and Beyoncé, but are equally engrossed in tales of love gone wrong in the cases of the Gosselins, Steve McNair, Tiger Woods, Governor Sanford, and Senator Edwards. In essence, we want love and relationships of great worth, but we are increasingly less willing to put in the hard work and personal sacrifice it takes to get there. Flanigan writes,

> "The fundamental question we must ask ourselves at the beginning of the century is this: *What is the purpose of marriage?* Is it—given the game-changing realities of birth control, female equality and the fact that motherhood outside of marriage is no longer stigmatized—simply an institution that has the capacity to increase the pleasure of the adults who enter into it? If so, we might as well hold the wake now: *there probably aren't many people whose idea of 24-hour-a-day good times consists of being yoked to the same romantic partner, through bouts of stomach flu and depression, financial setbacks and emotional upsets, until after many a long decade, one or the other eventually dies in harness.*

> Or is marriage an institution that still hews to its old intention and function—to raise the next generation, to protect and teach it, to instill in it the habits of conduct and character that will ensure the generation's own safe passage into adulthood? Think of it this way: the current generation of children, the one watching commitments between adults snap like dry twigs and observing parents who simply can't be bothered to marry each other and who hence drift in and out of their children's lives—that's the generation who will be taking care of us when we are old" (emphasis added).[2]

Ms. Flanigan concludes her article with an assertion that essentially expresses the need for this text. She writes, "what we teach about marriage will determine a great deal about our fate"[3]— affecting not only this generation, but also the generations that will follow. Our fate is questionable at best, as the definition and purpose for marriage, much like the definitions of love and relationship, has been lost in translation; its value forfeited for the past few generations.

Each day, I am reminded that we live in a society—that we were born into a generation—where the vast majority of individuals believe that an honest, wholesome, holy, committed, sexually pure, empowering, edifying relationship is completely unrealistic. Our lessons in relationship and marriage have taught us to survive, to conquer, to seek pleasure in the moment (even at others' expense), to accept "what we can get," to reject what we don't want anymore, and to make relationships work to fit our needs.

 Marriage is described as a "prison sentence" to young men who learn to drink milk without buying the cows.

Marriage is described as a "prison sentence" to young men who learn to drink milk without buying the cows, moving throughout the pasture and never seeming to be satisfied. Girls "play house" well into middle age, using their bodies and their affection to manipulate boys into men who will meet them at the altar in the wedding they have planned in their minds since they were six. For many, cohabitation has replaced marriage as the ultimate step in a relationship, and none of the people I know (and none of the people they know) live in a family that hasn't been affected by divorce. Here's the nuptial narrative our society presents: Two people got married. It sucked. They got divorced. Life got better. Therefore, marriage is bad. You want to get married? You don't know what you're getting into. One of you, if not both, will be miserable. You'll get divorced, too. It's inevitable. Therefore, stay single. Already married? That's okay. Just have an affair. You can always just divorce if you get caught....

I'm consistently amazed by the discouraging reports concerning marriage. The lessons are convincing, and "for better or worse, for richer or poorer, in sickness and in health, to love and to cherish, 'til death do us part" is a decreasingly attractive proposition. At times, it seems like the only folks fighting for marriage are waving rainbow flags! This is definitely not God's purpose for relationships. The world cites all the statistics that encourage people to stay single or justify divorce and infidelity. Guess what? The Church quotes Paul's writings or points to church leaders' examples and encourages people to do the same thing.

 People wait, and wait, and wait...and no one tells them what they are waiting for.

People wait, and wait, and wait...and no one tells them what they are waiting for, what to expect, or how to prepare for it. I know singles who have read so many books on marriage and dating that they could design and teach a doctoral dissertation on it, but they are no closer to being married than they were when they began. Married couples are far more willing to share their horror stories than their happiest times. If the nation's leaders (politicians and preachers) are willing to forsake the idea of lifetime commitment, why should the rest of us hold on to it?

We should hold on to it because it is God's plan for us, because His desire is for us to receive and then to share the love and commitment that He created for us to walk in. I know what it is like to truly desire the God-love described in Chapter 3 and to believe that it is somewhere beyond your reality as you find yourself stuck in the counterfeit again and again. Our connections are in critical condition, and if there was ever a time for us to seek the Lord and to know His plan for love, that time is now. The whole world, and all of creation, is awaiting the revelation of the sons and daughters of God, who will truly reflect the love and commitment of the Father (see Rom. 8:22-23).

Godly marriage is intended to be a portrait of the redemptive process, and Lord knows that it is time for a revolution in our lives and our relationships. God's answer to the Fall of mankind, and the fall of the marital relationship, is sacrificial covenant, built through a process of courtship in which husband and wife are joined as God and His chosen people are united. In creating an image of redemption and reconciliation in the earth, not only has God designed the product of marital commitment, but He has also designed a process for entering covenant. In this chapter, we will overthrow the enemy's attempts to confuse the purpose of relationship and reclaim marriage as a reflection of reconciliation.

Understanding the Problem: Commitment Phobia, Polytheism, and Polygamy

After receiving and researching much of the revelation contained within the second half of this text, I conducted my first workshop on *God's Divine Design and Courtship* with the single adults and college students in our local assembly. God was definitely glorified through the results, including the end of several relationships that were not ordained by the Lord and the engagement of two couples whose union was solidified by the process described in this book. I was most surprised by the reaction of one of the young men in our fellowship.

Damien, one of our most dedicated and most outspoken members, had provided comic relief and surprisingly honest insight into the urban male mind throughout our sessions. At the end of one of the workshops, he approached me with a unique contribution to our discussion. "People *don't* get married no more," he said matter of factly. Intrigued by the implications, I spoke with Damien at length about relationship trends, including the tendency toward multiple sexual partners, out-of-wedlock childbearing and child rearing, and cohabitation. "Before you are able to tell some people *how* to be married," Damien reasoned, "you may have to convince them to walk down the aisle."

Damien's argument echoes the sentiment of the *Times* article—that within the past few generations, people (both male and female) have embraced "living single" and find no need to embrace long-term commitment. My response to Damien and to any self-confessed or diagnosed commitment phobic is this: *Individuals are not living single at all!* In contrast, people are marrying over and over and over again.

The Commencement of Marriage

When we first encounter Adam in the Garden, he is single, completely separate from any other creature. The sexual act was the mechanism through which he was united with the helpmate God had created and presented to him, and a marriage bond was solidified! For proof, we need only revisit the story of the original man and woman and their marriage ceremony. In Genesis 2, Adam looked at Eve for the first time and embraced her as his own, saying, *"This is now bone of my bones and flesh of my flesh; she shall be called 'woman,' for she was taken out of man"* (Gen. 2:23). Eve was pulled out of Adam, and in the consummate act, Adam placed himself inside of her, completing the circle of life that allowed them to reproduce themselves.

> *For this reason a man will leave his father and mother and be united to his wife, and they will become one flesh. The man and his wife were both naked, and they felt no shame* (Genesis 2:24-25).

She transitioned from *"woman"* in verse 23 to *"wife"* in verse 25 as a direct result of Adam's pronouncement and God's authorization of their sexual union. Adam, likewise, accepted all the responsibilities as husband. Outside of marriage, Adam would not have the responsibilities of marriage—protection, provision, direction—but he also would not have access to its benefits—understanding, assistance, companionship, shared experience, and physical pleasure. The same is true for Eve, as marriage added a set of expectations from her and for her.

 God's marker for marriage is not a rented tuxedo, a wedding cake, or a flower girl.

God's marker for marriage is not a rented tuxedo, a wedding cake, or a flower girl. According to the type set in Genesis 2, the marriage ceremony features three distinct components: the presence of a governing authority, the declaration of covenant agreement, and the consummation of the marital bond through sex. A pronouncement of "love" and the making of plans for a future did not equal a marriage. And neither did having sex.

Instead, sex was the physical marker and bonding agent of the spiritual and emotional union of two individuals for one purpose. Sex did not create a marriage, but it was designed as the seal of a marriage, and God never intended for sex to exist outside of the union of man and wife. God created mankind to be both monotheistic (in relationship with Him only) and monogamous (in relationship with one mate only). Sex was intended to be a sacred experience; an act of giving and receiving that mirrored the intimacy created by God with His people. Sex, and the other benefits of covenant, are established by God and connected to marriage from the very beginning.

An individual who participates in activities designed for marriage should be prepared to make the type of commitment that God created that expression of love to consummate. God expresses His desire in His original commandments, instructing His chosen people that *"if a man seduces a virgin who is not pledged to be married* *and sleeps with her, he **must** pay the bride-price, and **she shall be his wife**"* (Exod. 22:16). According to First Corinthians 6, you become "one in body" with the person you have intercourse with.

Far too many people today want the seal of marriage without the substance of it. They give and receive the benefits of marriage, while rejecting the government's approval and without waiting on a sanction from God to make a true covenant in the presence of a spiritual covering that will formulate a lasting commitment. Consequently, people are content to go from relationship to relationship, or from marriage bed to marriage bed, seeking, demanding, and trying to offer the kind of satisfaction that can only come from a true relationship with God and should only be reproduced through a true commitment to one person who is also committed to you. Love, sex, and selfless devotion are far more damaging and dangerous when handled incorrectly than driving or fishing, and if you need a license to do either of those, you should also need a license to enter someone's heart, body, and spirit. Breaking the seal of one's heart or one's body without commitment and the approval of a higher authority, can produce disastrous effects.

 Breaking the seal of one's heart or one's body without commitment and the approval of a higher authority, can produce disastrous effects.

When mankind was seduced into an affair with the enemy, choosing to worship satan through intimate communion and obedience rather than the God of creation, they introduced the concept of polytheism (relationship with more than one god), and as a reflection and a result, polygamy (relationship with more than one mate). The true obstacle to modern marriage is not the desire to remain single; it the conflict presented by a body created for monogamous pleasure and a sinful nature that hides from commitment and seeks out multiple, successive relationships, yet can never be satisfied.

The Cause of Multiple Marriages

After mankind's fall, human beings got further and further away from the intentions of God in regard to their relationships with one another in the same way that they got further and further away from Him. Through Adam, sin and death are introduced to earth and are inherited by Adam's sons. In Genesis 4, we see the results as Cain kills his brother Abel and immediately suffers the consequences. Like his father Adam, Cain attempts to hide his sin, and like his father Adam, Cain is cursed—forced away from the land and destined for failure. Cain cries out, *"Today You are driving me from the land, and I will be hidden from Your presence; I will be a restless wanderer on the earth…"* (Gen. 4:14). Further separation from God produces an incessant, consistent, unsatisfying habit of *wandering*.

Cain, building upon the curse of his father and passing it onto his sons, establishes a derivative of our sin nature that makes running from the presence of God and wandering from place to place more comfortable but also less satisfying. The same can be said for the nature of modern relationships where the emphasis is on quantity, but the quality leaves far more to be desired. Society teaches that if you are not satisfied, it is acceptable for you to move from place to place, from person to person. Such a mentality is connected to a curse following disobedience.

 Society teaches that if you are not satisfied, it is acceptable for you to move from place to place, from person to person.

As early as the sixth generation of the human race, we see the results of the wandering nature of humanity. In Genesis 4, we are also introduced to Lamech, who marries two women, Adah and Zillah, whose names translate from Hebrew as "dawn" and "shadow," or "light" and "darkness." Lamech liked opposites, needing a taste of both sides of the equation in order to be satisfied. The fathers of those who "live in tents and raise livestock," and those who played musical instruments were products of the original polygamous relationships. In other words, the shepherds and musicians of the Old Testament are direct descendents of polygamy, and it is no wonder that the enemy has launched such great attacks against the pastors, politicians, and musicians/entertainers who have such enormous influence in terms of their messages and the standards they uphold.

In the eighth generation of the human race, we encounter another Lamech,[4] who was the father of Noah and who represents the generation prior to the great flood. Describing the days of Noah and the days before the *"coming of the Son of Man,"* Matthew tells us that the people were *"eating and drinking, marrying and giving in marriage"* (24:37-38). In other words, they were focused on their own pleasures; they were controlled by hunger and sexual desire to the extent that they were completely disconnected from God and His plan for mankind. Paul further describes this generation and the modern moment:

> *Although they claimed to be wise, they became fools and exchanged the glory of the immortal God for images made to look like mortal man and birds and animals and reptiles. Therefore* **God gave them over in the sinful desires of their hearts to sexual impurity for the degrading of their bodies with one another.** *They exchanged the truth of God for a lie, and worshiped and served created things rather than the Creator— who is forever praised. Amen.* **Because of this, God gave them over to shameful lusts...** (Romans 1:22-26).

Just as Adam and Eve exchanged intimacy with God and its benefits for momentary pleasure with the serpent and its consequences, the generation of Lamech and Noah, and the generation out of which we are being called, chose to follow lust rather than love, to seek shameful pleasure and greed over the satisfaction and contentment that comes from alignment with God's divine plan. Noah's generation was polytheistic and polygamous, seeking and responding to false gods and inanimate objects, and the modern moment is no better—controlled by markets, microchips, and text messaging.

Romans 1:28 states that because the people did not think it was important to maintain a knowledge, or an intimate relationship, with God, He *"gave them over to a depraved mind, to do what ought not to be done."* When individuals continue to reject the love and relationship that He offers, God releases them to deal with the consequences of their own sinful hearts. The practices of polytheism and polygamy are always linked, as a failure to uphold a standard in one's relationship with God always produces a failure to uphold a standard in one's emotional and physical ties to other human beings. When a nation embraces a god other than Jehovah, its families and its people suffer the consequences. The same is true for an individual and his or her household. The refusal to commit in marriage (or to complete singleness) is an outgrowth of a refusal to commit and submit to God.

The practices of polytheism and polygamy extended beyond the Book of Genesis to the nations of the world and continue into the modern moment, as they have been woven into the fabric of our American culture. We are living in the days of Noah! We have been taught that it is acceptable to claim Christ as our Lord and our Savior, while still being controlled by and dedicating our time and our attention to "created things," the pursuit of the wealth, success, and status of this world. Many of us, like Adam and the children of Israel, know that we have been created and chosen by God, but we continue to seek satisfaction in areas of our lives that are displeasing to Him. We may love God, but we are controlled by our efforts toward relationships, or drinking and clubbing, or climbing the corporate ladder. We have other gods.

As a result, He has handed this generation over to its lusts, and it has produced a culture driven by pornography, sexual immorality, fornication, adultery, and general debauchery. We live in a society that celebrates promiscuity. Women are encouraged to offer their "pearls"—their time, their energy, their attention, their support, their homes, and their bodies—to men with whom they are *not* in covenant. Likewise, men follow the wanderings of their sinful nature, content to live single lives (even when married) and unwilling and unchallenged to offer themselves in commitment and devotion to a single woman. We are not entering and maintaining marital bonds as God intended because our sinful natures are content to act like we are married, over and over again.

In John 4, Jesus encountered a Samaritan woman at Jacob's well. He opened a conversation by asking her for water, and then offered her living water as an invitation into an intimate relationship with Himself. Jesus told the woman to go and get her husband, and then to come back to Him. She admitted to Him that she had no husband, that although she had been going through all the motions, she had never entered a marital covenant. Jesus' response to her was quite abrupt:

> *You are right when you say you have no husband. The fact is, you have had five husbands, and the man you now have is not your husband. What you have just said is quite true* (John 4:17b-18).

She immediately recognized that Jesus knew her. He could somehow see that she had extended herself and had given herself to men over and over again. She was searching for life, for revitalization, for intimacy that accompanies a covenant that she had not been offered nor was willing to wait for. Jesus offered her an alternative—a life with Him that would quench all of her thirsts and the opportunity to share the benefits of that relationship with her peers. She accepted His proposal.

Aren't you tired of going from well to well, from relationship to relationship, from bed to bed, seeking satisfaction that you know will fade before the sun comes up? Allow the Samaritan woman's testimony to transform your relationships. God is able to deliver you from a life of going through the motions of intimacy and seconds of climax without experiencing a lifetime of the pleasure that accompanies love's lasting embrace that affects and transforms every part of your being.

The Curse of Multiple Marriages

Practicing polytheism, polygamy, promiscuity, or "acting married" produces the kind of results that destroy destinies, families, ministries, and nations. For evidence, we need only revisit the dynamic royal father-son duo of King David and King Solomon from Chapter 2. David is described as a man after God's own heart in Scripture. He was a conquering warrior, a radical worshiper, a respected leader chosen and anointed by God to shepherd His people. David had control of an entire kingdom, but he couldn't control his own hormones! In Second Samuel 11, David (who was supposed to be on the battlefield, leading his men) was at home, walking around the roof of his palace.

He saw Bathsheba bathing and, intoxicated by her beauty, decided that his desire for her was more important than the fact that they were both married already. David sent for her, and she was so enamored by the attention of a man in power that she prepared herself in advance to sleep with him. The sex seemed simple and convenient—friends with benefits. She went to him, he slept with her, and then he sent her back home. At that time, they had no idea that their actions were producing consequences that neither of them could ignore.

David immediately sent for Bathsheba's husband, expecting to use his power to coerce Uriah into sleeping with her as well. Uriah, who was a man of integrity and valor, refused to seek his own pleasure at the expense of those who were still at war. David, in a final effort to cover his own sin, arranged for Uriah to be killed in battle. David thought he had escaped the eyes and judgment of people, marrying Bathsheba after her mourning and "legitimizing" her son, but the last verse of the chapter informs us that David never escaped the eyes of God. According to verse 27, "...*the thing that David had done displeased the Lord*" (2 Sam. 11:27).

David, the warrior and worshiper, was forced to deal with the God-ordained consequences of his sin. God, through the prophet Nathan, promised David that his sin would be exposed and that the sword would never depart from his household. In addition, the child born to David and Bathsheba was struck with a lethal illness. God saw David's affair as more than sexual sin—it was a perversion of the institution of marriage, a horrible misrepresentation of God's love and favor to the other nations before whom Israel and David were exalted. David and Bathsheba's indiscretion produced a curse in their lives.

 David's affair as more than sexual sin—it was a perversion of the institution of marriage.

Guess what? Our sins have equally damaging consequences. The curse of secret affairs, seduction, sexual sin, and multiple marriage may manifest in multiple ways: unplanned pregnancy, disease or death, guilt, shame, unreciprocated emotions, depression, an inability to commit in later relationships, fear or inability to trust, financial distress, forfeit of impending success, discomfort in worship, embarrassment, and ineffective ministry—which means potential power surrendered to the enemy.

Or it could be passed down to your children. David's curse took a generational turn, affecting his sons and the entire nation of Israel. Two chapters after this indiscretion, David's son Ammon was overcome by "love" and sexual desire for his sister Tamar. When she asked him to wait and marry her, he chose instead to rape her, taking her virginity and her value. Overcome by hatred that replaced his confessed love, Ammon then threw Tamar out of his bed and out of his house. Two years later, Absalom, Tamar's other brother, arranged for Ammon to be murdered. Two years after that, Absalom conspired to steal his father's throne and turn all of Israel against him, and he slept with all of his father's concubines. The sword remained in David's household, and eventually Absalom was killed in a battle with his father's army.

David and Bathsheba conceived a second son, whose name was Solomon. Solomon became the heir to David's throne. Solomon inherited his father's position and his problem. The Bible teaches us that the Lord loved Solomon even from birth, and that He gave him *wisdom and very great insight, and a breadth of understanding as measureless as the sand on the seashore*" (1 Kings 4:29). Men of all nations sought Solomon for his counsel, and women from all nations sought him for his power and his wealth. Solomon was not just anointed king; he was chosen to complete the building of God's temple.

God promised Solomon that he and his descendents would always sit on the throne of Israel as long as he walked faithfully with God and did not allow anything else to steal his heart. David charged his son, passing on a warning concerning the dangers of polygamy and polytheism by telling him to avoid intermarriage with women who were not in relationship with the God of Israel. Ungodly relationship, which eventually pulled Solomon's heart from God, was the only thing that could destroy his destiny.

In First Kings chapters 10 and 11, we learn that Solomon accumulated three things: wisdom, wealth, and women! Solomon, walking in the type of rebellion and disobedience that we have already addressed, *"loved many foreign women besides Pharoah's daughter— Moabites, Ammonites, Edomites, Sidonians, and Hittites"* (1 Kings 11:1). He amassed 700 wives of royal birth, with 300 concubines on the side, and he *"held fast to them in love"* (1 Kings 11:2). In the same chapter, we learn that Solomon, who completed God's temple, was now building altars and exalting all of the gods of his foreign wives. His polygamy and polytheism merged—and God knew that Solomon's heart no longer belonged to Him.

Herein lies the dilemma: when the curse produced by deviance is passed on generationally, the sin multiplies, and, consequently, so does the damage and the penalty. God warned Solomon about the consequences of a polygamous and polytheistic heart:

> *But if you turn away and forsake the decrees and commands I have given you and go off to serve other gods and worship them, then I will uproot Israel from My land, which I have given them, and will reject this temple I have consecrated for My Name...* (2 Chronicles 7:19-20).

Immediately, God began raising up the enemies of the nation of Israel, who began to plot to regain their territory. After his death, the kingdom was split between Solomon's sons Jeroboam and Rehoboam, and as a result became the separate nations of Israel and Judah. For the rest of the Old Testament, God's chosen people were at war with each other and with other nations. They were held in bondage and their temple and cities were devastated by battle, never to fully recover.

Even as we stand in grace, the consequences of multiple marriages—whether they are sexual affairs or "soul ties"—are assured. The most difficult consequence to bear is a life, or a generation, separated from the love and the will of God. My question for Adam and Eve, for David and Solomon, for fallen athletes and politicians and preachers, for you is, is it worth it? Is it worth destroying your future, or your family, for a stroked ego or the next conquest? Is it worth the pain of heartbreak for believing smooth words and following the butterflies in your stomach? Is it worth passing on curses to your children, and to their children, and to an entire nation because you can't fight the feeling anymore? What in your life is more important than maintaining your relationship with Him? What, or who, have you made your god?

 What in your life is more important than maintaining your relationship with Him?

The Cure for Multiple Marriages

Though the nation of Israel never completely turned their hearts back to Him, God never stopped pursuing. God couldn't choose another nation just because He was displeased; He had already sovereignly chosen Israel. Throughout Scripture, God continued to call Israel out of its promiscuity and idolatry, urging them to pursue Him with their whole heart, mind, and soul. God always wanted His people to understand real love. Because Israel refused real relationship with God, they sought forbidden and, ultimately, unproductive and unsatisfying relationships outside of Him.

Truth is, it is far more common for modern individuals to ignore warnings and run from the love and presence of God, engaging in sexual immorality and cycles of heartbreak or unhealthy addictions, rather than run into the arms of God. The key to escaping the curse of multiple marriages is in realizing its danger and in giving our hearts back to God and realigning with His plans for our lives and our relationships. God is still pursuing, waiting for His people to give their hearts and their relationships back to Him.

God gives King Solomon the cure for multiple marriages.

If My people, who are called by My name, would humble themselves and pray and seek My face and turn from their wicked ways, then will I hear from heaven and will forgive their sin and will heal their land (2 Chronicles 7:14).

We live in a land in which the concept of marriage—as a committed, monogamous, God-centered, lifelong union of two hearts, two minds, and two purposes (one male, one female) into one—has come under severe attack. But if we, as God's people, would take a stand and give our hearts back to our first love, if we would repent from bad habits, addictions, and cycles, not only will God heal our hearts and relationships, but we also would be powerful enough to change the culture in our land. When we return to Him, every curse, every demonic attack, every weapon formed against us (our relationships, our families, and our ministries) is broken! When we turn our hearts to Him, He fixes them and restores our relationships with one another back to His original plan.

 It is easier to hold on to doing things our way.

For so many of us, the decision to totally submit to God first, and then to a mate, has been complicated by fear, insecurity, anger, bitterness, pride, and selfishness. It is easier to hold on to doing things our way, to seek pleasure our way, to work things out (or not work things out) our way, to follow what seems natural, to set up defense mechanisms, and so on rather than to truly give our hearts to Him and allow Him to work in our relationships. I know what you're thinking: "Doing this relationship thing God's way just seems too confusing and too hard." And I know how you feel.

It will take more than work; it requires the sanctifying power of the Holy Spirit to expose and to correct our mindsets, our attitudes, and our habits. It begins in our relationship with God, and when we are willing to surrender to His processes, submit to His way, and study His Word to know His standards and promises, God will take care of everything else. We must be willing to learn and to follow God's plan in order to inherit the blessing, the favor, and the benefits of relationships built according to His design.

Clarification for the Commitment Phobic

When I began writing this section, I thoughtfully revisited Damien's suggestion to convince people of the value of marriage again. When I couldn't figure out how to do that, I prayed and sought a response in the Word of God. In Matthew 19 Jesus is having a very similar discussion with the Pharisees and His disciples about the difficulty of maintaining godly relationships.

As the chapter opens, Jesus is healing multitudes in Judea, and the Pharisees are challenging and testing Him by asking about the lawfulness of divorce. Jesus answers their questions, revealing God's heart toward marriage.

> *"Haven't you read," He replied, "that at the beginning the Creator 'made them male and female,' and said, 'For this reason a man will leave his father and mother and be united to his wife, and the two will become one flesh'? So they are no longer two, but one. Therefore what God has joined together, let man not separate"* (Matthew 19:4-6).

According to the text, a man and a woman should unite *because God created them to do so.* When a man and woman unite as a result of God's divine will, they become one flesh...no longer separate, no longer alone! The force released in their agreement, in that union, is supposed to represent a bond that only death can break. That force is supposed to be stronger than financial struggle, more resilient than sickness, triumphant over conflict and suffering, capable of outrunning the passage of time and of overcoming changing body types and graying hair. The marriage vow is more than a promise; it is a declaration of defeat to the enemy. The bond of husband and wife is a constant reminder of the power of love and of covenant over any other principality or power in this world.

Like many of us, Jesus' disciples failed to truly understand the beauty of marriage or to discern its significance. As a result, they responded to Jesus' description of commitment and challenge for accountability the same way that many of us do. In light of the unselfish motivation, the responsibility to remain, and the forfeiting of independence required for marriage, the disciples decided it wasn't worth the effort. They answered Him saying, *"If this is the situation between a husband and wife, it is better **not** to marry"* (Matt. 19:10). Jesus sympathetically responds to His disciples, *"Not everyone can accept this word, but only those to whom it has been given"* (Matt. 19:11).

Based on Jesus' word, I have come to accept that every individual in the world will not change his or her attitude or approach toward relationships based on the revelation contained in this book. I have neither the words nor the authority to convince people to marry. It's a desire that God has to weave into one's heart. Marriage is a calling, a divine ordinance, a holy office, and those who walk into it can be, and should be, prepared. God is faithful to mold one's heart toward marriage if He so desires. How do I know? Because He did it for me, and he did it for Damien, the young man whose question opened up this section.

The first time that I met Damien, he was a college football player eagerly pursuing one of my roommates with one thing on his mind. Two years later we met again on a university campus. After making several excuses, he eventually accepted my invitation to join me at our church's collegiate Bible study. Today Damien is a beautifully saved man of God, eagerly pursuing God's will for his life and his relationships. He openly shares his testimony of transformation with other young men, especially his teammates. Damien walked into a real relationship with God, and when he gave his life to the Lord, God changed his heart. I am continually amazed by his growth.

 Before you can understand and submit to God's plan for relationships, you must enter a relationship with Him.

When he stopped focusing on females and sex and his next high/buzz, he was able to focus on his academics and graduation, on God's will for his life, on pursuing his goals, on opportunities to minister, and on taking steps to purposefully prepare for his wife. Before you can understand and submit to God's plan for relationships, you must enter a relationship with Him. Those who love Him desire to do His will and to walk uprightly before Him, and they enjoy relationships according to the purpose and pattern for which they were created. If God can turn Damien's heart toward the desire for a marriage and ministry built and maintained according to His blueprint, I know that He can do the same for His sons and daughters around the globe.

In His treatise on marriage to the Corinthian church, Paul offers his wisdom to the unmarried and to the widows: *"It is good for them to stay unmarried….But if they cannot control themselves, they should marry, for it is better to marry than to burn with passion"* (1 Cor. 7:8b-9).

In other words, being single is not a curse, and it should not be condemned. It is a valid choice, or an important season in one's life, because of the opportunity to devote one's heart, plans, and time to knowing God and one's self. Paul describes it as the best option because your interests and devotion are undivided (see 1 Cor. 7:35).

In this passage, however, Paul acknowledged that there are individuals who are born with passion, which if unshared, will consume its host. Paul encourages those individuals to marry—not shack up, not become "friends with benefits," not make false promises, not "fall head-over-heels"—but literally to become one flesh and share one life. The passion, the fire, that some feel to connect with another human being is a God-given desire. It is a calling, like any other ministry, and God's desire is that those who are called to marriage will marry, and remain married, and those who are called to be single will remain completely devoted to Him—in mind, heart, spirit, and body.

Singleness is a blessing, designed to provide the opportunity for self-discovery and growth and service to God and to the Kingdom. Marriage is also a blessing, designed to invite companionship, pleasure, partnership, and the power of agreement into the lives of those who are chosen for it. So instead of convincing individuals to marry, I am writing for the individuals who have the desire to lead godly lives and to create godly unions, but who have never seen the instruction manual for the marriages they want to build. Walking into a marriage designed by God is a supernatural experience. How awesome is it to know that God chose you and your spouse (here, or on the way) to reflect His love on the earth, and to demonstrate to the enemy that he is destined for destruction! God, in His grace and His mercy, sovereignly chose you to replicate and reveal His redemptive work and the power of reconciliation.

Finding a Solution: Three Principles of Covenant

Relationship is a God term, as are love, sex, and marriage. He doesn't leave us to our own devices to figure out how to understand and live out those concepts; instead, He gives us the pattern for marriage in His Word. If we can fully understand the love story that He describes for Himself and His bride, we will better understand the love stories that He has written for each one of us. In order to reflect His love, we must know His love and how it operates. In order to walk in His ministry of reconciliation, we must understand the process of reconciliation and what it requires. God has never left reconciliation to mankind. He Himself has been the initiator, the guarantor, the guardian, the custodian, and the mediator of our connections to Him and to one another. In other words, we don't have to fix them! God has always had a plan, always had a purpose, and always had a pattern. The center of that plan has been *covenant relationship.*

A covenant is a legally binding agreement, a promise that binds two parties together with behaviors and/or actions that are specified, agreed upon, and required from both.[5] Any relationship built on a foundation other than the pattern for covenant that God describes and exemplifies is *out of order.* It is a counterfeit. Here are the basics of the pattern, which we will explore in practical detail in Chapters 5, 6, and 7: sacrificial process, holy pursuit, and righteous response.

Sacrificial Process

A covenant is a "binding agreement" that is made and kept under a "seal." A covenant is established when both parties agree to the terms of the covenant and are bound in relationship to one another. In previous chapters, we learned that satan's first attack was an assault on relationships as he introduced sin to separate God and humanity. Though satan came to steal, to kill, and to destroy, God's plan was to restore, to reconcile, and to redeem the human race and the marital bond. God had already made a commitment and a promise to humanity. Even after mankind's fall, God remained connected and, bound by love to fulfill the plan He had already written for the people He had foreknown and predestined. His plan for reconciliation is *sacrificial covenant.* Throughout the Old Testament, into the tabernacle, and all the way to our love story's climax at the cross, sacrificial covenant is God's tool for maintaining connection with His people.

 His plan for reconciliation is sacrificial covenant.

Adam and Eve, and all of their descendents, found themselves walking under a curse as a result of their disobedience. Even as they were banished from the manifested presence of God and His provision in the Garden, God Himself ensured that they remain covered and protected. We learn in Genesis 3:21 that Adam and Eve tried to cover themselves with leaves, but that God, in His infinite love, made a covering for them out of animal flesh that would not wither, or tear, or be inadequate. Adam and Eve experienced death for the first time as a means through which they would be provided for. God sacrificed the first animals to seal His relationship and His covenant with the human race despite their fall.

The commentator Matthew Henry writes about this passage,

The beasts, from whose skins they were clothed, it is supposed were slain, not for man's food, but for *sacrifice, to typify Christ, the great Sacrifice.* Adam and Eve made for themselves aprons of fig-leaves, a covering too narrow for them to wrap themselves, as in Isaiah 28:20. Such are all the rags of our own righteousness. But God made them coats of skin, large, strong, durable, and fit for them: such is the righteousness of Christ; therefore put ye on the Lord Jesus Christ.[6]

God uses this sacrifice to set a pattern of covenant that we see all the way through Scripture, a covenant that climaxes at the cross and is sealed by the Holy Spirit, according to Ephesians 1:13-14.

Though Adam's fall instituted death, God always had a plan to reconcile us to Himself and to give us life. In *A Biblical Theology of the Old Testament*, essayist Eugene H. Merrill writes,

...the life [Jesus] lived demonstrated by its power and perfection all that God created Adam and all men to be. In other words, Jesus fulfilled in His life the potentialities of unfallen Adam just as by His death He restored all mankind to those potentialities.[7]

In other words, our relationship with Jesus Christ restores our ability to do all the things that God intended for mankind to do, including walking in beautifully blessed communion with God and with one another!

With the first sacrifice in the Garden, and with the final sacrifice of His Son on the cross, God sealed His promise to Adam, and to all of humanity, that we will walk in righteousness, dominion, and as the image of God in the earth. Because of Christ's sacrifice, the believer is completely redeemed from the penalty of sin, and we inherit *all* of the dominion, authority, and power that God intended for us to walk in. We can reclaim relationships as God intended, as portraits of His reconciliation with mankind.

We see the pattern of sacrificial covenant throughout the Old Testament with the covenants extended to Noah, Abraham, Moses, and the nation of Israel at Mount Sinai. During the days of Noah, when wickedness and perversion covered the whole earth, God spared this righteous descendent of the third son of Adam and his family, intent on fulfilling His covenant with humanity. He warned Noah about the impending rain and called him into an ark of safety, protection, and provision.

As the waters receded, Noah sent out a dove, whose return indicated that there was safety and provision beyond the ark. As soon as Noah descended from the ark, he built an altar to the Lord and sacrificed animals on the altar. According to Genesis 8:21, God smelled the *"pleasing aroma"* of the sacrifice and marked it by a renewal of His covenant to the human race. The Noahic covenant is found in Genesis 9 and God echoes the instruction and promise He gave to Adam in Genesis 1. God established an everlasting covenant with Noah and the generations to come and signaled that covenant with a rainbow in the clouds.

God's plan for mankind, as expressed in His covenant with Adam and Noah, was revisited and expanded with Abraham, a descendent of the third son of Noah. In Genesis 12, God promises productivity—to make Abram into a *"great nation,"* the agent of His determination of blessing and cursing, and the means through which all the peoples of the earth would be blessed. God promised a land to his offspring, Canaan, which represents a new Eden and a New Jerusalem. When Abram left the lands of Sodom and Gomorrah, he refused to take anything from the territories marked by sin, and God reestablished His covenant with Abram again. In Genesis 15, God called for Abraham to gather a heifer, a goat, and a ram, each three years old, along with another dove. Abram killed the animals, splitting them in two, and immediately God put him into a deep sleep. The Bible tells us that, *"…a smoking firepot with a blazing torch appeared and passed between the pieces. On that day, the Lord made a covenant with Abram…"* (Gen. 15:17-18).

God's covenant to Abram was sealed by this act of sacrifice, but God also required sacrifice from Abraham. In Genesis 17, God renewed His covenant with Abraham and gave him circumcision as a sign of the covenant. All of Abraham's male descendents were circumcised, and even today the process is not considered complete without the shedding of blood. He tells Abraham that the covenant *must be kept*, instructing, *"You are to undergo circumcision, and it will be the sign of the covenant between Me and you"* (Gen. 17:11). This covenant of the flesh represented purity. It echoed Abraham's requirement under the covenant to *"walk before [God] and be blameless"* (Gen. 17:1). Circumcision is an outward sign of an inward righteousness, a devotion to God as His children, and a commitment to following after His commandments because of this love relationship.

Later, God instructed Abraham:

... Take your son, your only son, Isaac, whom you love, and go to the region of Moriah. Sacrifice him there as a burnt offering on one of the mountains I will tell you about (Genesis 22:2).

Abraham walked in complete obedience to God by gathering wood, fire, and preparing to worship in the place that God was leading him to. Abraham trusted that *"God Himself will provide the lamb for the burnt offering..."* (Gen. 22:8). He was willing to give up the thing that meant most to him in order to please God.

The Bible says that Abraham bound his son to the wood, laid him on the altar, and prepared to slay his son. Because Abraham was willing to sacrifice everything, God stopped him in the process and provided a ram for the sacrifice instead. God reiterated His promise to Abraham when He saw that there was nothing that Abraham would withhold from him. The Abrahamic covenant is echoed to his son Isaac, and to Isaac's son Jacob, and to Jacob's son Joseph, and it is extended to the nation of Israel through Moses, and to the Church in the New Testament through Christ.

Abraham was willing to sacrifice everything.

A covenant must be made and kept under a seal, and flesh and blood had to be shed in order to seal the covenants between God and man. Sacrifices were also offered as atonements for sin, and the aroma of sacrifice drew God to mankind and made union, habitation, and reconciliation with His people possible. Likewise, sacrifice is required in the development of a covenant between man and woman. Both parties must be willing to accept the sacrificial love of Christ and to kill off anything in their flesh (intellect, habits, attitude, behavior, speech, emotions, thoughts, will) that is contrary to God's will and His instructions. Salvation, sacrifice, and sanctification (the cutting away of fleshly motives and actions) is a necessary practice in the heart of a believer and, consequently, in the life of an individual who is entering courtship or maintaining a covenant. That's right, you have to die to yourself! In Chapter 5, we will discuss the necessity of sacrifice and sanctification, along with practical examples of habits and attitudes that must be surrendered, cleansed, or transformed in the process of courtship.

Spiritual Roles

In the Book of Exodus, the covenant relationship given to Adam, Noah, and the descendents of Abraham were extended to the entire nation of Israel. On the mountain of Horeb, the angel of the Lord spoke to Moses from the burning bush and introduced Himself as *Yahweh*, the God of the covenant, the God of Abraham, Isaac, and Jacob. God told Moses that He has,

> *...surely seen the affliction of My people which are in Egypt, and have heard their cry by reason of their taskmasters; for I know their sorrows; and I am come down to deliver them out of the*

hand of the Egyptians, and to bring them up out of that land unto a good land...flowing with milk and honey... (Exodus 3:7-8 KJV).

God identified the nation of Israel as His people, sympathized with their plight in Egypt, and committed to delivering them from Pharaoh by His own strong hand. God initiated Israel's deliverance and used Moses as His chosen vessel to perform miracle after miracle to ensure their release so that they could take possession of the land that He had promised them. As a part of the covenant extended to Moses, God told him that the Israelites needed to take three days in the wilderness to worship Him and to make a sacrifice (see Exod. 3:12). The Hebrew term for worship is connected to service.[8] In exchange for delivering Israel from Egypt, God expected Israel to pledge her devotion to Him by serving and worshiping Him wholeheartedly.

Those are the terms and expectations of the covenant for both parties. The covenant given to Moses details roles and responsibilities for God—lover, initiator, protector, redeemer, and provider—and His chosen people—beloved, benefactor, devotee, caregiver, and worshiper. In the Old Testament, God is the *covenantor*, who is responsible for performing the covenant, and Israel is the *covenantee*, in whose favor covenant has been made.[9] In the New Testament, as prophesied in Jeremiah 31:34 and explained in Hebrews 8, those roles and responsibilities are now written upon the hearts and minds of the believer who is grafted into a better covenant with greater promises by faith in Jesus Christ.

 God is the covenantor; Israel is the covenantee.

The chosen people of God, the nation of Israel, were incapable of following His commandments, of chasing Him with their whole hearts, in and of their own strength. They were also unable to establish and maintain relationships that would reflect God's image. Though demonic influence and human decision introduced the curses of death, broken relationship, forfeited inheritance, polytheism, and polygamy into the earth, an act of divine love was powerful enough to break all of those curses. Though man refused to keep his commitment by completely and wholeheartedly serving God, He remembered His promise and never stopped protecting and pursuing the heart of humanity. His desire was to reconcile us to Himself and to one another. His plan was fulfilled through Christ, the Mediator of the New Covenant.

In Ephesians 5, we learn that God desires that men and women who marry fulfill the same roles and carry the same responsibilities as are laid out in His covenant with the believer. The apostle Paul wrote,

> *Be imitators of God, therefore, as dearly loved children and live a life of love, just as Christ loved us and gave Himself up for us as a fragrant offering and sacrifice to God* (Ephesians 5:1-2).

God's expectation is that His chosen people—male and female— would serve Him by living holy lifestyles, fleeing "even the hint" of sexual immorality, impurity, greed, foolish talk, coarse joking, and the *"fruitless deeds of darkness"* that have no place in the Kingdom of God. He even warns us not to "be partners" with anyone who exhibits those characteristics (see Eph. 5:11-12).

In the second half of Ephesians 5, Paul clearly articulated the roles and positions of both parties in marital covenant. The husband becomes a representative of Christ, charged with headship, sanctification of his partner through the Word of God, provision and care of his partner, and all of the responsibilities of love (see Eph. 5:25-32). God transforms the man into His image as the covenantor—the lover, initiator, protector, redeemer, and provider of all of his wife's physical, emotional, intellectual, and spiritual needs. The wife becomes a representative of the Church, charged with submission, respect, and honor of her husband (see Eph. 5:22-24,33). God transforms woman into His image as the covenantee—the beloved recipient of the husband's love and promises, the agent of praise and adoration, and the devoted body equipped to flesh out and carry the vision of her head.

 It is the responsibility of the bridegroom to win the respect, the adoration, and the trust of his bride.

Christ is separated from His bride for a season, but He actively pursues her—from Eden to Gethsemane and beyond. Guess what? The same should be true for our relationships. It is the responsibility of the bridegroom to win the respect, the adoration, and the trust of his bride. Men, you are charged to love as God loved, and you should be prepared to do whatever it takes to demonstrate that love to the woman God has gifted you to spiritually cover, including laying down your life, your feelings, and your desires for the weaker vessel. Women, you should expect no less, and you must open yourself to the practices of quiet submission, trust, vulnerability, and appreciation of a man who is being led by God.

Without a relationship with Christ, it is impossible for men and women to understand, let alone walk out, the roles that God established for them. Even with a relationship with God, it can be difficult to walk outside of societal norms, to break habits, reactions, and mechanisms that seem natural to us, or to escape behaviors, practices, and assumptions that we have learned from our mothers and fathers, or from their absences, or that we have developed in light of our own failed relationships. Recognizing and walking in our God-given roles is necessary for the building and maintenance of successful relationships. God's way, even when it is uncomfortable and challenging, is the only way. More about the God-ordained roles and responsibilities of men and women during courtship and marriage will be discussed in Chapters 6 and 7.

Sovereign Plan

A friend of mine, lovingly concerned about my extended season of singleness, recently forwarded a popular magazine article to me by email that encouraged single Christians to begin to "settle." The article claimed that Christians stay single for too long because we are waiting on an ideal instead of choosing from the vast number of available men or women around us. The article's advice: look at your options, choose the best one, and hope for the best. I was completely frustrated that a "Christian" writer would give such ungodly counsel.

To those of you who have questioned if there is more than one possible person for you, or who want to know where all the "available" men and women are, or who have wondered if you married the right person, or who are questioning a current relationship and want to know if it is from God, or who are floating through relationships hoping that one of them will work out, here is my counsel.

We serve a God of order and not of confusion. The choice of a spouse is a matter of discernment, not of human decision, and it requires prayer, not practicality. The choice of a spouse is a sovereign one! You were created uniquely, and the person God designed for you is equally unique. His bride, the Church, was sovereignly chosen out of Himself. Guess what? The same is true for your mate. God created you on purpose, with purpose, and for purpose, and He knows whom He has established on the earth to join to you to fulfill that purpose. He or she is designed to be a mirror image, an equal opposite who shares your dream, your destination, and your goals, but differs enough from you to cover your weaknesses and draw out your strengths. It is critical in this process that you know and trust God as your Father who knows what is best for you, and that you fully know yourself and the direction God is taking you.

 It is critical in this process that you know and trust God as your Father who knows what is best for you, and that you fully know yourself and the direction God is taking you.

If you don't believe me, just ask Isaac and Rebekah whose love story is written in Genesis 24. There are four characters in this story: the father Abraham, the servant Eliezer, the son/bridegroom Isaac, and the bride Rebekah. Each character's role is divinely connected to the love story of Christ and the Church, and they shadow our roles in the process of divine courtship. Isaac and Rebekah are with their families in two different geographical locations. Abraham decides that it is time for Isaac to marry, and sends his servant to choose, challenge, and relocate a bride based on the qualifications and instructions he provides. Rebekah serves Eliezer and follows him back to the estate. Isaac is working and praying in a field when he sees them approaching. Rebekah stops and veils herself, and Isaac goes to her and claims her as his wife.

Abraham stands in the position of God the Father—he owns and rules his estate, teaches and grooms the son, decides when the time is right for his son to receive his bride, determines the characteristics that she must possess, and sends his servant to prepare her. The servant Eliezer, whose name translates "God of help," "helper," or "comforter" is a type of the Holy Spirit.[10] He knows the will of the father, he identifies the bride whom God had already chosen, he communicates with the bride, and he brings the bride and the bridegroom together. Isaac is a type of Jesus Christ. He was born miraculously as a manifestation of a promise, was offered in sacrifice, and then resurrected back to life (see Gen. 22). Both Isaac and Christ worked to harvest a field and meditated in prayer prior to their bride's arrival, preparing a place for her. Rebekah is a type of the Church. She was chosen before she even knew it; she was willing to serve and follow the "helper." She demonstrated devotion to someone she had not yet been united to, and she was willing to leave everything that was familiar to join someone in a life of promise.

The sovereign plan for marriage is demonstrated through this story, as it is God who works through Holy Spirit to choose a wife for the son and to prepare two people and bring them together. Isaac and Rebekah had nothing to do with their own process. They didn't choose each other. They didn't pick the timing. They simply submitted to the will of the Father operating in their lives, walking by faith as they were led. It is God our Father who uses the Holy Spirit in our lives to prepare us and unite us with our mates. In other words, the pressure is off! All we have to do is work the ground and serve in the places where we are, trusting God to develop us, and trusting the Holy Spirit to lead us where He wants us to go.

 God uses the Holy Spirit to prepare the Church as a bride awaiting the return of Christ.

It is God who owns the whole world and orchestrates time, and He uses the Holy Spirit to prepare the Church as a bride awaiting the return of Christ—her bridegroom who prays for her and who will return to claim her. The questions of preparation, timing, and choice should be left to God, who has already written your love story. We are challenged to

> *Trust in the Lord with all your heart and lean not on your own understanding; in all your ways acknowledge Him, and He will make your paths straight* (Proverbs 3:5-6).

If you focus on Him, His guarantee is to order all of your paths straight to His promise, including the one toward your mate. You cannot choose (or leave) a mate based on circumstantial evidence. Trust God and draw close enough to Him so that you can follow wherever He leads you, with whomever He has created for you. Knowing God and His will for your life will help you eliminate fakes, but when making (or remembering) that decision, wait for and rely upon God to grant His permission and His blessing. Allow Him to lead your heart.

Not only is the choice of a spouse a sovereign decision, but so are the steps in the process. According to Psalm 37:23, *"The steps of a good man are ordered by the Lord: and he delighteth in his way"* (KJV). Still not convinced? Proverbs 16:9 tells us, *"In his heart a man plans his course, but the Lord determines his steps."* The God whom we serve not only watches over us as we walk, but when we trust in Him, He also shows us the direction, speed, and technique. We serve a detailed God who illustrates and orchestrates every specification in the design of the relationships He built to reflect His love and to manifest His glory.

Applying the Pattern: The Tabernacle as a Blueprint for Godly Courtship

In the last section, we discussed covenant relationship as the tool that God uses to reconcile Himself to humankind and to unite man and woman as a reflection of the love that Christ and the Church share. Nowhere is covenant relationship better illustrated than at Mount Sinai in the Book of Exodus. God promised Moses that He would deliver His divinely chosen people, who would worship and serve Him on the mountain, and He fulfilled His part of the covenant. From Exodus 19 to Exodus 24, God shared His expectations of Israel with Moses, including the Ten Commandments and regulations regarding feasts, property, justice, and social responsibility. In exchange for Israel's promise to live up to His expectations, God promised to bless them, increase them in number and health, destroy all of their enemies, and give them provision and prosperity in a land that He had already prepared for them. God, as a husband, paid a bride-price for Israel in the form of their deliverance from Egypt, which demonstrated His ability to provide for them and was an offer of engagement to her. Moses accepted God's proposal, recording the agreement in a written document described in Scripture as the *Book of the Covenant* (see Exod. 24:7).

In Exodus 24, Moses began preparation for the union of God and His people. He invited the priests and 70 elders of Israel as witnesses (see Exod. 24:1). He built an altar at the foot of the mountain and set the scene with worship and offerings (see Exod 24:5). God Himself stood at the altar with His people and communed with them. Moses read from the Book of the Covenant, and the people repeated their vows in response, *"We will do everything the Lord has said; we will obey"* (Exod. 24:7b). Immediately, the covenant was sealed by sacrifice, as the blood of the covenant was sprinkled on the people. This ceremony was immediately followed by a "honeymoon" during which the presence of God rested on His bride in a flame of passionate fire. God Himself set the pattern and type for a wedding ceremony and for the opening of a marriage!

Modern couples follow the same exact process as they write out their vows as promises to one another (book of the covenant), invite witnesses to testify to the sharing of those vows, meet at an altar after a period of sanctification and separation, give and exchange rings (sharing of offerings and gifts), seal their relationship with sex (blood covenant and consummation), and build a home and a life together after their honeymoon. Pretty amazing, huh?

In the next chapter of Exodus, immediately after the honeymoon, God began to give Moses the instructions for building a home to share with His people. For 40 days and 40 nights, Moses communed with God and received a blueprint for transitioning God's presence from visitation to habitation. The tabernacle, which literally translates "residence," "dwelling place," or "sanctuary" from the Hebrew, is the house for God's glory, which He desired to share with His beloved people.[11] In Exodus 25:8-9, God said, *"Then have them make a sanctuary for Me, and I will dwell among them. Make this tabernacle and all its furnishings **exactly like the pattern I will show you.***" For the first time since Eden, God prepared to live among a people He sovereignly chose, and the tabernacle was built from the wealth the Israelites carried out of Egypt when He delivered them from bondage. God was the owner and the architect of the tabernacle, and He desired that it be built according to His design and for His purpose. He provided every detail, and the tabernacle became a picture to the world of His love and commitment to the people He had set apart for Himself (see Exod. 25–31). He allowed Israel, His beloved, to build and prepare a home for Him.

The tabernacle was a tent constructed in the center of the Israelite camp during their wanderings in the wilderness. There was a seven-foot fence of white linen that set its boundaries, and it had only one entrance called the gate. The covering for the tabernacle was animal flesh stretched across pillars of wood. Inside the tabernacle were three sectioned-off areas, known as *courts*, that contained seven pieces of furniture arranged in a divine interior design:

1. The outer court—with the brazen altar and the bronze laver,

2. The inner court, also known as the holy place—with the golden lampstand, table of showbread, and the golden altar of incense, and

3. The holy of holies—with the ark of the covenant and the Mercy Seat.

The layout and design is significant because it is an illustration of God's grace and His sovereign plan to approach Him. God specifically laid out the measurements, the materials, and the men whom He wanted to build every aspect of His home, and failure to comply with God's building plans would have meant destruction for the people. You couldn't enter the tabernacle in any way you wanted to—the nation had to go through the tabernacle God's way. Every part of the tabernacle was a picture of God's grace and His sovereign plan for salvation and redemption through Christ, and God's desire was for the tabernacle to perfectly illustrate that message to mankind.

God designs the Old Testament tabernacle to establish a pattern and a type for covenant, salvation, reconciliation, and worship in the earth. The tabernacle was a "copy" and a "shadow" of things to come (see Heb. 8:5). In the New Testament, Christ fulfilled the pattern established in Exodus that prophesied of His coming for generations. Jesus mediates the new covenant, and mankind becomes the house for God's glory. According to First Corinthians 6:19-20, we no longer belong to ourselves; Christ paid the bride-price, and our bodies are now the *"temple of the Holy Spirit."* That's right—God lives within us! The first covenant and tabernacle came with *"regulations for worship and also an earthly sanctuary"* (Heb. 9:1). Now it is the believer, the Church, who offers herself in praise and worship unto God, and becomes the sanctuary where God dwells in the earth.

 Christ paid the bride-price, and our bodies are now the "temple of the Holy Spirit."

Marriage, the union of two believers, is a dwelling place for the glory of God, and it should also be built according to the instructions and the design He gave us in the Book of Exodus. Just like the tabernacle, marriage is an illustration of God's love, eternal covenant, and a portrait of Christ's redemptive and reconciliatory work. Just like the tabernacle, a believer should not enter the courts of a relationship with God, a friendship, a ministry, or a marriage leaning on his or her own plan or understanding. God provided the tabernacle as a blueprint for creating a dwelling place for His glory, and our lives and relationships should be based on God's divine design for His pleasure and for our own good!

Are you ready to learn how to experience the glory of God and reflect that glory in your relationships? For the next three chapters, we will be walking through the Old Testament tabernacle, exploring its furnishings as the pattern that God instituted in the earth for covenant relationship and the progression toward intimate worship with God and intimate commitment to a spouse. Each of the courts in the tabernacle represents a stage in courtship. In Chapter 5, we will discuss the outer court, which represents the season of singleness and/or the individual preparation that is needed to build, repair, or sustain a relationship. In Chapter 6, we will progress to the inner court, which represents the development of true friendship and intimacy that progresses through periods of dating and engagement. In Chapter 7, we will climax our discussion in the holy of holies, where God's glory is revealed through His covenant with you and extended into the covenant relationship of marriage through the seal of sexual intercourse.

 God's Word has challenged, opened, pressed, stretched, cut, healed, encouraged, and strengthened me.

I feel that it would only be fair to warn you: the journey through the courtship is not for kids! Even as I have studied and prepared this text, God's Word has challenged, opened, pressed, stretched, cut, healed, encouraged, and strengthened me. I have been my most vulnerable, my most honest with God, with myself, and in my relationships. I've learned things about myself that I needed to know, and I discovered a few things I wanted to forget so that I could avoid accountability for them. And God continues to show me new things about myself, and the world, and His people. The courtship's journey is an active one—reading by faith is not enough. You must be ready to walk. Writer Maria Robinson said, "Nobody can go back and start a new beginning, but anyone can start today and make a new ending."[12] As you turn to the next page of this text, I challenge you to make a commitment in your heart to start a new page in your life. No matter where today finds you, you can purpose in your heart a new direction for tomorrow. Let's develop a new goal. A new vision. A new plan. Let's turn the page.

Endnotes

1. Marriage has been the topic of several feature articles and news features in popular media sources including *Time, Newsweek,* CNN, et al. at the time of this book's publication. This particular article can be accessed online. Caitlin, Flanigan. "Is There Hope for the American Marriage." *Time* magazine, 2 July 2009. *Time.com.* 2 July 2009. Web. 6 July 2009. http://www.time.com/time/nation/article/0,8599,1908243-4,00.html.

2. Ibid.

3. Ibid.

4. Other scholars debate if the two Lamechs of Genesis 4 and 5 are the same individual, based not only on their names but on the similar names of their fathers and occupations of their

progeny. Whether they are the same individual or not is less important for this study than the concept of the expanding practice of polytheism and polygyny, producing a progeny that was offensive to God.

5. Paraphrased from the entry on "Covenant." *The American Heritage® Dictionary of the English Language, Fourth Edition.* Houghton Mifflin Company, 2004. 7 December 2009. Dictionary.com http://dictionary.reference.com/browse/covenant.

6. "Genesis 3." *Matthew Henry's Commentary on the Whole Bible* (1706). BibleStudyTools.com. 10 March 2011. http://www.biblestudytools.com/commentaries/matthew-henry-complete/.

7. Roy B. Zuck ed. "A Theory of the Pentateuch." *A Biblical Theology of the Old Testament* (Chicago: Moody Press, 1991).

8. Strong, *Strong's Exhaustive Concordance of the Bible*, #H7812.

9. The online entries for "covenantor" and "covenantee" can be accessed in *The American Heritage® Dictionary of the English Language, Fourth Edition.* Houghton Mifflin Company, 2004. 07 December 2009. Dictionary.com. http://dictionary.reference.com.

10. Strong, *Strong's Exhaustive Concordance of the Bible*, #H461.

11. Ibid., #H4908.

12. Quote found online at http://thinkexist.com/quotation/nobody_can_go_back_and_start_a_new_beginning-but/174633.html. For more information on author Maria Robinson, see http://www.maria-robinson.com/.

SECTION 3

*The Courtship: A Systematic Approach
to Dating and Marriage*

Chapter 5

THROUGH THE GATE: SALVATION, SANCTIFICATION, AND SANITY

"Vision without action is a daydream. Action without vision is a nightmare." —Japanese Proverb

"Vision," wrote satirist Jonathan Swift, "is the art of seeing what is invisible to others."[1] In other words, true vision is not the ability to see what is seen; it is the ability to distinguish between what is readily seen and to grasp a concept, a picture, an image, or a revelation that lies beyond what the eyes can perceive. When I was growing up, I loved puzzles and games, especially brainteasers and word games, which would stretch my vocabulary and my critical thinking skills. (I admit, I was a little bit of a nerd!) I was coming of age in the '90s, and as I was matriculating through middle school, "Magic Eye," a new puzzle phenomenon, invaded scholastic book fairs, libraries, and classrooms.

Magic Eye books contained colorful, repeating 2D patterns, which contained hidden 3D images. The Magic Eye books were extremely popular, and they spent weeks on the *New York Times* best-seller lists. My friends loved these books, and we passed them from person to person and eagerly found the hidden images. As much as I enjoyed a good puzzle, I hated Magic Eye! No matter how hard I looked at the pictures, or how desperate I was to see what was concealed, I was unsuccessful. People would try to help me by showing me how to hold the book or admonishing me to cross my eyes or gaze at a certain distance, but their efforts and advice were to no avail. I would stare at the pictures for hours, becoming more and more frustrated with each attempt, turning page after page determined to find a puzzle that I could figure out.

I didn't know it at that time, but it is absolutely impossible to "figure out" a Magic Eye puzzle. The key to Magic Eye lies not in one's critical thinking or logic skills, in one's ability to copy what worked for someone else, or in one's knowledge or experience. The viewer has no control in Magic Eye, for it is the creator who placed the hidden image beyond the pattern. In order to be successful, a viewer has to cultivate the ability to look past the pattern and to focus his or her gaze on the image in the distance beyond what he or she can see.

When one is in the correct posture and position to view the image, the muscles controlling the focusing lens of the eye actually relax and stretch out! Once the viewer's gaze is fixed in the right direction and he or she is no longer distracted by the busyness of the pattern, the image will simply appear! I thought that I could figure the puzzles out, or that if I looked hard enough or did everything that I was told, that I would be able to see the image. In contrast, my efforts to view the hidden image were thwarting my ability to see it. Because I refused to relax, to look past the pattern and ignore the distractions, and to just allow the image to come to me, I was frustrated over and over again, until I simply gave up on the concept altogether.

In the previous chapters, we uncovered the dysfunctional nature of our relationships and traced the source of our individual failures and generational curses to their origin. We stared at the patterns of relationship in this country, staring straight at song lyrics, statistics, and other examples from Scripture, our modern society, and from our own experience. We also revisited God's plan for love and covenant and realized that God never intended the pictures of brokenness that we gaze upon in the media and in mirrors. Beyond our failures and our frustrations, God has displayed an image of Himself that He has been waiting for us to discover.

 Beyond our failures and our frustrations, God has displayed an image of Himself that He has been waiting for us to discover.

Today, I challenge you, as God has challenged me, to cultivate your vision, your ability to see beyond what you have seen, to know and receive and offer the type of love that can only have its origins in Him. When we relax and release our expectations and frustrations, and we focus our gaze on God in the midst of our circumstances and situations, we can trust that the image that He created will emerge in our lives. We don't have to fix our vision or our relationships. If we keep walking toward Him, He will produce a new vision, and in time a new standard, from within us.

When we encounter Moses and the Israelite nation at the end of Exodus 24, they had just consummated the covenant ceremony, and Moses remained in the presence of God for 40 days and 40 nights. It is during this period that God provided Moses with a vision for the tabernacle and gave him the exact pattern, measurements, required materials, and even the names of the builders! The tabernacle was to become God's dwelling place, a portrait of Christ and a paradigm for His glory in the earth, and God gave precise and detailed instructions and admonished Moses to build *exactly according to the pattern* that He was showing him (see Exod. 25:9,40; 26:30; 27:8; Num. 8:4; Heb. 8:5). In his text, *Seeing Christ in the Tabernacle*, Ervin N. Hershberger makes an amazing point that proves just how important the tabernacle is to God.

> God used two relatively short chapters (Gen. 1 and 2) to record the creation of the universe. But he used fifty chapters (13 in Exodus, 18 in Leviticus, 13 in Numbers, 2 in Deuteronomy, 4 in Hebrews) to explain the construction of the Tabernacle....[2]

Moses didn't have to figure out the vision for himself; he did not have to fail or get frustrated in his efforts to produce the vision that God had placed before him. Not only did God give Moses an exact pattern for the tabernacle, but He also made advance provision. God had favored Israel in their exodus from Egypt, instructing and allowing them to take gold, silver, and cloth from the Egyptians. When God told Moses what to use to build the tabernacle, He only asked the Israelites for what He knew He had already given to them.

 Contrary to popular belief, God wants more from us than patience!

Before Moses could build anything, he had to receive a clear vision, and before they could produce the vision, the Israelites had to be willing to offer up things that they considered valuable. Contrary to popular belief, God wants more from us than patience! He expects us to follow His instructions and to be willing to do and/ or give up anything in order to benefit from His presence in our lives and in our relationships. There is a God-ordained process for receiving and manifesting vision. Before the Israelites could take one step into the courts of the tabernacle, they had to know the process. And before you take one step into the courtship, it is important that you do the same. You must spend time with God in prayer and in His Word, count the cost of true discipleship and commitment, and seek revelation of God's divine purpose for your life and for your relationships.

 One of the things that has frustrated me the most during my season of singleness is that no one seems to be able to tell you what you are supposed to be doing while you are single.

Going to the Mountain: Understanding the Season of Solitude

One of the things that has frustrated me the most during my season of singleness is that no one seems to be able to tell you what you are supposed to be doing while you are single. I've heard every bit of advice that one could possibly receive from well-meaning church mothers, concerned relatives and friends of both genders, and from seasoned pulpiteers, and most has been so contradictory, or so ambiguous, that it hurt rather than helped. I've been told that I was too picky, and that I was not picky enough. I've been told that you should accept someone who has most of the qualities you want in a mate and that any relationship will take work, and I've been told that you should never compromise for anything less that all the qualities that you want and deserve and that anything that you have to work at is not sent by God. I've been told to marry and have children early for obvious biological reasons, and I've been told to delay starting a family to pursue my career and education and ministry for economic and social reasons. My all-time favorite word of advice (written in my most sarcastic authorial tone) is that singles should just "Wait." I promise you, if I ever hear any variation of the phrase, "Wait on the Lord" again in regard to the issue of relationships, I'll just scream!

For any of you who have wondered what you should do about loneliness or boredom, or how to know if you should date someone or if he or she is "the one," or how long you should date, or how far is too far, or if you married the wrong person, or how to fix your marriage, let me give you only piece of advice that has rung true for me in my experience. It's not a clever, repeatable phrase, a catchy sermon title, or an easily remembered acronym. It is a clear, direct, biblical truth: You must seek God! Not just wait on Him, but also pursue Him, His heart, His plans, and His time line. And when you seek Him, He answers you with the revelation you need to fulfill the vision that He has preordained and planned for you. Just as God spent over 50 chapters detailing His plan for the tabernacle, God has written and is ready to reveal to you His plan for your life and your relationships.

In James 1:5, we learn that if we lack any wisdom, we should seek God, who gives to us all generously without finding any fault. Jesus, speaking to the disciples, said that the friends of God do what God commands.

> *I no longer call you servants, because a servant does not know his master's business. Instead, I have called you friends, for everything that I learned from My Father I have made known to you* (John 15:15).

The disciples walked beside, listened to, served with, and followed Jesus for three years, and in the process of developing relationship with them, Jesus revealed to them who He is, who they were, and what God's plans were. In First Corinthians 2:7-10, Paul extends this concept, revealing to us that we have, speak, and live by a secret wisdom that God destined for our glory before time began. If we want to live and love in ways that produce glory, we can't depend on our own experience or expertise. It can only come through divine revelation. According to this text, *"No eye has seen, no ear has heard, no mind has conceived what God has prepared for those who love Him'—but God has revealed it to us by His Spirit..."* (1 Cor. 2:9-10). The vision that He has placed in your heart—the one that you haven't seen, or ever heard about happening, and that you don't even understand yourself—will only be produced through the Spirit. God has been waiting to reveal His plans and release His promise to His children, but we must leave the realm of the familiar and climb to new heights of faith and expectation in order to receive this type of revelation.

Discipleship—Seeking God Through Your Singleness

To receive the revelation of the tabernacle, Moses had to climb up and remain on Mount Sinai. He had to walk away from people he loved and who depended upon him. He had to leave the comfort and familiarity of the valley, pass through the wilderness, survive treacherous terrain, and adjust to changing climate and increasing pressure. He had to trust God for even his basic needs, while submitting to a 40-day period of testing, teaching, and rebuke. He had to be patient and willing to wait and continue to seek God until the fullness of the vision was received.

To receive the revelation you need for your life, your relationships, and for marriage, you will have to climb your own mountain. You will have to submit to solitude, accepting that time alone with God is not just a part of the process—it is absolutely necessary for the process! You will have to cut some relationship ties and re-prioritize others. You should prepare in advance to leave behind places and habits and defense mechanisms that have been comfortable, and to endure trial and temptation, which will produce patience and perfection in you. In your mountain expedition, you will be stretched in your faith, and you will have to learn what it is to depend on God and allow Him to mold and to shape you into who He created you to be. And when God begins to speak to you, you must resist the urge to make the vision come to pass in your own way, choosing instead to stay in His presence in a posture of prayer until you have not only the promise, but also the ordered steps in the process that will lead you to that promise.

 Courtship is a process that begins with and prioritizes what you do by yourself and with God.

There is a major difference between terms like dating, engagement, sex, marriage, and courtship. Dating or marriage refers to actions that you take with another person. Courtship is a process that begins with and prioritizes what you do by yourself and with God. The real reason that most of us are not successful in our relationships is that we do not spend the time and make the effort in our relationship with God that will produce a vision for and develop the love that we will need to maintain our other connections. Rather than running to our mountain and spending time in the secret place with God, we run into multiple relationships, into busyness in careers or ministry, to Facebook, or to our cell phone so that we have someone, anyone, to talk to. Instead of studying His Word for guidance, we turn on cable television or our iPods to drown out the sound of His voice. Married couples would rather argue, work extra hours, or stay busy with the kids than fast and pray and seek God together. We are often willing to do anything to avoid being alone with God, when alone is exactly what we need to be in order to obtain the purging, healing, strength, focus, favor, and vision that we need to be successful in our relationships and in life.

The problem with most relationships is that people enter them expecting a mate to be their God—to heal their hurts, to help them overcome their pasts, to provide for them, to lead them, to always be there for them, even when they aren't holding up their end of the bargain. Or they are downright determined to play God in someone else's life by trying to "fix him" or "help her" and become more and more co-dependent as the days go by. No human being can do all that! Marriage is a partnership of two humans, who together create more impact in the Kingdom than they could produce alone. It is not substitution for counseling, a quick fix, a way to satisfy lust, or a financial arrangement. Until people are willing to let God be God in their lives, they will continue to experience frustration in their relationships based on unrealistic expectations of themselves and of potential or current mates.

Before I started writing this text, I made a conscious decision to stop allowing stuff in my life to interfere with my relationship with God. For the first time in my adult life, I was determined to make Him my priority. I was tired of investing in people and activities where I was giving my all with nothing (no difference and no appreciation) in return, so I repented of my "God complex" and refocused my energy on taking care of myself and cultivating a love relationship with God. He was the first person I spoke to in the morning and the last voice I heard at night. I told Him everything about my day, asked Him for what I needed, shared my frustrations and my joys. I set date nights, specific times for prayer and study. I gave myself a curfew, a time when I stopped receiving phone calls or visitors so that I could take care of myself and my home, and could open myself up to His presence. He listened to me, and I listened when He began to speak. I took a lesson from Moses who recorded the commandments and the Book of the Covenant, and I wrote down the things that He told me for two reasons: 1) I didn't want to lose or forget anything, and 2) I knew that there would be a day when God would want me to share those words with others. Today, you are reading those words.

You have to stop running. Nothing else will satisfy the empty place or time in your life. If you allow Him to, God will commune with you right now. He'll bring you joy in your solitude and peace in the midst of your storms. He'll give you instructions and vision and a promise for your future. If you're single or widowed or divorced, maximize this season and get everything from God that He wants you to have right now. You have no excuses, no other demands on your attention that you are obligated to fulfill. Give that attention to yourself and to pursuing God and His purposes for your life, for there will be a time when your attention will shift back to those to whom you will be connected. If you're married, but you know that your life and relationship is headed in the wrong direction, go back to the mountain, seek God's face, and allow Him to give you a new beginning. He's waiting.

Stewardship—Giving God What You've Got

In Exodus 25:2, God said to Moses, *"Tell the Israelites to bring Me an offering. You are to receive the offering for Me from each man whose heart prompts him to give."* Immediately after the covenant ceremony, and prior to the fulfillment of the vision that God gave to Moses about the tabernacle, God checked the heart of the people by challenging their giving. God itemized the building materials for the tabernacle and requested that each person be willing to offer whatever they had in order to contribute to the establishment of a dwelling place for God's glory. God asked for items of different economic and emotional value: gold, silver, bronze, goat hair, fabric, wood, oil, spices, and gemstones. The people were asked to give according to what was in their hearts and what they had in their house.

 Love can always be measured by one's willingness to give.

Love can always be measured by one's willingness to give. God loved the world so much that He was willing to give up His only begotten Son, and Jesus loved us so much that He was willing to give up His life. The Israelites had to take inventory by searching their storehouses for gifts that would demonstrate the love and desire in their heart to establish a home for the glory of God. What are you willing to give to Him? God never requires more from us than what we have, so perhaps the better question to ask is what do you have to give to Him? Have you been blessed with financial resources or time or obedience or gifts and talents? Are you ready to give Him your pain or your bitterness or your failures? Are you a tither, a worshiper, a servant?

Before God trusts you to demonstrate His love to another person, God is going to measure your giving and your commitment to Him. It is a question of stewardship. God entrusted the Israelites with the spoils of Egypt, allowing them to bring the goods through the Red Sea and wilderness with the foresight and understanding that those goods would be used to build His dwelling place. Are you mature enough to recognize that everything you have—your time, your testimony, your wealth—all belongs to God, and that He has made you a steward?

Until you are willing to place what you have back in the hands of God and trust Him with every area of your life, you are not ready to walk into the type of relationship that will house His glory. God never calls us to give, or to do, or to endure, or to become, anything that He hasn't already prepared and provided for. As you enter the courtship process, you should be willing to give God whatever He asks of you, trusting that it is not only for His glory, but also that it all works for your good too. Loving God with all of your heart, mind, and soul is excellent preparation for learning to love yourself, and, in time, to love another person. It is, in fact, the only preparation that works.

Foresight—Gaining a Perspective With Purpose

Not only did God give Moses a vision for the tabernacle that he and the Israelites were to build, but He also gave him an exact pattern and a step-by-step process. In Exodus 25, God began revealing the pattern and instructions to Moses for the final piece of furniture within the tabernacle: the ark of the covenant. The ark was symbolic of the humanity and divinity of Jesus Christ, and it was covered by the mercy seat, which represented holiness and atonement and was the place where the glory of God descended and remained. We'll discuss the ark in our discussion of the holy of holies in Chapter 7, but for now it is important to note that God told Moses to start building with His goals in mind, so that everything else that Moses built would be constructed with the ark of the covenant and with the mercy seat in the forefront of his thoughts.

Why did God tell Moses to build the last piece of furniture first? I'm so glad that you asked. God always shares a vision by revealing the final product and then walks His chosen vessels through the rest of the process. God doesn't just want us to blindly follow His instructions. He has called us His friends, sons and daughters, kings and priests, and He wants us to know and to walk in His purposes. True faith is not just blindly following God; it is seeking His face and trusting that God will do what He has said that He will do, even when circumstances and situations may dictate otherwise. In Isaiah 46:10, God said, *"I make known the end from the beginning...what is still to come. I say: My purpose will stand, and I will do all that I please."* God always declares the end of a thing prior to its beginning, and He reveals that end to those who love Him and will pursue Him.

Delight yourself in the Lord and He will give you the desires of your heart. Commit your way to the Lord; trust in Him, and He will do this: He will make your righteousness shine like the dawn... (Psalm 37:4-6).

So many of us are willing to settle for so much less than the life God wants for us and that we want for ourselves. We have given up on the idea of being truly happy, pursuing our dreams, and having the type of loving relationship and family that we have always wanted. God knows the plans He has for us, to prosper us, to let us see no harm, to give us hope, a future, and an *expected end* (see Jer. 29:11). Do you have a vision, a dream, a goal for your future and relationships? Do you have faith to believe that God is able to give you the desires of your heart? If you don't know what you desire, how can God bless you with it? How will you know that man, or woman, or job opportunity, or ministry position, came from God (or didn't come from God) when it arrives and claims to be for you?

As you begin your own journey through the courtship, you must start with the end, your destination, in mind. Whether you are single, divorced, widowed, dating, engaged, or married, it is absolutely critical for you to have a clear vision for your life and a clear objective in your relationships. You must develop a personal vision statement, writing down the vision for your life and your relationship as God gives you the revelation. Developing your vision will require you to answer some of the most difficult questions you'll ever have to ask: Who are you? What is your place in the world and in the Kingdom? What are your likes/dislikes? What do you enjoy doing and what brings you joy? What are your goals and what do you want out of life? When you have reached the end of your journey, how will people remember you?

 You must develop a personal vision statement, writing down the vision for your life and your relationship as God gives you the revelation.

Your vision, as contained in that statement, will provide accountability when you are about to stray off the path toward

God's purpose and your goal, motivation when you're not sure that the process and the pain is worth it, and documentation of your testimony when the vision comes to pass and you are ready to share your praise report to build the faith of others. It will guide you as you start making preparations for ministry or for marriage. Just as Moses saw the blueprint for the ark of the covenant first, it is critical that the start of your journey be God-centered and Christ-focused. To truly walk through the courtship, and to see God's grace and favor rest upon your life and your relationships, holiness must be your goal, and His manifested glory must be your ultimate aim. Settling for less than what God wants for you is no longer an option. You have no more time, energy, or love to waste.

Avoiding Golden Calves: Overcoming Impatience, Temptation, and Other Vision Pitfalls

When Moses descended from Mount Sinai, he was greeted with an absolute mess! The same Israelites whom God had delivered from the hand of the Egyptians, who had depended on God for food and water in the wilderness, who had entered covenant with God at the mountain, and who were challenged to consecrate themselves and prepare for His habitation had chosen instead to build another object for their affection. By Exodus 32, the Israelites had grown impatient with God while waiting on Moses to come to them. They gathered together and made a decision to make new gods to go before them. Because their promise didn't come fast enough in their opinion, they decided to create an idol and built altars to worship their new god. They stripped naked and participated in an orgy complete with food, drink, dancing, and singing. God's wrath moved Him to want to destroy the nation in their adultery, but instead God sent Moses back to correct the *"stiff-necked"* people who corrupted themselves in worship and sexual immorality with false gods they created instead of trusting the God of creation to meet their needs (see Exod. 32:7-9).

There were immediate consequences for the nation of Israel: they had to drink of their own sinful decisions (Exod. 32: 20) and they had to endure shame among the other peoples (Exod. 32:25). And there are immediate consequences for us when we decide to move outside of God's instructions and timing. Impatience, doubt, and rebellion in covenant are dangerous constructs. It is simply impossible to produce or maintain a supernatural promise through natural or sinful actions or by responding to fleshly desires.

Just ask Abraham, whose efforts to produce an heir out of his own flesh led to Ishmael and an entire nation that continues to war against the people of God to this day. Consult with Lot's wife, who was rescued from sin-filled circumstances but who was destroyed when she continued to look back and refused to move forward. Inquire of Esau, who forfeited his birthright for a bowl of soup because he couldn't control his appetite. Your biggest mistakes were probably moments when you pursued your own cravings without any consideration of doing things God's way, waiting on His timing, or when you doubted Him. Sometimes we even get angry with Him because we forget that God promised to give us the desires of our heart if we will delight ourselves in Him.

Be careful…the times in your life when you feel like giving up and forgetting about the consequences are the times when you most need spiritual accountability and a true relationship with God that will give you strength in the midst of your weakness or frustration. We are not surprised by the devices of the enemy, who will watch your walk for evidence of weakness or vulnerability and will present you with temptation based on sin in your heart and who is hoping that you engage in activity that is contrary to God's will. The phone will ring with an invitation to come over, or an illicit website will pop up, or a co-worker will begin to flirt with you, and the danger is that the immediate thrill will overshadow the threat to your life and your relationships. You must be aware. You must be patient. You must be prayerful. You must stay close to the mountain and keep your eyes on God and on your vision.

You must stay close to the mountain and keep your eyes on God and on your vision.

When Moses descended from the mountain, he stood in the gate of Israel's camp and asked a simple question: "Who is on the Lord's side?" Those who had decided to take a stand gathered themselves around Moses, and they were challenged to gather their swords and kill their brothers, their spouses, and their neighbors who refused to take the stand. Three thousand people died that day because their hearts were so hardened by their sin habits, or by anger or disappointment, that they could not recognize the opportunity that they had to experience God's blessing. When you decide to really take a stand for God and to walk in holiness in your relationships, there are some ties that absolutely, positively must be cut off. If you really want to live a saved, sold-out, sanctified lifestyle, you cannot continue to walk with people who continually reject Christ.

If you have decided live by God's Word and live a sexually pure lifestyle, your best friend or new love interest can not be a person who has an extensive collection of pornography, who insists on one-night stands, or who tells you he or she "can't live without sex...." If you have decided that you want to make your marriage work and you will not participate in adultery, you can no longer associate with single or married friends who will use your complaints about your current relationships to tempt you into relationship with them, who remind you of your past, or who brag about their sexual conquests and point out that you could get away with the same thing. If you have decided to have joy in your season of singleness, or as you face a new beginning as a widow(er) or divorcee, you must cut off anyone in your life whose conversation invokes or provokes anger, bitterness, jealousy, distrust, or fear.

Surround yourself with individuals who will take a stand with you and when they see you struggling, who will take a stand for you. Now is the perfect time for you to get rid of the dead weight that you have been trying to drag into your destiny. If they don't trust God the way you trust Him, if they don't believe as you believe, if they aren't walking toward the same destination, cut them off so that there will be room in your life for blessed relationships with people who are.

In Exodus 33, Moses and the people who made the decision to truly follow God are forced away from the mountain. Moses pleaded with God in the tent of meeting, acknowledging that there was nothing more important to Israel than having the presence of God. Not only did God show Moses His glory, but He also invited him back on the mountain to renew His covenant. By Exodus 35, all of the Israelites who were willing brought what they had to begin construction of the tabernacle. Now is the time for you to walk away from anything and anyone that is keeping you from God. You aren't waiting on God to receive His promises; He is waiting on you to get ready for them. The moment that you run to God with your whole heart and with no hidden agenda, He will release what He has already planned for you and restore your relationship with Him and your opportunity to forge relationships according to His blueprint. Let's get ready to build.

 The moment that you run to God with your whole heart and with no hidden agenda, He will release what He has already planned for you and restore your relationship with Him and your opportunity to forge relationships according to His blueprint.

Through the Gate: Building Fences and Changing Perspective, Posture, and Position

I grew up in the home of a Church of God in Christ (COGIC), Pentecostal, "Holiness or Hell" pastor. When I wanted to date before age 16, or go to parties on the weekend, or wear pants to church, my parents' answer to my demands and whining was always Second Corinthians 6:17: *"Therefore come out from them and be separate, says the Lord. Touch no unclean thing, and I will receive you."* I have always loved God, and I have always loved His Word, but there are certain passages that I just didn't want to understand or submit to, and this was always the chief! I did not like this Scripture.

I considered myself close to God, but I was definitely attracted to the world. I felt like I was missing out on something—everything on the other side seemed so much more fun, more exciting, with a lot less struggle and a lot less pain. When I turned 18, I prayed to God, and I told Him that living for Him hurt too much and that it cost too much to be a disciple. I talked to my parents, and told them that I had demonstrated that I was responsible and could make my own decisions. I was tired of being different. I wanted to fit in.

Several years later, I changed my mind! Unfulfilled by weekend after weekend in the clubs looking at the same people and dancing to the same songs, and unsatisfied by relationships with men who were incapable of loving me the way I wanted to be loved because they had no relationship with the God of love, I found my prodigal self humbled and repentant before the Lord. I was exposed to the deception, the selfishness, the manipulation, and the downright evil of this world, and it sent me running back to my Father, where I belong.

Today, I teach the young people that I lead that we were never designed to fit in. In fact, God called us out. We speak a language the world does not understand. We believe things by faith that the world cannot see. We walk in favor that is contrary to the laws of nature. We refuse sin that other people are completely controlled by. I understand Second Corinthians 6:17, and Psalm 1:1-2, and Ephesians 5:11, in a way I refused to understand them in my youth. We don't do things the way the world does because we don't want the world's results. There are patterns and behaviors that are simply beneath who we were created and chosen to become. We are special…and that is a good thing.

Have you ever wondered why the Israelites built the golden calf? I believe in my heart that they built an idol because that was the pattern and the standard that they were used to. The Egyptians, and all of the surrounding nations, worshiped idolatrous gods, so Israel, even when given a promise and a warning from God, reverted back to the patterns that were so pervasive in the culture. They had a vision for something different, but in that moment, it seemed easier and more exciting to just do what everybody else was doing. They were delivered from bondage, but not from the baggage.

 God's goal in delivering the Israelites, in bringing them to the mountain, and in giving them instructions for the tabernacle, was to be able to dwell among them.

The same is true for us. Before we take a step into a relationship with another person, we have to get rid of the mentality, emotions, and the behaviors that we developed while we were in bondage and that are so prevalent in our culture. God's goal in delivering the Israelites, in bringing them to the mountain, and in giving them instructions for the tabernacle, was to be able to dwell among them. In order for that to happen, they had to be separate and they had to release the weight and the sin that they had been carrying through the wilderness. They had to go through the gate.

Separated, Liberated, and Protected

The tabernacle was a tent and enclosed area constructed in an open field at the center of the Israelite camp. The tabernacle has been described as the most expensive worship center ever made for its size, estimating the value of the materials used in its building (minus the labor costs) at approximately $10,000,000.[3] The frame of the fence that established its boundaries was made of 60 pillars of wood, which God specified should be standing *upright*, with hangings of *fine linens* forming its walls (see Exod. 27:9-19; 36:8-34). The tabernacle had two types of outer covering: badger skins and ram skins dyed red (see Exod. 26:14).

The camp of the Israelites and the tabernacle itself stood out from the other nations and their tents. Not only was Israel's camp set up in divine order, but the tabernacle's linens were made of a brilliant white fabric with gold, silver, and jeweled accents. The holiness of God who dwelt in the tabernacle and the people who gathered there were in stark contrast to the darkness of the world and the camps around them. When I began studying the tabernacle, God began to minister to me the importance of living sanctified, separated lives from the rest of the world. We must change our focus.

What we have in our relationships with God and with our brothers and sisters in Christ is far more valuable than anything you will find in this world. If we would stop looking at the world and allow God to be the center of our lives and our relationships, then we could build the kind of lives and see the glory of God in such a magnificent way that the world would have to look at and envy us. When the people of the Kingdom of God stop being distracted and drawn by the world, we can live and love in a manner that brings the light of glory to God in a world searching for an answer and for hope. We are set apart!

The five cubic (seven and a half feet) high walls of the tabernacle were made of wood and white linen, held together by bronze bases and silver bands at intervals of five cubits. The tabernacle's fence controlled both access and approach, and it stood as a picture of God's grace. The walls excluded those who were not in covenant relationship with God. Those who were not in covenant couldn't even see what was happening inside! Entrance in the courts was reserved for a special people who were called and chosen; the walls formed a shield, a shelter, and a new start.

The tabernacle was a place of safety and security—once inside, the people were free from fear and danger, and they were liberated from the pull of the world and from their sins. It is no wonder that King David longed and fainted for the courts of the Lord (see Ps. 84:2). Entrance into the courts was a privilege! The walls and coverings, along with everything else in the tabernacle, pointed to the redemptive work of Christ: the brass base and the silver bands and caps representing mankind and the processes of refinement and redemption, the linens representing holiness, the red-dyed skins providing shelter from storms representing the blood. In fact, the tabernacle only had one entrance, called "the Gate." In John 10:7, Jesus Himself proclaims, *"I am the gate,"* and in John 14:6, Jesus lets His disciples know that He is *"the way and the truth and the life."*

The courtship is a path to true liberty: freedom from your past, from fear, from anger, from frustration, from heartache, from disappointment, from guilt, and from shame. Christ Himself is our entrance, and once we have stepped inside the gate, we can experience newness in life and in our relationships. We have a new grace-purchased beginning, and in Christ we are blessed with every spiritual blessing in heavenly places. Our righteousness is as filthy rags, but Christ sacrificed His life to cover us in His linen, His righteousness.

Our righteousness is as filthy rags, but Christ sacrificed His life to cover us in His linen, His righteousness.

Our hearts, our lives, and our relationships may have been bruised, battered, and broken before, but once we enter courtship and covenant with Christ, He makes us all over again. *"Therefore if any man be in Christ, he is a new creature: old things are passed away; behold, all things are become new"* (2 Cor. 5:17 KJV). When you step into the outer court, into Christ, everything about you becomes new—your attitude, your mentality, your focus, your identity, your behavior, everything! When the enemy tries to show up in your life and remind you of your days in the wilderness, rebuke him and watch him flee. He no longer has access to you or control over you. You are free.

Let it Burn: Sacrifice, Justification, and the Death of Your Sin Nature

The first piece of furniture that an Israelite would encounter in the tabernacle was called the brazen altar, or the altar of burnt sacrifice. The brazen altar was the largest piece of furniture in the tabernacle, absolutely unavoidable to those who entered the outer court.[4] The altar was made of acacia wood, described as the strongest and most enduring type of wood, and it featured four horns made of brass (see Exod. 27:1-8). The Hebrew root word for altar means "to slay" or to "slaughter," and the altar was a raised platform used for burning the animals of sacrifice.[5] The blood shed at the altar represented the atonement, or the paying of the penalty for sin.

In Exodus 12, God decreed the beginning of a new year for the nation of Israel, marked by a feast known as the Lord's Passover. Every household and family was to slaughter a lamb and place the blood of the animal on their wooden doorposts, and then they were to completely consume the lamb by roasting it over a fire and eating it and burning any of it that was left over. The Israelites were to stay within their homes, within the walls that had been covered by the blood. God promised that the plagues and death that struck Egypt would pass over any home where the blood was found.

The children of Israel knew the significance of sacrifice—it was a continual reminder of their covenant with God, and the altar within the tabernacle reminded them of the Passover and how God had saved Israel from death in Egypt when the plagues affected the rest of the world. When they placed their sacrifices at the altar, retaining the blood and completely burning the flesh, they understood that the death of an innocent animal was paying the price for their sin. God explained this principle in Leviticus 17:11, when He instructed,

For the life of a creature is in the blood, and I have given it to you to make atonement for yourselves on the altar; it is the blood that makes atonement for one's life.

The sacrifices that Israel offered were temporary coverings for sin and shame, but Christ paid the penalty for our sin once and for all. He was placed on an altar, raised on a wooden cross, and made a sacrifice for us. He was without spot or blemish, a lamb slain even before the foundations of the world to give us abundant life through His blood. The tabernacle sacrifices could only offer the people a reminder of their sinfulness, but Christ came to free the people of God from the power and the penalty of sin forever.

As a result of God's will, *"we have been made holy through the sacrifice of the body of Jesus Christ once for all"* (Heb. 10:10). By His one sacrifice, Christ established perfection and righteousness for those who are walking toward holiness. Because Christ was willing to exchange our sin for His righteousness, He forgets all of our sin and our mistakes and our failures. When you enter relationship with Christ, you are redeemed by His blood (see 1 Pet. 1:18-19)! Just as God saved the Israelites from bondage in Egypt, Christ died to free us from bondage to sin and the enemy. You are a new creature with the opportunity to start a new life.

Consuming the Lamb

During the Passover, it was not enough for the Israelites to see the lamb or to stand in the doorway of their homes; they had to kill and cook and consume the whole lamb and remain within the house. Likewise, it was not enough for the Israelites to just see the gate to the tabernacle or to gaze upon the sacrifices offered. The Israelites only experienced the presence and forgiveness of God when they *completely entered* the gate and brought a sacrifice. Within these types, God was trying to show us that He does not want us to miss out on anything that we have access to in our salvation. Consuming the lamb of God, receiving Christ into our hearts, is designed to produce a change in our lives. If there is an area of your life where you are continuing to struggle, it is probably an area that you have not surrendered to God and allowed Him to consume. When you hold on to sin in your life, you deny the power and grace of God to deliver you in that area, and you make the sacrifice of no avail.

 God was trying to show us that He does not want us to miss out on anything that we have access to in our salvation.

When Jesus died for our sins, He didn't just die for its consequences. He died so that we would no longer have to experience sin, so that we could walk in dominion over it. It is not enough for you to be saved eternally but dying physically or spiritually. God does not just want to give you eternal life; He wants to give you abundant life. God does not just want you to have a healthy relationship with Him; He wants you to have blessed relationships with other people. In order to escape cycles of sin and shame, you must consume Him, and allow His Spirit to consume you. It is Christ *in us* that is the *hope of glory* (see Col. 1:27). It is only when you allow Christ to live and to grow within you that you have the opportunity to see the glory of God rest on your life, on your finances, on your ministry, on your family, and on your relationships.

Salvation through Christ not only allows us to escape death as a penalty for our sin, but it also gives us the power over sin in our lives. There are four horns on the corners of the brazen altar, and horns in Scripture symbolize power! Christ's blood paid the penalty for our sins, but His resurrection gives us life and power and authority over death, the grave, our lusts and flesh, and all of the enemy's tricks and deceptions. According to Second Peter 2:19, *"a man is a slave to whatever has mastered him."* If you do not master your flesh or your sin habits, they will master you. No man can serve two masters— either you will be controlled by the Holy Spirit and submitted to God, or you will be controlled by your flesh and your lusts and submitted to the bondage of the enemy.

In Romans 6:1, Paul asks the believer if we should continue to sin just because we have grace, and the answer is *"God forbid"* (Rom. 6:2 KJV). We are new creatures in Christ Jesus, but our old man, with his old desires, must be slaughtered. Salvation gives us the power to kill off the habits in our lives that used to kill us. The apostle tells us to take the time, energy, money, and the parts of our body that we used to serve the devil in our sin, and commit those things completely to serving God and then watch what is produced in our lives.

The Principle of Atoning Sacrifice

The altar is the first stop for the Israelites within the tabernacle, and the altar is the first step for the believer in the courtship. You must be ready to surrender anything in your life or in your heart that is contrary to God, and the altar is the perfect place to make the alterations needed for your life. When a man in Israel was ready to offer a sin offering, he would take a male calf or sheep that had no blemish, and he would lay his hand on the head of the sacrifice. The man would say, "I accept you as my substitute," and the gesture would be symbolic of the man transferring his sin to the innocent animal. He would then kill the animal by his own hands, recognizing that the animal was dying as a result of sin that he himself had committed, and the animal bearing the sin would be presented to the priest to be burned on the altar. The altar is still available to us, and Christ has already offered Himself as the ultimate scapegoat.

 God wants us to live lives without guilt and shame.

God wants us to live lives without guilt and shame, and to be able to fully experience His glory without fear of the consequences of our sin. All that He wants us to do is to accept Christ as our sacrifice—to present and transfer our sin to the already slain Savior, and to allow it to be purged out of our lives as we live by the Spirit of God. Paul wrote in Romans 6:11-12, "...*count yourselves dead to sin but alive to God in Christ Jesus. Therefore do not let sin reign in your mortal body so that you obey its evil desires.*"

My grandmother expresses the same sentiment through the lyrics of an old blues song. She says, "Don't let the devil ride. Cause if you let him ride, he'll want to drive...Don't let him ride!" You do not have *any* room in your life or in your vision for sin! If it looks like sin, smells like sin, sounds like sin, reminds you of sin, you have to kill it out of your life. Sin produces death...even if it is not an immediate physical death, as in the case of Adam and Eve. Sin causes separation, shame, and the type of consequences that can change the course of your life and the generations that will follow you. It is impossible to kill something that you love, so you have to begin to hate sin. If you can't hate the sin, hate the consequences enough to kill the cause.

You have to recognize the behaviors and patterns in your life that are killing your relationship with God and that will kill any relationship that you enter. Paul lists the obvious acts of the sin nature, including discord, jealousy, fits of rage, drunkenness, and selfish ambition in his letter to the Galatian church (see Gal. 5:19-21). And Paul urged the Colossian church to *"put to death, therefore, whatever belongs to your earthly nature: sexual immorality, impurity, lust, evil desires and greed, which is idolatry"* (Col. 3:5). In other words, kill off the stuff that is trying to kill you. That means throw away your dirty magazines, toys, and videos and put a block on adult content on your computer. That means delete any sex texts, stop sleeping with the person you are not married to, and clear your phone book and Facebook friend list of any temptation. That means that you immediately discontinue the lying, the manipulation, the selfishness, the stealing, the gossip, the jealousy, and the excessive spending. Stop running from the truth! Acknowledge and confess anything in your life that you feel the need to hide or cover up—first to yourself and God, then to anyone else you may be hurting.

 Falling into sin does not make God love you any less.

Deliverance is not an easy process, but you cannot and will not be successful in life, in ministry, or in marriage by causing, inviting, or participating in drama, avoiding conflict, and pursuing your own desires. It is impossible to walk in the anointing, power, peace, or joy when you are still operating in your flesh and your lusts. The world tries to convince you to get away with your sin; I'm trying to convince you to get rid of it. Falling into sin does not make God love you any less, but He will leave you at the altar of sacrifice until you grow up and decide that you are not going to keep resurrecting and enslaving yourself to the stuff that Christ gave His life to give us victory over. He will let you to make the same mistakes over and over again until you are ready to surrender to Him. Your inheritance, in life and in relationships, is on the line.

Stay in His presence and allow His glory to reveal the sin hidden in your heart and to consume your own nature. The desires of the Spirit and the desires of our nature are in conflict with one another, so if we pursue the desires of our flesh we automatically exempt ourselves from the promises God has given to us in His Spirit. If we live by the Spirit and stay in pursuit of God, it becomes impossible to follow after the desires of our sin nature and we automatically qualify for our inheritance. The rules are simple: If you can say no to the stuff that will please your flesh momentarily, God will bless you in a way that will feel good to your soul and your spirit in the long term. When we successfully move on to the other steps in the courtship, our time at the altar will remind us of God's love and grace and will empower us to walk in forgiveness and humility with the goal of extending the reconciliation and the righteousness that has been given to us, to those with whom we enter covenant.

Stopping to Reflect: Self-Awareness, Self-Esteem, and Sanctification at the Bronze Laver

Though anyone in the nation of Israel could access the brazen altar, only the priests were allowed at the second piece of furniture in the tabernacle. The bronze laver was a water basin used for ceremonial washing. It was placed between the altar and the door to the holy place, and its positioning represented the intersection of service to man and service to God. It was a completely reflective surface, made from the bronze mirrors that women brought as an offering, and it was filled with water. The priests washed themselves at the basin in preparation for duty, as God required a daily walk of consecration and purity from His servants.

In *the courtship*, the bronze laver is absolutely unavoidable. The Bible declares that the priests had to wash with water before they could make any further progress *"so that they will not die."* Spending time at the bronze laver daily was critical for the survival and the advancement of the priest and the people (see Exod. 30:17-21; 38:8; Num. 19). In the outer court, we learn that there are sin habits in our life that we must kill off, but there are also contaminants to our destiny that we must wash off. Water in Scripture speaks of the Word and the Holy Spirit, and as believers and members of a royal priesthood, God expects us to avail ourselves to wash and to be washed by one another (see Eph. 5:26; Titus 3:5; Isa. 44:3; John 7:38-39).

The mirrors used for the bronze laver would need to be broken, melted by fire, and molded into their new shape for their new purpose. Brokenness, and trial by fire, and being rebuilt and re-purposed are all a part of courtship. We cannot carry our old man, our old habits, and our old attitudes into new lives, new vision, and new relationships. According to Psalm 51:16-17, God does not take pleasure in sacrifice or burnt offerings, but *"the sacrifices of God are a broken spirit; a broken and contrite heart."* Preparation for any ministry, including marriage, will require brokenness. God will allow whatever He chooses in our lives to break us out of old patterns and old molds—He wants to break you out of your independence, break your pride and self-will, break you away from your past in Egypt and in the wilderness, and if it brings you back to Him, He does not mind you having to experience a broken bank account or a broken heart.

God never asks us to be perfect in and of ourselves—but He begins perfecting us when we leave the sin and the weight that we often carry, so that we can look unto Him as the author and finisher of our faith. God wants us to walk in repentance and in His Spirit, and to fully comprehend and take hold of the liberty and power that He purchased for us by His sacrifice. Trials and tribulations lead to brokenness, and brokenness produces faith and patience in us that lead to maturity and perfection. The amazing thing about God is that He only breaks us to make us. He takes pleasure in our broken spirit because it prepares the way for us to be filled and controlled by His Spirit.

Prepare for an Extreme Makeover

A mirror is a reflective surface designed to produce an image of the same shape and size as the original object. The priest's progress in the next dimension, the inner court or the holy place, required that he walk in purity and righteousness. The brazen laver gave the priests the opportunity to take a critical look at themselves so that they could remove anything that should not be with them when they progressed to the next place. As servants and representatives of God, they were careful to make sure that the image they reflected in the mirror was the one that God required. My question for you at this point in your journey is a simple one: "What do you see when you look in the mirror?" We have already learned that we were made in the image of God and in His likeness, and blessed to be productive and to walk in dominion and authority.

 What do you see when you look in the mirror?

Though we understand this truth intellectually, most of us have been through so much that we no longer see ourselves the way that

God sees us. Do you see yourself as a victim or as victorious? Are you a sinner, or are you a saint? Have your experiences made you bitter or better? Are you capable and deserving of a glorious life and lots of love, or do you feel doomed to spend life alone and unhappy? Are you royalty or a reject? Our image, first distorted by sin and satan in the Garden of Eden, has been continually misshapen by our experiences, by our mistakes, and by other people's opinions. Perhaps the question we should ask ourselves is not what do we see, but what do we want to see, and how do we recreate our image?

Here is a biblical truth: Whatever you behold, you become! My initial sermon, birthed out of my own identity crisis and transformation, was based on that truth.

And all of us, as with unveiled face, [because we] continued to behold [in the Word of God] as in a mirror the glory of the Lord, are constantly being transfigured into His very own image in ever increasing splendor and from one degree of glory to another; [for this comes] from the Lord [Who is] the Spirit (2 Corinthians 3:18 AMP).

When you take your focus off of what happened to you, what they said, who left, your past, and your flaws, and choose instead to make the glory of God and His Word your mirror, God promises to make you a reflection of His splendor so that you are progressing from glory to glory. It is impossible for you to meet, greet, and know how to treat the person God created for you if you don't even know who God created you to be.

Before you move forward in this process, you'll need time for reflection. Take a day, a week, a month, or a year away from pleasing or criticizing other people to take a critical look at yourself. Even if you choose not to write everything down in a journal, you must come to some realizations about who and where you are, how you got there, and what you can do *now* to eliminate anything preventing you from becoming the person you really want to be.

The Israelites survived bondage in Egypt and wandered through the wilderness and, as a result, they picked up some habits and thought patterns that had to be sanctified before they could walk into their Promised Land. The same is true for us. As you continue through your journey toward purpose and toward God-centered relationships, you must be willing to leave behind and wash away *everything* in your memory, your personality, or your habits that will deter or delay you from destiny. You may have carried it to get to this point, but if it can't help you get to your destination, it's got to go! How do you fix a distorted reflection? I'm glad you asked…

Bathed and Born Again

When a priest was sanctified for the priesthood, he was washed from head to toe in the water of the bronze laver. This complete washing is symbolic of our baptism, as we are immersed in water from head to toe and, consequently, cleansed from our past and unrighteousness because of our placement in Jesus Christ. The ceremonial washing of the priest marked a new beginning in his life, a change from his roles in Egypt and the wilderness to preparation and consecration for service unto the Lord. Baptism does the same thing in the life of a believer, as we are buried with Him in baptism and raised with Him through faith in the power of God (see Col. 2:12). The bronze laver and baptism are both stages in covenant, as one dies to the past and begins a completely new life consecrated to God. You must be willing to give up and wash away your old man to walk in the newness of life and to have access to the things of the Kingdom (see Rom. 6). Consecration is the act that completely removes a priest, and a believer, from the system of the world and assigns him to a new set of standards connected to God. In John 3, Jesus was talking to a Pharisee named Nicodemus who was amazed at the miracles He performed. Jesus told him that a man cannot see the Kingdom of God unless he is born again. To clear up Nicodemus's confusion, Jesus explained, *"I tell you the truth, no one can enter the kingdom of God unless he is born of water and the Spirit"* (John 3:5). In order to progress in the courtship and to experience a love and a life and a relationship connected to advancing the Kingdom of God and walking in its promises, you must be willing to be born again. Your rebirth cannot stay in the spirit realm—God wants a new beginning for you in your heart, mind, emotions, actions, will, speech, and relationships.

 Your rebirth cannot stay in the spirit realm.

The priest's consecration, and the believer's baptism into water and the Spirit, is so complete that it need only occur once to produce a total transformation. It is a complete change in nature and in identity. When you are preparing to walk in purpose in relationships and/or in marriage, your whole mentality has to change. Your old attitude, your old temper, your old insecurity, your old personality has to shift in preparation for the service that you will offer to God and to the person He places in your life. Whatever pattern of behavior or speech or thinking you identified yourself by prior to this moment can be sanctified and changed, simply by you allowing God to wash your hurts and your disappointments away so that He can replace them with His love.

Denetria, one of my best friends, is a perfect example of the benefits of the bronze laver. She remembers growing up and facing "innocent" ridicule and teasing from her family and friends, which the enemy used to develop insecurities about her height, skin, and facial features. She felt empty and unattractive, until she started getting attention from older guys. Denetria changed her standards and her physical appearance to gain and keep their approval, losing her virginity at an early age to a guy whom she immediately discovered was cheating on her. Denetria's first relationship set up a pattern of relationships in her life in which she looked to men for attention and approval, adjusted her standards to keep them happy (even when she was not), and continued to develop insecurities and trust issues from cycles of lies, manipulations, and cheating. Denetria was a college freshman when she found out she was pregnant and facing life as a single mother.

At this point in her life, Denetria started pursuing a personal relationship with God. She had always been involved in church, but this was the first time that she truly turned to Him for answers and strength. She connected to a church family and fell in love with His Word and with worship. Denetria says that as she started falling in love with Him, He helped her fall in love with herself. As she pursued God, her "issues" were revealed and came to the surface of her life. She says that emotionally, physically, and spiritually, she "felt like she was being purged."

She had to end an emotionally abusive relationship, delete old phone numbers from her contact list, forgive the people who had hurt her and let her down, throw away pictures and gifts that reminded her of previous mates, and get rid of anything connected to the pain of her past. She could no longer see herself as a victim. She could not hold a grudge. She could not continue to walk in insecurity or in fear. God had to cleanse her heart. Denetria reached a turning point when she could no longer afford to purchase the colored contact lenses she had been wearing since she was a teen. Stripped of this mark of beauty and the makeup she had hid behind, Denetria had to find the beauty within herself.

Today Denetria is an awesomely anointed minister of the gospel and praise and worship leader who is married to an equally anointed minister of the gospel and praise and worship leader. They are united in love, in purpose, and in parenting their amazingly gifted daughter. Denetria is the founder and CEO of Girl Talk, Inc., a non-profit organization designed to help teen girls navigate the issues she has overcome.[6] As she learned to love and accept herself, her testimony propelled her into a ministry that will change a generation and into the promise God gave her for a man who would love and accept her.

The water of the basin—the Word and Spirit of God in operation in our lives—produces the transformation needed for consecration. I could spend the entire book discussing things that you picked up in your Egypt and carried through your wilderness that need to be released and transformed in your life as you progress toward promise: sexual abuse, emotional abuse and teasing, physical abuse, abandonment and neglect, insecurity, fear, manipulation and control issues, jealousy, anger, the need to know everything or have the last word, pride and ego, doubt and unbelief, and the list goes on and on. I feel your pain, but I refuse to validate it.

God promises to turn every bad thing that you've done, and that has been done to you, into something good because you love Him and are called according to His purpose. Whatever your issues are, you have held on to them for long enough. I am praying that, even as you read, God will reveal to you the issues of your heart, so that you will recognize that it's time to let them go. As we prepare to develop godly relationships, we can look forward to a completely clean slate, with absolutely no baggage. As we progress into the courtship, God tells us to *"forget the former things; do not dwell on the past. See, I am doing a new thing!"* (Isa. 43:18-19a). Whether you are single, divorced, widowed, dating, or married, God is starting your life, your heart, and your relationships over again.

 Whatever your issues are, you have held on to them for long enough.

Holy = High Maintenance

The priests in the tabernacle were consecrated, purified, and washed from head to toe, but in their daily walk and service they would come into contact with people, the ground, and sacrificed animals while inside the tabernacle, which soiled and defiled them. The priests were not just required to wash one time—the process of sanctification had to be progressive! According to Exodus 30:20-21, *"...when they approach the altar to minister...they shall wash their **hands** and **feet**."* The priests had already been consecrated, but the dirt they had to walk through when fulfilling their responsibilities left them open to contamination. Because they had already been clean, they only had to wash the parts of their bodies that had been exposed. They had to wash their hands and their feet daily in order to be prepared for and effective in their service.

 Just like the priests, we must keep the things that we experience externally from corrupting who we are internally.

Just like the priests, we must keep the things that we experience externally from corrupting who we are internally. For the Israelites (and for us), hand washing is a ritual to keep germs and contaminants on the outside of our bodies from getting on the inside. The priests washed their hands in the morning and at night, prior to meals and after, when using the restroom, and anytime they came into contact with anything dead. The priests' hand washing was representative of our need to act righteously.

In Scripture, hands and feet always symbolized what was happening inside a person's heart. Clean "hands" and "feet" are an indication of pure motives, right actions, and clear direction, all necessary for moving to the next place in the courtship. Washing our hands will keep our hearts pure even when we come into contact with things that could defile us or make us sick. King David wrote,

Who may ascend the hill of the Lord? Who may stand in His holy place? He who has clean hands and a pure heart....He will receive blessing from the Lord... (Psalm 24:3-5).

Maintaining clean hands gives us access to the holy place, to greater heights and depths of God, and to divine blessing.

 Sometimes we encounter people or situations with innocent intentions, but the enemy is trying to place a contaminant in your heart.

Have you ever picked up something with your hands without realizing how dirty it was? Or realized that something that looked clean was far more rusty or dusty than it appeared? Sometimes we encounter people or situations with innocent intentions, but the enemy is trying to place a contaminant in your heart—a negative thought, doubt, ill will, anger, fear—that doesn't belong there. As soon as you identify it, get rid of it, prioritizing your purity over anything else. Job 17:9 states, *"Nevertheless, the righteous will hold to their ways, and those with clean hands will grow stronger."* Those who bounce back from their issues, who continue to seek God and pursue righteousness, get stronger and stronger, and so do their relationships.

The priests and the people, in their travels to and through the tabernacle, were barefooted or wore sandals. As a result, their feet came into direct contact with the dust and the dirt of the ground on a continual basis. The priests washed their feet so that the places they had to walk through or stand in would not keep them from serving in holiness or fulfilling their purpose. They had to wash their feet

196 ∞ *God's Divine Design for* DATING *and* MARRIAGE

before they could progress into the inner court and holy place. We see the same thing in the New Testament. We should continually walk in repentance and forgiveness—though we have been saved and delivered, we must also be cleansed in our daily walk. Not only should we request forgiveness and cleansing as we serve God, but we also must be willing to offer forgiveness to those we serve. We see examples of this in Matthew 10:14, when the disciples are told to *"shake the dust off* [their] *feet"* whenever anyone rejects them for carrying the gospel. As you pursue God and relationships based on His love and righteousness, you will have to shake off any rejection, criticism, or misunderstanding you face for living and choosing to express love God's way.

We see other examples of foot washing in Scripture when Mary washed the feet of Jesus in Luke 7 and when Jesus washed the feet of His disciples in John 13. In both of these examples, the washing of the feet is not only an act of cleanliness; it is preparation for divine purpose. The disciples were told not only that having their feet washed was a requirement, but also that they were required to wash one another's feet. In other words, a believer must continually walk in humility and in service, placing others above him or herself while remembering that he or she too will make mistakes and will need the service of others. In your journey, eliminate any pride or arrogance that has tried to set itself up in your heart. We all make mistakes, we all fall short, we all need forgiveness and grace, and we all have the opportunity to offer those gifts to others who need to see and understand that love truly does cover a multitude of sins.

Newness of life and hope for the future of our relationships is a free gift from God, but when you receive it, you should recognize that the gift must be maintained. The enemy is always trying to find ways to sneak in and remind you of the past, and the desires or sin that can hide behind your heart will give him opportunity. Even after your breakthrough, please be aware that the enemy will try to bring those issues back up and that you must resist him. Your deliverance will be tested, but those moments are just opportunities for you to prove to the enemy, to your past, and to yourself that you are completely new and pressing toward your future. You must do everything in your power to guard your peace, the purity of your heart, and your faith and hope in God and in your present or future spouse.

 You must do everything in your power to guard your peace, the purity of your heart, and your faith and hope in God and in your present or future spouse.

When insecurity, fear, and unforgiveness try to sneak back in, you must seek God and allow Him to cleanse the area of your life in which the enemy is trying to reestablish a stronghold. Put away your detective gear, your little black book, and your weapons. Take your issues, your concerns, your hesitations, and your pains to God. If you keep your mind on Him, He has promised to be your protector, the lover of your soul, and to keep you in perfect peace. I've learned to ask God to wash me on a daily basis, to fill me with His Spirit, to *"search me, O God, and know my heart: try me, and know my thoughts: and see if there be any wicked way in me, and lead me in the way everlasting"* (Ps. 139:23-24 KJV). He knows me, and He loves me. He has never let me down.

Setting the Mood: The Preparation Required for Inner Court Intimacy

In the second chapter of the Book of Esther, a young lady named Hadassah was brought into the courtyards of the king's harem. She and the other young women were assembled to begin preparation for intimate relations with the king. Hadassah was submitted to those placed in authority over her, Mordecai, her adoptive father, and Hegai, who was the king's servant, and she followed every bit of guidance and counsel they gave her without question or challenge. Each of the young women had to complete 12 months of prescribed beauty treatments, *"six months with oil of myrrh and six with perfumes and cosmetics"* (Esther 2:12). When Esther walked into the inner chambers of the king, she carried only what the servant of the king told her to carry, and she walked in favor with everyone, especially the king. Beauty treatments can be painful, expensive, and time consuming—between the burn of a hair straightener, the pain of waxing, cutting yourself while shaving, the cost of a haircut or extensions, poking yourself in the eye to put in or remove contact lenses, gym memberships, and so on, but they are often worth the ordeal once you see the results.

 Esther had no knowledge of how to get herself ready for relationship.

When the priests were called to service in the tabernacle, it was Moses' responsibility to guide them, wash them, dress them, and anoint them—they could not do it alone. Esther had no knowledge of how to get herself ready for relationship—it was Mordecai and Hegai who led her into the king's favor. Likewise, God doesn't leave it up to us to assemble everything that we need to be prepared to walk into relationship. As we make ourselves available to Him, walk by faith, and begin to focus on His love and faithfulness rather than on our pasts, problems, and our imperfections, He makes sure that we are washed, clothed, and anointed to be fruitful and productive in our love lives, which will reflect back to the love that He has for us. Esther stayed focused on her goal—intimacy with the king, and so did the priests in their desire to experience the glory of God. When you walk through the process of preparation for a relationship and a marriage that looks like God, reject frustration and discouragement and stay focused on the love and intimacy that you know God is preparing you to walk into. Now here are the final stages of the priests' preparation.

Dressed Up: Inner Court Apparel

In Exodus 28, God tells Moses to make new garments for the Levites that would give them dignity and honor. The priests' new uniform included a breastpiece, ephod, robe, tunic, a head turban, and a sash. The priests' garments were to be of fine white linen, with accents in blue, purple, and scarlet yarn woven with pure gold—the same materials with which the curtains of the tabernacle itself were made. The priests' garments were representative of their role within the kingdom and of their calling to represent God and the people. The priestly attire is a shadow of the spiritual identity and the fashion and style that a believer should walk in when progressing into ministry and/or covenant relationship.

You were taught, with regard to your former way of life, to put off your old self, which is being corrupted by its deceitful desires; to be made new in the attitude of your minds; and to put on the new self, created to be like God in true righteousness and holiness (Ephesians 4:22-24).

Your new identity in Christ must be put on; it must be worn.

The fine linen was made from flax, in a tedious process in which the plants were uprooted, combed, stretched, watered, beaten, washed, and then spun into beautiful white thread. When the process was finished, the handmade linen was softer and stronger than any other fabric; it was naturally stain-resistant; and it did not shrink. The priests' undergarments, outer robe, head turban, and waist sash were all made of this fabric. This fine linen, and the garments of the priests, represent modesty and righteousness. The white linen covered their entire bodies, but especially their private parts, their hearts, and their heads. The linen garments show us that we must continually walk in humility and in the confidence that accompanies being covered in the righteousness of God, wearing thoughts, mindsets, habits, and, yes, clothing that demonstrate our commitment to be holy and set apart for God.

The high priest's ephod was an apron-like garment worn over his robe. On the shoulders of the ephod were two plates that had to be joined, and connected to the shoulder pieces was a breastplate covered in 12 jewels that represented the 12 tribes of Israel. When the high priest entered the holy place, or the inner court, this "breastplate of decision" covered his heart. It held the memorial stones, as well as the Urim and Thummim, which represent revelation and truth (see Exod. 28:29-30). The high priest kept the kingdom on his heart, and he inquired of God while carrying revelation and truth with him. As we walk into the next dimension of our relationships, we must do so with our hearts focused on the Kingdom of God, basing our decisions on the light of His Word and on truth. We must wear honesty and purity of purpose on our hearts, seeking God and His Kingdom first with the expectation that everything else will be added unto us (see Matt. 6:33).

 We must wear honesty and purity of purpose on our hearts.

The hem of the ephod was an unbroken circle of golden bells and pomegranates. The craftsmen designed the bells to be heard whenever a priest went into or came out of the holy place, and they speak of joy and praise. The pomegranate is a fruit that, when opened, contains seeds that produce more fruit. Psalm 100 opens with the charge to *"make a joyful noise unto the Lord...serve the Lord with gladness: come before His presence with singing"* (Ps. 100:1-2 KJV). At all times, a priest should wear praise, and that praise will produce joy, and that joy will ultimately produce strength. A priest should also be productive—growing in the fruits of the Spirit: *"love, joy, peace, patience, kindness, goodness, faithfulness, gentleness and self-control"* (Gal. 5:22-23). When we remain connected to God, He produces fruit through us, and our productivity and praise should be evident to all people at all times.

Not only were the priests' garments spiritually attractive, but they also were visually beautiful and expensive. Like our Levitical counterparts, you must begin to dress and to carry yourself in a manner that denotes your royalty. Invest in yourself! When I was a college student, my mentors always told me to dress for where I want to go. While other students were coming to class in pajama pants and flip-flops, I wore causal dress attire. When I accepted a call into ministry, I purchased dress suits and heels and made a decision to keep my hair and nails done because I was representing not only myself, but also God. I changed my appearance to make sure that it lined up with my identity, and I challenge you to do the same. It has nothing to do with the money you spend (most of my suits were department store clearance specials). It is about you taking the time to present your best self and gaining confidence for yourself and from others in the process. The priests' attire opened the door to the inner court, and what you wear (both naturally and spiritually) will open doors in your relationships.

Smelling Good: Inner Court Anointing

When the priests prepared to go into the inner court, or the holy place, they not only dressed well, but they smelled good too! Moses was to *"take the anointing oil and anoint him* [the priest] *by pouring it on his head"* (Exod. 29:7). To *anoint* translates as "to smear," which means that the priests were so covered in the anointing that it covered their head and, eventually, their entire body. The oil was rubbed into and absorbed into their clothing and skin. The sacred oil used for anointing was *"a fragrant blend...the work of a perfumer"* (Exod. 30:35). God gave specific instructions for the blending of the oil. Olive oil was used as the base and it was mixed with *"500 shekels of liquid myrrh, half as much...of fragrant cinnamon, 250 shekels of fragrant cane, 500 shekels of cassia..."* (Exod. 30:23-24). The anointing has always been rare, expensive, valuable, and reserved for God's very best.

The practice of "anointing" in Jewish culture represents a formal elevation in a person's status, as in the consecration of a priest, the engagement of a bride, and the crowning of royalty. In the case of priesthood, the anointing operated by "removing him from the realm of the profane and empowering him to operate in the realm of the sacred."[7] The anointing conferred on a king, known as the *ru'ah YHWH* ("the spirit of the Lord"), was a gift from God that provided spiritual support (see 1 Sam. 16:13-14; 18:12), strength (see Ps. 89:21-25), and wisdom (see Isa. 11:1-4) necessary to fulfill the divine assignment.[8]

 Relationship is a calling.

Relationship is a calling, and as you continue in courtship, please know that your friendship, your ministry, your marriage will ultimately belong to God, who entrusts it to your hands so that you can cultivate it and make it fruitful. As you move from living and making decisions based on what you have seen or experienced to an understanding of ministry and relationship based on its sacredness to God, He anoints you for ministry and for the witness your relationships will become. Contrary to popular belief, it is impossible to build or maintain a divine relationship unless God anoints you to do so. When the Spirit of the Lord rests upon you, it empowers you to love, to provide, to submit, to protect, to forgive and to forget, to hope, to teach, to inspire, to heal, and to restore—to do all of the things you may be asked and assigned to do in your relationships. Pray for God to increase your ability to walk in His anointing—that is, His support, His strength, and His wisdom. And if you are feeling pressed or stretched—or stressed—count it as joy, knowing that it is a part of the process.

It was necessary for the priests to be anointed because all of the vessels that they came into contact with were anointed. The vessels were holy, and God required anything that touched them to be holy too (see Exod. 30:26-29; 40:9). If a vessel came into contact with something that was not anointed, it ceased to be anointed. The Israelites, and individuals like Achan and King Saul, were anointed until they made decisions that caused the power and favor of God to be removed from their lives, causing them to lose battles, possessions, and territory. Because the anointing can be removed, it is critical that you guard and protect it. The vessels in the tabernacle were so sacred and precious to God that He refused to allow anything to come into contact with them that would wipe off or tarnish their shine. You are a vessel, chosen and anointed by God, and you must be careful if there are people and/or things in your life that pose a threat to your anointing because they are not connected to the Spirit of the Lord.

During my period of consecration and separation to God, I noticed that there were two things that would always activate frustration and depression and loneliness in my emotions: listening to love songs and watching wedding shows on television. I enjoyed listening and watching, but afterward I would find myself wondering when my time would come—which would evolve into jealousy and questioning God and losing faith because I thought I was ready for love. When I identified the source of those feelings, I gave away my CDs and unplugged my television. When a priest's head was anointed, the oil covered his eyes, his nose, his ears, and his mouth. Guard your gates! If listening to Teddy Pendergrass makes you want to "turn off the lights" or hearing R. Kelly takes you back to who you were with in 1994 or convinces you that "ain't nothing wrong with a lil' bump and grind," you need to let the batteries die on your iPod.

If your co-worker's scent makes you think about her all day instead of your wife, walk the long way around the office to avoid her desk. If your friends' dirty jokes or gossiping tendencies start to pull you in, cut off the conversations. Kissing a frog will not give you a prince or a princess, but it will give you warts! Watch your mouth—use the power of your tongue to glorify God. Complaining or talking about the devil will decrease your anointing as it exalts the enemy over the strength of your God. The anointing upon your life is precious and valuable. It will protect and cover you, but only if you guard and protect it.

 The anointing upon your life is precious and valuable.

In Exodus 30:31-33, God made sure that Moses understood that the anointing should never be poured on the "flesh" of men, or those not consecrated as priests, nor should anointing oil be used for any other purpose than what God intended it for. The word for the holy anointing oil in the Greek is *chrisma* and the word for the anointing itself is *charisma*, both of which speaks of a supernatural empowerment flowing from God's presence and favor on an individual's life.[9] The modern term *charisma* is defined as a "trait found in persons whose personalities are characterized by a personal charm and magnetism (attractiveness), along with innate and powerfully sophisticated abilities of interpersonal communication and persuasion."[10] The anointing produces charisma, which is the ability to use charm and persuasion to draw people or attract them to you. God, knowing the power of the anointing to produce attraction, tells Moses that the anointing should never operate outside of His order, His presence, and His will. It was never intended to fuel the fleshly desires of man. Before we move any further, I am compelled to issue two warnings:

1) You should not misuse your anointing. Your gift should not be used to "run game," to manipulate people into doing things for or with you, or to get people to like or love you. When God anoints you, people will be drawn to your gift for the purposes of ministry. You cannot confuse (or allow them to confuse) who you are as a person with what you are called to do. If you are anointed to win the lost, perhaps you should avoid blurring the boundaries between developing intimate relationship with you and the relationship that those you minister to may need to develop with God. "Missionary dating" is normally a pretty bad idea. The same could be true for prophets, musicians, teachers, preachers, and others who are called to positions of service and authority. Eliminate conflicts of interest. Before initiating any relationship, check your motives and your methods to see if it is connected to the purposes of God, or if it is designed to distract you, deter the other person, or to destroy your anointing. If it is an assignment from the enemy, minister and move on. You must die to your flesh—pray against your pride, insecurity, ego, any need to be needed, and any tendency you have toward flattery or flirtation. Bonding with the wrong people or spirits will mess up your anointing. And trust me when I say that the enemy has sent them to distract you. *"Dead flies cause the ointment of the apothecary to send forth a stinking savour: so doth a little folly him that is in reputation for wisdom and honor"* (Eccles. 10:1 KJV). If your anointing has started to stink, get rid of the flies… you can only hide your foolishness for so long!

2) You cannot base your attraction to someone on his or her anointing. When the oil of anointing is applied, it leads to overflow (see Ps. 23:5), and it demonstrates and invites affection and devotion (see Ruth 3:3; Song of Sol. 4:10). Although wealth, influence, visibility, and the ability to inspire are all admirable qualities, they do not reveal the true measure of a person, nor do they tell you a person's maturity, commitment, or how compatible he or she would be with you. There is a distinct difference between a person being admirable because he or she is gifted, talented, blessed, or anointed, and a person being a good candidate for marriage or being sent from God to walk in assignment and purpose with you. I cannot begin to tell you the number of broken hearts I have witnessed because a person "fell in love" with someone or "claimed" him as her spouse based on what she saw on a Sunday morning without ever getting to know the person for who he really is. Just because a vessel has a big dream, vision, charisma, or is anointed to sing, play an instrument, preach, or to run a business, does not mean that he or she walks in integrity, that you have anything in common, that you have the same ideas about relationships, that you share the same goals, or that he or she will be attracted or devoted to you! In the words of Public Enemy, "Don't believe the hype!" Nurture your own anointing and, in time, God will draw the person who you're supposed to be connected to, and you'll know it because you'll walk through the steps in the rest of this chapter to learn and discover who he or she really is and to discern if God is calling you to walk and serve with him or her!

Feeling Great: Finally Ready to Advance

In 2000, recording artist India.Arie released an album featuring one of the most beautiful songs I have ever heard. With only the mellow strumming of a guitar accompanying her voice, she sang, "I am ready for love/ why are you hiding from me/ I'd quickly give my freedom/ To be held in your captivity…." My college girlfriends and I would play the song over and over again on repeat, and it never failed to produce a substantial amount of tears from us. We were 18—just beginning the journey to discover who we were and what the world was really like—but we were all convinced that Ms. India had just given voice to the inner workings of our minds and the readiness of our hearts. We were persuaded. We were determined. We were waiting. We were wrong.

And so was Ms. India. There was a logical fallacy in her lyrics that I did not recognize until I started researching and writing this chapter. When you are ready, truly ready, love cannot hide from you, and you don't have to seek it out. It emerges from a place within you, and it draws the love that God has simultaneously birthed from within the person He created for you. The Spirit of the Lord prepares you both and orders your steps to a place where your walks, your visions, and your identities will merge into one. If it sounds impossibly amazing, too good to be true…that's because it is. That's what makes the process so special. That's how you know that it is God who orchestrated it, and that's how He gets the glory.

 We confused desire for preparation, and the lack of an established process to walk through made us impatient.

It was easy for my friends and I to think that we were ready for love because there were no benchmarks in place for readiness. We confused desire for preparation, and the lack of an established process to walk through made us impatient. If you are wondering about whether you are ready for serious relationship, or if a person who you are considering as a mate is ready, all you have to do is evaluate your progress. When a person has consecrated him or herself to the Lord, that person leaves behind the influence and control of the enemy and the world by developing a loving, personal relationship with God, accepting Christ's sacrifice, and rejecting sin. Such people allow the Word and Spirit to wash away their past and leave behind their baggage. They dress up in righteousness and walk in joy and gratitude. They develop a heart that works toward a vision to enhance or serve the Kingdom of God. They submit to spiritual and natural authority. They walk in anointing and power along with the Christ-like nature of Kingdom confidence and humility. That person will carry a testimony that is absolutely undeniable.

You can evaluate your readiness for relationship based on your testimony. Your testimony is the greatest tool you have in ministry and in building relationship. It is the substance of priestly bonds, as shared process and purpose produce the type of intimacy that grows into meaningful relationship. It is a trustworthy saying that you will attract who you are. When you walk out your priesthood, you will be surprised by how God connects you to the people who look, sound, talk, and believe just like you!

The outer court is the dimension of introspection and transformation. During your season of singleness, or after a divorce, a lost spouse, or during a needed break or separation in an existing relationship or marriage, you have a unique opportunity to learn about yourself and to evaluate chances for growth and change. Change never begins with a new idea or a word of advice. Change begins when we discover that the way we have been doing something is no longer working, or when we figure out that a minor adjustment can produce greater effects. Change happens when we evaluate our lives and our relationships and admit that what used to work is no longer working, is no longer making sense, and is no longer comfortable. Change only occurs when you get sick and tired of being sick and tired. Before you can move to and be effective in the next stage of your life and your relationships, you'll have to change your direction. But before you can change your direction, you have to change your decisions. And before you change your decisions, you have to change your attitude—about God, integrity, sanctification, relationships, marriage, sexuality, and yourself.

Your time, experiences, and decisions while in the outer court allow for deliverance from the contamination of this world and from the defilement of your past, and prepare the way for your inner court relationships to be based on truth, honesty, wholesomeness, and the blessing that follows holiness. Anything that you do not kill or cleanse at this point in your life will follow you and contaminate your relationships. "One" is a whole number, and before you join yourself to another person, it is important that you are healed, whole, and holy. If, after your time in the outer court, you realize that God's plan for you is to remain single (for a season or for a lifetime), there is absolutely nothing wrong with that. In fact, Paul advocates singleness because it allows for undivided devotion to the Lord and to your own desires (see 1 Cor. 7). Don't allow anyone else pressure you into something you are not ready for or are not called to do.

 Don't allow anyone else pressure you into something you are not ready for or are not called to do.

The inner court is a dimension of service and ministry, and any relationship is a call to both. Before you approach an altar (for marriage or ministry), it is important that you are truly prepared to walk in priesthood. In the next chapter, we will focus on building and maintaining relationships, but before you can build a life or a ministry or a marriage with another person, it is critical that you take the time to get yourself together—your credit report, your work history, your time management, your spending, your ability to be faithful, your ability to communicate effectively, your relationship with God and with people—*everything!*

Even as you progress in your relationships, the consecration and commitment that you have made with God will continue and expand. Your life, your ministry, and your relationships will be better because you took the time to love God and yourself. Because of your pursuit of God, you'll never have to walk or build relationships alone. The Holy Spirit will lead, comfort, convict, and empower you, and I am *"confident of this, that He who began a good work in you will carry it on to completion..."* (Phil. 1:6). As building relationship with God and seeking His Kingdom become the most important things in your life, He has promised to bless you and the works of your clean hands.

Endnotes

1. Jonathan Swift (1667–1745). http://thinkexist.com/quotes/jonathan_swift.

2. Ervin N. Hershberger, *Seeing Christ in the Tabernacle* (Harrisonburg, VA: Vision Publishers, 2007).

3. From "The Tabernacle," a lesson taught by Dr. James Modlish. *The Bible Study Page.* http://www.thebiblestudypage.com/taber_fence.shtml.

4. Ibid., http://www.thebiblestudypage.com/taber_altar.shtml.

5. Strong, *Strong's Exhaustive Concordance of the Bible*, #H4196, #H2076.

6. To learn more about Denetria's organization, Girl Talk, Inc., visit http://www.girltalkinc.com.

7. Louis Isaac Rabinowitz. American-Israeli Cooperative Enterprise. "Anointing." Jewish Virtual Library from Encyclopedia Judaica. http://www.jewishvirtuallibrary.org/jsource/judaica/ejud_0002_0002_0_01124.html.

8. Ibid.

9. Strong, *Strong's Exhaustive Concordance of the Bible,* #G5545, #G5486.

10. The online entry for "charisma" can be accessed in *The American Heritage® Dictionary of the English Language, Fourth Edition*. Houghton Mifflin Company, 2004. 7 December 2009. http://dictionary.reference.com.

Chapter 6

PAST THE CURTAIN: FELLOWSHIP, SERVICE, AND (UN)EQUAL YOKING

"Love is the force that ignites the spirit and binds teams together."
—Phil Jackson

Contrary to popular belief, loneliness is not a trick or device of the enemy. It is not a spiritual attack, and it cannot be rebuked, "bound," or prayed away. Loneliness is defined only as the state or condition in which one is without companionship. It is simply the state of being alone. Before you change the state of your relationships and eliminate loneliness in your life, you have to change your mindset about them. In her poem, "Alone," Poet Laureate Maya Angelou wrote:

Lying, thinking
Last night
How to find my soul a home
Where water is not thirsty
And bread loaf is not stone

I came up with one thing
And I don't believe I'm wrong
That nobody,
But nobody
Can make it out here alone.

There are some millionaires
With money they can't use
Their wives run round like banshees
Their children sing the blues
They've got expensive doctors
To cure their hearts of stone.
But nobody
No, nobody
Can make it out here alone.

Now if you listen closely
I'll tell you what I know
Storm clouds are gathering
The wind is gonna blow
The race of man is suffering
And I can hear the moan,
'Cause nobody,
But nobody
Can make it out here alone.

Alone, all alone
Nobody, but nobody
Can make it out here alone.

God's plan was never for mankind to live in isolation, but one of the enemy's devices is to deceive us into believing that life or ministry would be easier if we stay independent, private, and alone. It is his goal to separate us from God, from meaningful relationships, and ultimately to force us into solitary confinement. Solitary confinement, the denial of human contact and companionship used as a punishment, is a type of psychological torture. It is so unnatural for human beings to live in isolation that extended periods of solitary confinement produce physical, mental, and emotional illness that can conclude in death.[1]

 ### Loneliness is not permanent, nor is it a punishment.

Loneliness is not permanent, nor is it a punishment. It is a gift from God, a human emotion designed to make it uncomfortable for us to exist outside of the relationships for which we were created. Without loneliness, we would remain emotional islands, refusing to reach out to God or to anyone beyond ourselves. We would remain closed-minded, selfish, and independent, even when it would be to our advantage to build relationships with others. If you are experiencing any level of loneliness right now, it is an indication that God has placed in you a desire to connect with Him and/or with other human beings. That desire should no longer force you into nights of tearful fits, one-night stands, or bouts of depression. Instead, it should encourage you as you pursue God and His type of love. Break out of solitary confinement! Reestablish connections with God and the people around you—call your family or a friend, join a church and attend service regularly, go on a date and spend time talking to your spouse. I challenge you to start resisting your own loneliness and start building and renovating relationships with those whom God is connecting to your life.

God only uses periods of solitude to give us time alone *with Him!* During those periods, it is His desire to commune with us so that we grow closer to Him and so that we can reflect upon our own lives and needs and desires. Even during those periods we are not alone, as He has promised to never leave us and never forsake us. And God even places an expiration date on those seasons of our life. In fact, no one in the Bible had to endure a season of isolated consecration that lasted longer than 40 days! The quickest way to defeat the enemy's hold on your life is to come into agreement with God and to reach out to another believer who will also agree with you.

There is a power released in unity and agreement at every level of divine relationship.

> *Again, I tell you that if two of you on earth agree about anything you ask for, it will be done for you by My Father in heaven. For where two or three come together in My name, there am I with them* (Matthew 18:19-20).

 ## God's presence and His favor rest on relationship.

God's presence and His favor rest on relationship—that is why the enemy tries to initiate division and isolation. When we allow God to heal our hearts, when we escape the pain and mistakes of our pasts, and when we enter (or reenter) friendships, relationships, and marriages based on love, respect, honesty, commitment, and pure motives, God promises to be with us and to answer our prayers. Solomon makes the need for relationship even more clear:

> *Two are better than one, because they have a good return for their work: if one falls down, his friend can help him up. But pity the man who falls and has no one to help him up! Also, if two lie down together, they will keep warm. But how can one*

keep warm alone? Though one may be overpowered, two can defend themselves. A cord of three strands is not quickly broken (Ecclesiastes 4:9-12).

Divine relationship provides assistance, accountability, comfort, safety, and protection.

The Triune Nature of Divine Relationships

God has ordained a blessing for those who walk in unity, which is impossible without the participation and agreement of more than one party. It was God Himself who said, *"It is not good for the man to be alone"* (Gen. 2:18). True friendship and real love are a gift from God, and building relationships that stand the test of time require His strength, His grace, and His love! Developing relationship is a process—there are steps and stages to walk through, and a love established by God will grow and mature over time.

There are three levels of relationship described in the Book of Proverbs. *Friendship* is the first type of divine relationship, setting the foundation for all others. Proverbs 17:17 says, *"A friend loves at all times, and a brother is born for adversity."* In this passage, *friend*, or *rea* in Hebrew, can be translated as "an associate (more or less close): brother, companion, fellow, friend, husband, lover, neighbor."[2] Building and maintaining relationships of any type—associates, friends, neighbor, or spouse—requires the commitment and ability to walk in love and promises the same in return.

Fraternity, or brotherhood and sisterhood, is the second type of divine relationship. *Brother* in Proverbs 17:17 is translated *'ach*, which refers to one with whom one is connected in kinship or resemblance, by birth or by a recognition of equality and similarity.[3] Proverbs 18:24 gives us a recipe for both friendship and an even closer type of bond: *"A man that hath friends must shew himself friendly: and there is a friend that sticketh closer than a brother"* (KJV).

In this passage, the phrase *"sticketh closer"* is translated *dabeq*, which means "to cling, cleave, or adhere."[4]

The third dimension of relationship is *fidelity*, which encompasses lifetime commitment and matrimony when man and woman cleave to one another and become "one flesh." Within our tabernacle blueprint, friendship is outer court relationship, fraternity is inner court relationship, and fidelity is the relationship to be patterned after the holy of holies.

 Within our tabernacle blueprint, friendship is outer court relationship, fraternity is inner court relationship, and fidelity is the relationship to be patterned after the holy of holies.

The outer court was known as the *"tent of the congregation"* (Exod. 39:40 KJV). It was the place where the Israelites assembled for worship. The tabernacle was not only built to establish relationship with God, but also to encourage interaction and fellowship among the people of Israel. As you separate from the world and truly begin to seek and develop relationship with Christ, His desire is for you to grow in your relationships with your brothers and sisters and neighbors in Christ. The Israelites in the outer court may have had different backgrounds and different struggles. They would not have been perfect, but in entering the tabernacle and bringing their sin offerings to the altar, they all shared the same goal. The same is true for you. As you walk through and emerge from the outer court of your own life, you will encounter people at every stage of their own journeys. Use this time to allow God to expand your horizons and to give you a picture of and a heart for His Kingdom, which includes peoples of every race and ethnicity, every socioeconomic status, every educational background, every family type, and who all have their own unique story to share with you.

The outer court is a birthing place for divine friendship, and as you pursue God, you can expect Him to begin placing people in your life who have the same heart, vision, drive, and struggles as you do with whom you can share testimonies and tears, encouragement and accountability. If you open yourself up to the process, God will use your new network of friendships and your spiritual family to build and restore your faith in people who are also driven by His purposes. God will use those same relationships to assist you through your processes at the altar and the bronze laver.

Some will be there to activate your flesh and show you sin that may still be active in your heart, and others will be there to point out things that you need to kill off and to hold you accountable to leaving them at the altar. Some may act as mirrors, people with struggles that you can identify with, and others may act as cleansers, people whose testimonies may assist you as you wash away your past, your insecurities, and your baggage. You can build outer court relationships in any environment: work, church, organizations, online, your neighborhood, etc. As you begin to open up to others (and vice versa), you grow to see different aspects of God's Kingdom and experience a deeper dimension of God's love. These friendships may challenge you, build you up, pull out strengths that you did not know you had, or humble you, but you will be a better person because you developed God-directed and purpose-centered relationships in your life.

Within the circles of people with whom you may associate, there will be a smaller group of people with whom you find a true affinity or affection for. These are the individuals with whom you share common interests, purpose, and direction. The inner court, or the holy place, is reserved for the select individuals with whom you share a bond of admiration and respect. The inner court is the dimension of service, fellowship, prayer, and revelation. It is a safe place in which you can share your dreams, your hopes, your passions, your time, your vision, and your prayer requests with people who you can trust to understand, to support, and to help.

Within the inner court, you will develop your closest friendships, including your romantic relationships. In this dimension, you grow with people whom you can call your brothers and your sisters, your "besties" and your "homies." It is the realm reserved for the people you love, and eventually your mate should emerge from the individuals within this dimension of relationship. This chapter focuses on building the bond of intimacy in your inner court relationships, with a specific focus on how to handle romantic relationships. In the next chapter, we will talk about expanding and protecting the bond of intimacy toward the one (and only) person sovereignly chosen to walk with you into the holy of holies within the covenant of marriage.

Creating Bonds: Understanding the Principle of Equal Yoking

Within the outer courtyard of the tabernacle was a tent, known as the tabernacle proper. This tent contained the inner court (or the holy place) and the holy of holies. Although the outer court was open to the entire nation of Israel, the inner court was reserved for the priests. The priests were all taken from the tribe of Levi, descendants of the third son of Leah and Jacob/Israel. Leah called her third son Levi, which means "jointed unto," because she hoped and prayed that bearing three sons would cause her husband Israel to join to her as a companion (see Gen. 29:34). The Levites were called to connect God and humanity, but they were also connected to one another by bloodline and in service. They looked alike, talked alike, grew up together, shared experiences and trials— they were brothers. Within the nation, they were connected by birthright, by common purpose, by shared identity, and by shared mission. A man couldn't choose to become a priest, nor could he be made one. He had to be a Levite, called into the priesthood from birth.

Peculiar and Particular: Covenant-Based Relationships

But ye are a chosen generation, a royal priesthood, an holy nation, a peculiar people; that ye should shew forth the praises of Him who hath called you out of darkness into His marvellous light (1 Peter 2:9 KJV).

In other words, once God has called us, chosen us, and sanctified us, we are set apart as a generation of priests—set apart for praise and to walk in the purposes of God very much like the Levites.

Seeing ye have purified your souls in obeying the truth through the Spirit unto unfeigned love of the brethren, see that ye love one another with a pure heart fervently: being born again, not of corruptible seed, but of incorruptible, by the word of God, which liveth and abideth for ever (1 Peter 1:22-23 KJV).

Once you are saved, you are inducted into a new fraternity, a brotherhood of believers who are born again through the Spirit of God and the Word of God. We look alike—growing daily in our resemblance to Christ and to our heavenly Father. We talk alike, professing the Word of God and the vision He births out of us, which is like foolishness to those outside of the family. We share trials and tribulations, overcoming this world because the greater one lives within us. We are produced through the bloodline of Christ, connected by the divine love we share with one another. Christ, by His blood, *"has made us to be a kingdom and priests to serve His God and Father—to Him be glory and power for ever and ever!"* (Rev. 1:6).

 Those who reject Him, who do not believe as we do or walk in the faith that we live by, are consequently rejected from the priesthood.

This fraternity—more than any other in the entire world—is highly selective. We gain access to the priesthood because we believe and place our trust in Jesus Christ. Those who reject Him, who do not believe as we do or walk in the faith that we live by, are consequently rejected from the priesthood. They have no access to the inner court, and they are incapable of walking in the love of God or in a true bond of friendship because they are at enmity with God. God kept trying to get the Israelites to understand this principle, but they were more attracted to the "neighboring peoples" than they were to building relationships with the people they were related to (see Deut. 7:2-4; Josh. 23:11-13; Ezra 9:10-12; Neh. 13:25-27). Even when the other nations were at war against them, Israel maintained a strange attraction to their enemies! I can only imagine God's frustration and disappointment as Solomon, Samson, and an entire nation of the people He loved turned their affection to people who would hurt them over and over again while leading them away from Him. Sound familiar?

Most people are too picky about things that don't matter, and not picky enough about the stuff that should. Men have a list of requirements for the women they date—they know the age range, the measurements, and the number of sexual partners she can have to make her experienced but not "freaky." Women have a list that is twice as long—they have acceptable occupations and income, an acceptable height and build, and a time line that a man has to move along based on their biological clocks. I truly believe that God wants to give us the desires of our hearts, but He is waiting for us to desire the things that will matter in the long run. Evaluate your list and make sure that you are focused on the things that truly matter. How is his relationship with God? How does she interact with you, with family members, and with other people? What do you have in common? Do you have the same goals and vision? Physical attractiveness, wealth, or one's sexual chemistry should never outweigh a covenant relationship with God and the potential you share to build a life together. In Matthew 7, Jesus told the parable of a wise builder and a foolish builder. The wise man built his home on a rock, and it withstood the wind and the rain. The foolish man built his home on sand, and when the storm came, the house *fell with a great crash.* If you are walking in a cycle of crashing relationships, perhaps you need to check your building materials—what are you using as a foundation for your relationships?

Bonding and Yoking

As a believer, you should never establish a covenant, enter a commitment, or develop a bond (physical, emotional, spiritual, marital, business, or personal) with any person who is not already in covenant relationship with God. For your protection, there are no exceptions to this rule.

> *Do not be yoked together with unbelievers. For what do righteousness and wickedness have in common? Or what fellowship can light have with darkness? What harmony is there between Christ and Belial? What does a believer have in common with an unbeliever? What agreement is there between the temple of God and idols? For we are the temple of the living God...* (2 Corinthians 6:14-16).

God gave the same instructions to Israel when He warned them against planting two types of seeds in the same field, making garments with two different kinds of fabrics, and harvesting with two different breeds of work animals (see Deut. 22:9-11). In his letter to the Corinthian church, Paul described the threat of "unequal yoking," or the union of people from two different backgrounds of belief who simply should not come together, who cannot be productive, and who will never come into agreement because of their unequal foundations and dissimilar perspectives.

A yoke, also mentioned in the Book of Deuteronomy, is a wooden beam connected to the head or neck of two oxen to keep them in alignment as they plow a field or carry a load. Oxen always work in pairs, but when a farmer wanted to save money, he would purchase an ass instead of an extra ox and connect the ass to the yoke. Oxen are trained to follow the verbal command of their driver, to work hard and fast, and to have stamina for the long haul. Asses, on the other hand, are difficult to train and are stubborn by nature because they are far more driven by "self-preservation." When a yoke is applied to the ox and the donkey, they tend to go in opposite directions so that the ox, in addition to carrying the original load, also has to drag the jackass along.

Paul issued a command to the Corinthians using this analogy. He pleaded for the Corinthians to shift their affections from pagans and the ungodly back to God and His people. Paul instructed believers to not create any ungodly bonds and to end any that had already been created. Paul understood that an unequally yoked relationship will not only drain the strength of a believer, but that it also has the potential to continue to drag a believer further and further from God.

Paul is not telling us to completely avoid interaction with the world. In fact, we are encouraged in First Peter 2:12 to live such good lives among unbelievers that they see our good works and glorify God. Living those lives among them, however, requires separation from them when it comes to partnership. The divine love and respect that believers walk in and share is completely selfless, and God protects us from the hurt and disappointment we experience when we try to give that love to someone whose very nature is focused on pleasing him or herself at your expense. We have to trust God, turn our affections to Him and away from this world, and stop trying to make pagans into priests, donkeys into oxen, hustlers into husbands, or harlots into housewives.

We have to trust God, turn our affections to Him and away from this world, and stop trying to make pagans into priests, donkeys into oxen, hustlers into husbands, or harlots into housewives.

Identifying Relationship Types Before It's Too Late

Wouldn't our relationship decisions be easier if God gave us some type of secret password or a members-only handshake, something to identify people who love Him and who are trustworthy? We may not have a membership card to flash, but God has given us the Holy Spirit, who leads and guides us into all truth. If you are finding yourself attracting or attracted to the "wrong types" of people, perhaps it is because you have been ignoring God's Word, or quenching the leading of His Spirit, or have been refusing to walk in your own priesthood. You can always recognize a priest because the processes of regeneration and consecration produce an appearance, conversation, and a lifestyle that is completely different from what is found within the world.

Opportunities to meet new people and to strengthen existing relationships are all around you, but one of the classic mistakes in courtship is misidentification. Misidentification occurs when you take a person who belongs outside your camp and allow him or her into your inner court or holy of holies because she looks good or he says all the right things. It can also occur when you push away people who should be in your inner or outer court because you aren't ready or don't feel worthy of the friendship that they are ready to offer you. You can only identify where people belong in your life by watching their lifestyles and through conversation.

If people tell you that they do not believe in Jesus, or that they belong to another religion, or give you a reason why they stay away from church, believe them and place them in the appropriate category. Such a person is one with whom you should share an evangelistic relationship, living a life of example before him or her, explaining the gospel and offering the opportunity to know Christ as Lord and Savior, and shaking the dust off your feet if he or she rejects you. That individual is not a candidate for "yoking" or covenant-based friendship, relationship, or marriage because of the danger he or she poses to your direction, your momentum, and your destiny.

 When we demonstrate that we are prepared to be a friend, or a spouse, God will draw those who need to be drawn to us.

The distinctions between the other types of relationship (friendship, fraternity, and fidelity—or friendship, dating, and marriage) are a matter of discernment, and they are easier to recognize and classify through fellowship and prayer. In my experience, all that God requires from us is that we "show ourselves friendly." When we demonstrate that we are prepared to be a friend, or a spouse, God will draw those who need to be drawn to us, and our relationships will classify themselves. Emerging from the outer court will give you a fresh start and a sparkling new perspective on the possibilities for your life and your relationships. Walk where He leads you and look forward to sharing the days ahead with those who love God, love you, and share your goals and your outlook. If the people around you fail to fall into that category, it is time for you to leave them behind.

Through the Door: Building Intimacy and Preparing for Consecrated Contact

When a priest had been washed, dressed, and anointed, he was ready to walk into the second dimension of the tabernacle. The inner court, also called the tent of meeting, was a sanctuary where the priests would meet and gather for service. The door that provided entrance to the tent was made of *"blue, and purple, and scarlet, and fine twined linen, wrought with needlework"* (Exod. 26:36 KJV), which was the same material that was used to make the breastplate of decision that covered the priest's heart. It contained three pieces of furniture: the golden candlesticks, the table of showbread, and the altar of burnt incense, which we will explore as the next three steps in the courtship. The inner court, representing the second dimension of relationship building, was the domain of information exchange and bonding, fun and fellowship, prayer and evaluation, growth and service, action and intention, and testing and trial.

The purpose of this stage in courtship is interaction and the development of meaningful friendship and intimacy, which will serve as the springboard for success in a marriage. If you are single and uninterested in marriage, friendship remains a gift to you if you are willing to work toward developing it. You should maximize this stage, even if you plan to pursue life and ministry while remaining single. If you are single and interested in marriage, know that your potential spouse will emerge from the people you have made an effort to engage with, enjoy, serve with, and get to know. If you don't make connections, not only will you miss out on the opportunity to network and build relationships with the wonderful and interesting people around you, but you also will not be able to develop an intimate connection with a mate. If you are dating, engaged, or married, your marriage will be sustained and enhanced by your ability to cultivate friendship and ministry as its basis. When you can truly enjoy one another, trust one another, and serve one another, it makes loving one another a pleasure and a privilege rather than an obligation and a responsibility.

When a priest arrived at the door to the holy place, he had no idea what to expect on the other side. He had to trust that his preparation would serve him well as he progressed toward serving

God. Walking into a new relationship or marriage, or even into a new mindset about relationship or marriage, requires a great deal of courage and boldness. You will be leaving a realm where you are comfortable in order to engage intimately with someone whom you do not yet know or—if you are already in relationship—with someone you may no longer recognize. As you step through the threshold, you have two assurances: 1) You'll always be covered, and 2) it is God who orders your steps, and when you are submitted to His will and walking by faith, those steps always bring you closer to Him and to the promise He has given you.

It is God who orders your steps, and when you are submitted to His will and walking by faith, those steps always bring you closer to Him and to the promise He has given you.

Under Wraps: Spiritual Covering

As described in Exodus 26, the tabernacle proper had a covering of four layers made of different materials. The ceiling of the tabernacle was made of fine linen coupled with gold, which again speaks of the beauty of righteousness. The priests could always look up and know that they were standing in God's dwelling place, surrounded by His presence and His favor (see Exod. 26:1-6). Above the linens were two more layers—one made of black goat's hair, which was connected to the sin offering and was covered by a layer of ram skin dyed red, which represented the blood of the sacrifice (see Exod. 26:7-14). Together, these layers depict a picture of grace, as Paul describes in his letter to the Romans: *"Blessed are they whose transgressions are forgiven, whose sins are covered"* (Rom. 4:7). They placed a layer of skin from badgers or sea cows on the very top of the tabernacle, which was the toughest material used in the tabernacle's construction. This layer was weather resistant and protected the priests from the environment, seasonal conditions, and storms. They were always protected.

As you enter the next dimension and develop relationships, you need to know that you are covered. As you focus on serving and pleasing God, He takes on the responsibility of protecting you. It's not your job anymore. Always remember that choosing to walk in holiness and to live out a God-centered relationship is a beautiful and rewarding thing to do. Others on the outside may never understand, but it is only because they don't have access to the type of love that you desire to experience. You walk and serve and live and love under grace, which means that you are still covered, even if you make a mistake. As an individual and within a marriage, God promises to protect you and to keep you in the midst of your storms and hazardous conditions, as long as you stay focused on living a life and producing a love that glorifies Him.

It is so important that you continue to walk in covenant with Christ, so that He can provide a covering for you through His righteousness, strength, and blood. But it is also important for you to have a covering in the natural—to honor your parents (if living) and to identify and join a ministry and a body of believers who can provide a spiritual covering for you. You should be leery of walking into relationship with anyone who has no spiritual covering and no accountability, whether it is because of fear due to a previous church wound, an inability to walk in grace and accept the mistakes and humanity of other believers, a rejection of his or her natural parents, or a rebellion against spiritual authority. God calls believers to fellowship with one another, and there is a blessing in the corporate anointing that cannot be obtained by other means (see Ps. 133). Spiritual accountability and covering provides biblical instruction, counsel, prayer, encouragement, and so many other things that will be a lifeline for your relationships and your marriage.

God calls believers to fellowship with one another, and there is a blessing in the corporate anointing that cannot be obtained by other means.

My life completely changed the first time that I attended Overcoming Believers Church. I had never heard the Word of God preached so powerfully that it made the Scriptures come alive in my life and in my spirit. I was surrounded by people who loved God as much as I did. They are crazy worshipers with testimonies to back up their praise. For the first time in my life, I did not feel alone or empty, and today, I love the members of our congregation as I love my own family. I have a spiritual father and brothers and sisters in Christ who tell me when I'm wrong, who support me when I'm right, who listen to me when I ramble, and who pray for me without ceasing. They saw and encouraged potential in me that I wasn't ready to see. They wouldn't let me give up when I wanted to quit. They threatened the suitors I introduced them to, and they helped me learn how to trust. I know, beyond any doubt, that I would not be where I am in ministry, in life, or in my relationships, without my spiritual covering and the friendships that I know God assigned to my life through our church. I want the same for you, and for anyone with whom you enter relationship.

Safely Exposed

The inner court, or the holy place, within the tabernacle was completely enclosed with the exception of the ground. The priests, with their feet freshly washed, served barefoot in the second dimension, coming into direct contact with the earth. Though the high priest was covered from head to toe, God's desire was for his feet to be exposed. In Exodus 3, Moses was on the far side of the same desert at Mount Horeb, and a consuming fire, resting on an unconsumed bush, grabbed his attention and beckoned him closer. God called to Moses from within the bush, saying, *"Do not come any closer....Take off your sandals, for the place you are standing is holy ground"* (Exod. 3:5). From that moment forward, every time that Moses hid himself out of fear, revealed one of his weaknesses, or exposed a fear or a failure, God reminded him that He is the God of covenant and reassured Moses that everything that he needed for his assignment had already been placed in his hands.

The holy ground that Moses, and later the priests, stood upon represents a place of intimacy and vulnerability. Just as Moses removed his shoes and was safe in opening up before God, you must be willing to truly open up and allow yourself to be vulnerable in relationships. The inner court is not the place for macho men or defense mechanisms. Just as the sandals protected their feet and were not allowed in the holy place, you have to release all of the things that you have used to avoid being open in your feelings and your interactions. Perhaps it is your sarcasm, a tendency toward criticism, timidity, avoiding necessary conversations and communication, shutting down emotionally to avoid conflict, or lashing out when your feelings are hurt or to prevent them from being hurt.

 The inner court is not the place for macho men or defense mechanisms.

The inner court stage in courtship is a safe place for the believer to be vulnerable, and that vulnerability is necessary in developing intimacy. Because you have walked through your process, and because you have made a conscious decision to only create bonds with individuals who have demonstrated evidence of their own process, it is Okay for you to let your guard down. Every step that you are willing to take without your defenses brings you one step closer to the relationship you really want. Be yourself! It is the only way for you to draw and connect with people like you, and, ultimately, to the person God created for you.

The road through the courtship, in ministry and toward marriage, is difficult, but God in His sovereignty never intended for us to walk the road alone. The courts, and the Kingdom, are built upon the concept of unity. How can it be possible for you to love God and not love your neighbor whom you see daily? If you are looking to build a godly marriage, you must learn and practice the principles of godly friendship. Build relationships with your brothers and sisters in Christ. You will be better for the effort, and so will the individuals whom you befriend.

One of the questions that I am most frequently asked by singles is, "Where should I go to meet someone?" I love the looks of confusion when I give them my answer: "Everywhere and nowhere!" You should go to church to serve God and to enjoy worship and fellowship with other believers. You should go to work to make money to provide for your needs. You go to the grocery store or to the mall to make purchases. You should travel to experience new places and cultures. You go to the bowling alley, the gym, the pool hall, the library, a museum, or a bookstore because you are pursuing a passion or a hobby. You should visit a restaurant or attend a social event or concert to enjoy the food, music, ambiance, or your friends at a particular scene. Going to places and participating in activities that you enjoy will provide you the opportunity for you to meet believers with whom you hold shared interests, but you should never go anywhere intent to "pick up" a date. God has sovereignly chosen a mate for you, and He is faithful to present that person to you in His timing.

 God has sovereignly chosen a mate for you, and He is faithful to present that person to you in His timing.

For the courtship, the inner court is not a geographical location; rather, it is shift in mentality that you should carry wherever you go. A priest entered the inner court for the purpose of worship and service, and we should enter relationships with the same mindset. Once in the holy place, priests had responsibilities at three different places: the golden lampstand, the table of showbread, and the altar of burnt incense. Each of the pieces of furniture represents an essential ingredient in the making of a God-centered relationship. Relationships and marriages are as unique as the individuals who create them. As a result, it would be impossible to come with a set of dating how-to's and rules for you to follow, but the tabernacle's furnishings provide a blueprint for the elements of covenant relationship that must be a part of every relationship. For the when's, where's, and how to's, God has given us the Holy Spirit, who will lead us in all truth. Singles, walk as God leads you, to the places He leads you, to meet the people that He draws to you for the purposes He reveals, and make up your mind to enjoy yourself every step of the way.

Truth Be Told: Golden Sticks and Illumination in the Inner Court

The first piece of furniture that a priest would encounter in the holy place was the golden candlesticks, or the lampstand or menorah (see Exod. 25:31-39; 37:17-24). It was made of a single sheet of pure gold, weighing a talent—which equals about 90 pounds and today would be worth millions of dollars. The lampstand had seven lamps, one shaft, and six ornately constructed branches. The lampstand did not hold candles. The branches held bowls in which a lit wick was placed into oil. The light produced by the lampstand was enough to fill the entire tabernacle—there were no windows, no natural light, and no other candles or lamps.[5]

The light produced by the lampstand was enough to fill the entire tabernacle.

In Leviticus 24:1-3, God told Moses to command the priests to bring *clear* oil of pressed olives *"so that the lamps may be kept burning continually. ...from evening to morning, continually."* The high priest was charged with the responsibility of trimming the lamp consistently so that the light never went out. The ornate design of the lampstand was modeled after the almond tree, and each of the three branches on each side contained three items that represented three stages of maturity and development: a bud, a blossom, and a mature almond. The priests had to tend to the lampstand without ceasing. Like the process of gaining fruit from the almond tree, the lampstand would only produce light when its oil and wick were replenished and *cultivated.*

The lampstand itself represented the relationship of Christ and the Church. He is the central shaft of the lampstand, the chief cornerstone, and the branches extending from the shaft symbolize the Church (see John 15:5). The lampstand is used to illustrate God's Word in Scripture (see Ps. 119:105; Prov. 6:23), the Holy Spirit (see Rev. 4:5), and guidance or wisdom (see 2 Sam. 22:29; Ps. 18:28). Not only should your covenant relationships and marriage be built on a foundation of God's Word and communication with the Holy Spirit, but it also must be cultivated through clear and consistent communication with your friends and spouse who walk and live in agreement with you.

Open Exchange: Creating Genuine Dialogue

Within the courtship, the light of the lampstand represents truth—the type of honest, open, genuine dialogue and conversation that is essential to the building of intimacy in any relationship.

Dialogue can be defined quite simply as "a conversational exchange between two or more people."[6] Communication, at its best, is an equal trade of truths and sentiments. In his 1923 book, *I and Thou*, theologian Martin Buber creates and argues the "philosophy of dialogue," which he defines "not as some purposive attempt to reach conclusions or express mere points of view, but as the very prerequisite of *authentic* relationship between man and man, and between man and God."[7]

If you are working to build or to maintain an intimate covenant relationship, the ability to talk to one another is a prerequisite. It is dialogue, the exchange of information, thoughts, and opinions, that builds the bonds of relationship. As you read, ask yourself this updated version of the rhetorical question posed in Amos 3:3: Why would we even begin to think it is possible for two people to walk together, if they cannot discuss matters calmly and reasonably to the point of understanding and agreement? True dialogue is not about making a convincing argument or reaching some defined, final conclusion. Walking in intimate dialogue and, eventually, covenant relationship, is about sharing oneself (your day, your week, your past, your future, your successes, your failures, your dreams, your desires, your abilities, your weaknesses, etc.) while being equally open, respectful, and receptive to learning the same about another person.

Clear, honest communication with God (through study of His Word, worship, or in prayer) will build your relationship with Him and dispel any darkness that tries to reign in your life. Likewise, clear, honest, direct communication with another person will build intimacy between you and will eliminate any areas of darkness, division, or confusion in your relationship and in your understanding of one another. You can never be afraid to learn about others or to allow them to learn about you. Consequently, you should not avoid important conversations or the ability to grow in love through dialogue, even if the opportunity is disguised as conflict.

You can never be afraid to learn about others or to allow them to learn about you.

Speaking Truth, Building Trust

The design of the golden candlestick was based upon the almond tree, which is a symbol of the faithfulness of God's Word and divine timing to produce a promise.[8] In Jeremiah 1, God spoke to Jeremiah and emphasized the promise and divine timing of his prophetic calling. Their dialogue progressed when God asks, *"'What do you see, Jeremiah?' 'I see the branch of an almond tree,'* [Jeremiah] *replied. The Lord said… 'You have seen correctly, for I am watching to see that My word is fulfilled'"* (Jer. 1:11-12). By placing the imagery of that tree within the inner court, God was reminding His people that good fruit would be produced out of His Word in its ordained season. Whatever He says is the truth—for our lives and our relationships—and He is faithful to watch over His words and His promises. Whatever He has said to you, you can trust and believe it shall come to pass.

If God watches over His Word to perform it in His relationship with us, we should watch our words to make sure that we can perform them in our relationships! Be careful of the words you speak—make sure they are the truth. Be careful of the promises you make—they create the expectation of what you are to perform and fulfill in your relationship. So often, individuals begin a relationship with words and promises that they cannot or will not perform. Consider these phrases: "I'll always be there for you," "I'll do anything to make you happy," "I can give you whatever you need," "You're the only one," "I'll never hurt you or leave you," and so on. These lies, disguised as loving words of affirmation offered with the best intentions, are dangerous and damaging because they create false expectations.

Used recklessly, statements like those are verbal grenades, causing irrefutable damage when a person releases them and walks away. When building a relationship based on trust, you must be careful to speak out of a place of truth, clarity, and simplicity—and you should demand the same. Avoid fake or premature promises and vows—any "absolute" statements (always, never, anything, everything) are statements of covenant and should only be made in marriage. That includes the use of the word *love*, which is a word of promise and commitment and creates a bond that is not meant to be broken. Don't promise a lifetime of anything to someone until you are making a formal, financial, legal, lifetime commitment.

Growing in intimacy requires a foundation of the exchange of simple truths and a history of words kept.

Growing in intimacy requires a foundation of the exchange of simple truths and a history of words kept, which builds into levels of deeper understanding and connection. Genuine dialogue and conversation allows two people to build trust, and trust is initiated by dialogue that develops with nurturing over time. Romans 10:17 says that *"faith cometh by hearing, and hearing by the word of God"* (KJV). It is the progressive and continual hearing and meditation upon God's Word that produces our belief in who He is and what He can do. Likewise, it is the words shared in our communication with one another over time that allows us to establish intimate knowledge of and faith in one another. There are levels of communication, and advancement into the deepest levels requires trust and time.

Branches of Dialogue

The branches of the lampstand featured ornate detailing on the branches of the almond tree with three specific elements: the bud of the plant, a flower blossom, and the mature fruit of the almond.

Just as the fruit of the tree experienced three levels of maturity and development, so does dialogue and communication. First Corinthians 15:46 provides a simple, biblical truth: *"The spiritual did not come first, but the natural, and after that the spiritual."* The Message Bible says it like this: *"physical life comes first, then spiritual."* Human beings began as natural beings first—which means we experience and interpret things initially on a very natural and surface level. As our interaction increases, so does the depth of our understanding, until we reach the dimension of the spirit. Within courtship, the three elements of the lampstand branches represent the three levels of fruitful and productive dialogue: informal (casual), intentional (committed), and invested (covenant).

 Human beings began as natural beings first— which means we experience and interpret things initially on a very natural and surface level.

Informal dialogue is a natural exchange of basic questions and answers. It should focus on conversational topics that are foundational and factual, with a single goal of getting to know a person and building rapport. You should take the time to get to know people with no agenda and to allow them to get to know you with absolutely no agenda. Learn who they are, what they enjoy, what important perspectives they subscribe to about life and family, where they are from, what makes them laugh, and what their pet peeves are. You may discuss current events, sports, politics, alma maters, careers, and so on. Your dialogue with most people will never progress beyond this level, and that is perfectly okay.

You may develop an intrigue or an attraction to some individuals, and your conversations may advance to the level where you are purposely trying to explore a connection between you. This level of dialogue is intentional, as you are committed to investing the time and attention required to truly begin to understand someone and to allow him or her to understand you. In this level, the objective, fact-based conversations evolve into more personal ones, as you share revelation about your dreams, your goals, your pasts, your fears, etc. In this dimension, it is important that you accept the truths that you learn about someone without judgment or criticism, but with careful attention and evaluation. Both of you should be listening to learn what you share in common and what you can appreciate about the other person, while paying close attention to anything that may signal a mismatch of your personalities or your purposes.

 This level of conversation is connected to covenant.

There will be very few people with whom you move to the third level of communication: invested dialogue. When an individual is invested, they have developed enough trust to share intimate details of their lives and their emotions, and to share insight that creates a spiritual bond. This level of conversation is connected to covenant. You should keep the most sacred and intimate parts of yourself locked away until you encounter the person God has given a key to. This is a spiritual process, and you will need time and discernment to know with whom you should reveal the deepest parts of yourself. Even God keeps the deepest parts of Himself and the deepest revelation of His Word reserved for those who persevere through trial without walking away from Him. Never underestimate the value of testing within your relationship—in my experience, an individual's true nature, feelings, morals, and intentions toward you (and your intentions toward him or her) are most clearly revealed in seasons of difficulty or trial. The true test of a relationship is whether or not you can work back to a place of agreement in the face of internal or external difficulty.

Dialogue is an exchange, which means it must be equally shared. Both of you should have something to say, and both of you should know how to listen. You must learn when to speak up and when to shut up. In terms of relationship roles, the enemy has reversed the pattern God intended for conversation. In Eden, God spoke to Adam and challenged Adam to speak. Satan spoke to Eve and challenged her to. It was God's plan for Adam to lead in all things, and it is my sincere belief that a man should be comfortable taking the lead in initiating and maintaining dialogue and communication within the household.

Within the inner court, it was the high priest who tended the lampstand and, in order to walk as the priest of his household, a man of God may have to reject cultural norms and speak out and open up in order to keep his house in order. Women must be willing to submit in dialogue and communication—rejecting satan's plan to make us challenge our men, and ultimately, God's plan. Women were created for the purpose of helping, so when we take on a role of leading in our relationships, rather than assisting and supporting, we are operating outside of God's will. A woman must trust the man God placed in her life and allow him to find a voice within their home, and a man must stand up and speak. Ultimately, dialogue should involve both partners making an intentional effort to hear the other person, and in doing so, both people will be respected and heard.

Another word of advice: the deeper your level of dialogue, the more damage can be caused by inviting outsiders into your conversations. Be careful to keep the intimate details of your dialogue and your relationship between the two of you, and to only share intimate conversation and interaction with someone you truly know will do the same. Do not open up to someone who will not open up to you, and only seek advice or counsel from spiritual accountability you trust to be honest, understanding, and led by God.

Spending Time and Breaking Bread: Interaction in the Inner Court

The second piece of furniture in the inner court, placed directly across from the golden lampstand, was the table of showbread (see Exod. 25:23-30; 37:10-16; Lev. 24:5-9). The table itself was made from acacia wood covered in gold, and it had a golden crown that formed its borders at the top. Bread was to be placed upon the table continually, and the priests would enter the holy place with hot bread on each Sabbath. After placing the fresh bread on the table, they would gather together to break and eat the bread from the previous week. The bread could not leave the holy place and could not be shared with anyone outside.

The bread on the table is exemplary of Christ and His relationship with the Church. The gold-covered wood speaks of His humanity and His divinity, and He was crowned twice, with thorns on the earth and with His royal diadem and all power in the heavens. In John 6, Jesus identified Himself as the manna and as our living bread and living Word, saying, *"I am the bread of life. He who comes to Me will never go hungry..."* (John 6:35). At the Last Supper, Christ invited His disciples to take and eat of the bread, which represented His body. In First Corinthians 10:16-17, the apostle Paul explained that the bread that we eat at the table of fellowship represents our "communion" with Christ, and that our fellowship with Christ should produce a "communion" with one another. He writes, *"...The bread which we break, does it not mean [that in eating it] we participate in and share a fellowship (a communion) in the body of Christ?"* (AMP). The word *communion* in this passage is *koinonos* in Greek, translating *fellowship, partnership, participation,* and *communication.* Communion is sharing in such a way that individuals come together to form a union or a bond of oneness.[9]

Within the process of courtship, the table of showbread represents dating, intentional effort to participate in shared activities, and fellowship set for appointed times.

It is impossible to build relationship without consistent fellowship—which requires participation, communication, and sharing. God calls us to fellowship with Christ, and then He challenges us to walk in consistent fellowship with one another. Within the process of courtship, the table of showbread represents dating, intentional effort to participate in shared activities, and fellowship set for appointed times.

Defining Dating

To help you further understand the concept of "dating," we should probably look at its most basic definition. According to the *American Heritage Dictionary*, a *date* is a "time stated in terms of the day, month, and year…a particular point or period of time at which something happened or existed, or is expected to happen… an appointment."[10] *Dating*, in its very nature and definition, is connected to the establishment and assignment of a period of time to a particular purpose. It is defined in context as "an engagement to go out socially with another person, often out of romantic interest."[11] The priests in the tabernacle had an established and regular time to meet at the table of showbread, and as you build a relationship with someone, you should set and establish time to spend together. You should also make plans to participate in and share activities, events, meals, and other hobbies and interests of your choosing.

Showbread is literally translated from the Hebrew to mean "bread of the face" or "bread of presence."[12] It indicates both the watchful eye of God over the priests' fellowship, and that the priests were face to face in sharing and communing with one another. Genuine intimacy requires presence—both a physical presence and a mental/emotional one. Priests could only eat this bread at the table in the inner court because God did not want the priests to take sacred communion and spread it around. It is hard to be fully engaged in developing relationship with a person when you continue to eat at more than one table.

"Breaking bread" is a modern colloquial or slang term meaning:

> to engage in a comfortable, friendly interaction…to share a meal…social interaction where something is shared. This could be food, money, commodities, assets, or other various items…To break bread is to affirm trust, confidence, and comfort with an individual or group of people. Breaking bread has a notation of friendliness and informality…[13]

Breaking bread is, by its very nature, an enjoyable experience. Dating should include the sharing of hobbies and interests and events that both people enjoy, and will ultimately produce special memories that a couple will share. These may include a walk in the park, a victory in family bowling or a card game, a special "dress-up" dinner, a concert, or a worship service—anything that you share in common or that one partner wants to share with the other. It should also be a process that establishes expectations and builds trust.

I am often asked about online dating, and in anticipation of this book, actually registered and set up a profile on a couple of different sites so that I could speak of the experience without any unfair judgment. By definition and based on my own experience, the terms "online" and "dating" are mutually exclusive. Websites, forums, and social networking sites are great for meeting people, and even for engaging conversation and dialogue, but until face-to-face contact and "presence" are introduced and maintained, the interaction cannot advance to the level of relationship.

Without presence, any relationship, especially a relationship based on Internet or phone conversation, tends to build the tongue-based, counterfeit intimacy discussed in Chapter 3, and it fizzles out as quickly as it begins. Perhaps the most valuable concept and contribution of dating websites like Match.com and eHarmony.com are the personality tests and interest inventories that they use to match couples based upon their compatibility. The tests ask the types of questions that you should be considering in your own evaluation of yourself and of a potential mate. It is important that you enter and progress in your relationships with the goal of assessing and determining compatibility—not just intent on "making your relationship work" but discovering if the match is a "fit" when both individuals are acting as their "true" selves.

Though this book will not provide a complete "Do's and Don'ts" of dating, the table of showbread does provide some important and interesting guidelines.

#1. Priests Interact in Pairs and in Groups

On the Sabbath, the priests changed out the bread on the table, and together they ate the bread removed from the table. This event took place on the day set aside as sacred to God, indicating how important God considered fellowship. Other writers, preachers, and websites have taken up the debate of whether a couple should spend time alone or in groups, with family or at church. I think that all of the above are important and should happen in order as a couple advances through the process.

Early in the dating relationship, it is key for a couple to spend time alone together in public places *and* to meet and interact with all of the important people in the life of a potential mate (family, friends, church). This will give individuals the opportunity to "break bread" and to observe a potential mate in his or her most comfortable environment with the people he or she knows the best. The interaction in the early stages does not have to be prolonged, but as the relationship progresses, so should the amount and quality of time spent. For example, meeting briefly for coffee after work may progress into dinner and a movie and may eventually evolve into a meal prepared inside the home.

#2. Priests Stay Away From the Dirt and Out of the Dark

One of the other questions I often encounter about dating is, "How far is too far?" My simple answer is that anything that will defile (mentally, physically, emotionally, or spiritually) you or the person you are involved with is too far. Any intentional or unintentional act or conversation (whether in person, online, over the phone, or through text message) that produces temptation, guilt, shame, fear, or insecurity is too far. Priests didn't try to see how close to sin they could get because a priest knew that any sin or defilement on his part would not just affect himself, but also the other priests and eventually the whole nation. If a priest was unclean, through contact or by what was released from his own body, he was not only denied the opportunity to fellowship with another priest, but he was also completely cut off from the presence of the Lord (see Lev. 22).

If you find that you never meet or end up in relationship with a "good" woman or a "good" man, it is possible that the sin in your heart is separating you from the place in God where you will find him or her. Within a relationship, sin will not make you closer. In fact, it will make your interactions uncomfortable, and it will introduce division and discord. According to First John 1:6-7, anyone who claims to have fellowship with God but walks (or dates) in darkness is a liar. If we walk (and date) in the light, then He honors our fellowship with one another. Darkness in Scripture does not just symbolize sin; it is the very thing that covers it. Here is some practical counsel: Make sure that your dates, especially early in the relationship, are in public so that you are accountable for the visibility of your actions. Whenever you are alone together, make sure you keep the lights on!

#3. Priests Never Let the Table Get Empty

Priests prepared ahead—before they ate the bread on the table, they had already baked and placed 12 more loaves of bread in its place. The bread in the inner court speaks of satisfaction, provision, and supply. On a weekly basis, the priests made sure there was fresh bread, and they poured frankincense upon the table to make sure that the fragrance of the offering was pleasing to God. The time they spent together was sacred. Without the attention of quality time, your relationship is in danger of growing stale. In the business of modern life, it can be so easy to neglect the people who are closest to you. We often give our time, our joy, and our energy to our careers, to ministry, and to people pleasing, and we never stop to truly enjoy fellowship with God and with the people who mean the most to us. As you get closer to covenant relationship, resist the natural tendency to take the person you are in relationship with for granted and set aside time in your weekly schedule to keep what you share fresh and exciting. That way, you close a door to the enemy who wants to pull you or your partner away to another table.

Burning Incense: Intercession, Meditation, and Decision-Making in the Inner Court

The third and final piece of furniture that a priest would encounter in the second dimension of the tabernacle was the golden altar, or the altar of burnt incense (see Exod. 30:1-10,35-38; 37:25-29; 40:5,26-27). It was placed at the threshold of the holy place and the holy of holies, just before the veil that separated them. Just like the table of showbread, the golden altar was made of acacia wood and overlaid and crowned with gold, which also represents Christ. Just like the altar of burnt sacrifice, the golden altar had four horns on its corners, along with rings, on which blood from the sacrifice and the oil of anointing was placed. The high priest would bring coals from the altar of burnt sacrifice to the golden altar and pour incense upon them. As the incense burned, it produced a unique scent of love and worship that was pleasing and attractive to God. The high priest had to burn incense by morning and night when the golden lampstand was tended and while the burnt offerings were made. The incense was to burn continually, rising as an offering to God, *"a perpetual incense before the Lord throughout your generations"* (Exod. 30:8b KJV).

The altar of burnt incense is the place of prayer. In Psalm 141, David called upon the Lord and asked to be heard: *"May my prayer be set before You like incense; may the lifting up of my hands be like the evening sacrifice"* (Ps. 141:2). In both Revelation 5:8 and Revelation 8:3-4, we learn that the scent of incense rises and still fills the heavens, and the incense is the *"prayers of the saints."* Not only does the piece in the holy place represent our prayers, but it also demonstrates the love and the commitment that Christ has to us by praying on our behalf. Even at this moment, Christ is interceding for you and for your relationships; in fact, Hebrews 7 says that the very reason He lives is to pray for us (see also John 17:9-10; Heb. 7:25; Rom. 8:34).

 Even at this moment, Christ is interceding for you and for your relationships.

Jesus spent the last day of His life, the moments before His arrest and impending crucifixion, in prayer—essentially standing at the altar of burnt incense. His prayer can be separated into three distinct categories: prayer for Himself, prayer for the disciples, and prayer for other believers. In John 17:1-5, Jesus prayed for the Father to glorify Him, so that He could in turn give glory back to His Father. Jesus prayed for those whom God had given to Jesus to walk with Him—for protection, for unity, for full measure of joy, and for their sanctification through the Word (see John 17:6-19). Jesus expanded His prayer to include all believers—present and future—and prayed that we would all see glory and walk in unity and love as He lives inside of us (see John 17:20-26).

According to Matthew 27:50-51, the moment that Jesus yielded His spirit and gave His life on the cross, the veil of the temple was split, immediately opening up access to the holy of holies. Jesus gave us the ultimate example of what it takes to truly build intimacy. We should move into the holy of holies—the dimension of divine covenant relationship, complete intimacy, and marriage that invites and reflects the glory of God through prayer and submission of our spirits to the will and the sovereign plan of God. Just as Jesus' prayer in Gethsemane was focused in three dimensions, so should your prayers as you look toward building the final ingredient for intimacy and covenant relationship.

Individual Prayer for Guidance and Direction

Though every piece of furniture in the tabernacle was considered holy to God, it was the altar of burnt incense that He considered "most holy." No "strange incense," meat, or burnt sacrifice could be burnt there (see Exod. 30:9). God wanted incense made according to His instructions, and no flesh was to be placed on the altar, just as our prayers are to be offered unto God as led by the Holy Spirit, not according to our will or our sinful desires. The incense was made of equal measures of four pure spices, all types of gum or resin extracted from trees: stacte, onycha, galbanum, and frankincense. All of the spices carry a distinctive scent and have medicinal properties, and when combined together, the scent is pleasing to God.

As you make decisions for your life and your relationship, it is critical that you do so through prayer.

The Lord's Prayer, the model Jesus used to teach His disciples to pray, also had four distinct ingredients: praise and adoration, confession and repentance, supplication and request, and submission and silence. As you make decisions for your life and your relationship, it is critical that you do so through prayer. It undergirds, directs, sanctifies, and completes all of the other key elements of building a covenant. Your preparation for marriage requires a walk of continuous prayer, and through your quality time with God, He will equip you for marriage and ministry.

Prayer of Agreement for the Growth of One Another and for the Relationship

As an individual, you should be praying for yourself, but you should also pray for—and with—the person with whom you are in relationship and whom you will marry. Jesus demonstrated His love through prayer all the way until He breathed His last breath on this earth. He continues praying for His bride in anticipation of the day when the trumpet sounds and we are caught up to meet Him in the air. He prayed for the disciples who walked with Him, and He prayed for believers who had been given to Him before they were even born. If Christ can intercede for us, we should be interceding for the person who we will meet at the altar, whether we have met them or not.

I started praying for my husband-to-come when I was 12 years old as I committed the most intimate parts of myself to him. I did not know who he would be, or where he was, or what he was going through, but I knew that he was somewhere out there and that I wanted both of us to be ready when God brought us together. For years, I have prayed for his physical strength and that God would guard his heart and his mind. I have prayed for his career and his family, his finances, and for stability in his life. You don't have to wait until you meet the person. Begin to trust God for the person He has already created for you and start speaking life and interceding for him or her now.

Once you meet and begin to grow in relationship with that person, prayer is the essential ingredient in the formation of your spiritual bond. In Matthew 18, Jesus teaches the power of agreement in prayer:

> *...if two of you on earth agree (harmonize together, make a symphony together) about whatever [anything and everything] they may ask, it will come to pass and be done for them by My Father in heaven. For wherever two or three are gathered (drawn together as My followers) in (into) My name, there I AM in the midst of them* (Matthew 18:19-20 AMP).

The incense, prayers, unity, and agreement of the saints please God so much that hey invite His presence. He comes in as I AM, the God of covenant, who provides guidance, meets every need, and answers every attack and every word of the enemy. Through prayer, you will know when and how far to progress in your relationship. You can also come into agreement in regard to your individual needs and goals and ministries. Your relationship should also provide a safe place for confession, healing, and restoration.

> *Confess to one another therefore your faults (your slips, your false steps, your offenses, your sins) and pray [also] for one another, that you may be healed and restored [to a spiritual tone of mind and heart]. The earnest (heartfelt, continued) prayer of a righteous man makes tremendous power available [dynamic in its working]* (James 5:16 AMP).

As we open up to one another, we not only increase the intimacy of our bonds, but our earnest prayers also build and rebuild our hearts and our minds and produce the type of power in our spirits that causes dynamic results.

Prayer of Intercession for Family, Ministry, Career, and for External Situations

The priests were instructed to burn incense by morning and night, at the same time that the burnt offerings were made. Just as the burnt offerings covered the sins of the people of Israel, so did the prayers that were offered. The incense was never to stop burning; in other words, the priests were to be continually offering up intercessory prayer for the people they were connected to. Just as two or three can pray in agreement and expect God to show up in their midst and to answer the prayers they offer for themselves, a couple can come together and pray and watch God show up and move on behalf of the people around them. A couple should be interceding for their home, their families, their neighborhood, their community, their churches, their circles of influences, their workplaces, their government, and their nation.

 The priests were to be continually offering up intercessory prayer for the people they were connected to.

In Numbers 16, an entire family and 250 men were swallowed up into the earth alive and sent to hell for not considering the altar of burnt incense sacred. Soon after, God promised to send a plague through the entire camp of Israel because they refused to heed the warning issued by God. They were guilty of pride, iniquity, and complaining. When Moses and Aaron realized the plague had come, they fell to their faces in worship, and when the plague began to kill people, Moses told Aaron to run and burn incense to make atonement for the people.

The Bible says that Aaron stood between *"the living and the dead,"* and that the plague stopped the moment he burned the incense (Num. 16:48). In Second Chronicles 7:13-16, God makes a promise that in the midst of drought, famine, or plague, *"If My people, who are called by My name, will humble themselves and pray and seek My face and turn from their wicked ways, then will I hear from heaven and will forgive their sin and will heal their land"* (2 Chron. 7:14). When two or more of us who are called by His name come together and humble ourselves, pray, and seek God and repent, God promises to hear us, answer us, and send healing, forgiveness, and restoration to whoever we are connected to (see Luke 11:9-13; 1 John 3:21-22; 5:14-15). Prayer in relationship presents the opportunity to come into agreement and to make Kingdom impact. A couple who learns to pray together accesses the ability to restrict and release things from the spiritual to the earthly realms.

Deciding on "I Do": Looking Through the Veil to Commitment and Covenant

The other questions that I am frequently asked about dating and relationships are all variations of how and when to take the "next step." How do you know if you have found the one? How do you end a relationship that is not working? When are you ready to be married? To those I answer: Many priests passed the lampstand, served at the table, and smelled the incense, but only one (the high priest) could progress beyond that point, and only at the specific time and in the specific way that God established.

We may enjoy conversation, fellowship, or even prayer with different people, but only one person has been called to walk with us all the way through the process and to enter the covenant of marriage sealed by a sexual relationship.

We may enjoy conversation, fellowship, or even prayer with different people, but only one person has been called to walk with us all the way through the process and to enter the covenant of marriage sealed by a sexual relationship. I always ask married couples who appear to be genuinely happy and in love how they knew that they had found "the one," and I always get the same frustratingly simple answer. They just knew. Adam and Eve just knew. Isaac and Rebekah just knew. Boaz and Ruth just knew. I have to believe in my heart that when God brings the right person into your life you will know, too. The journey into covenant is a faith walk, and, ultimately, you will need to let God be guide, and you must trust what the Holy Spirit reveals to you. Whether He tells you to stop what you are doing with the person you are with, to remain where you are, to begin something new, or to progress to the next level, listen to Him.

If you are unsure, take the time to evaluate your place in the inner court and see if the time you have spent there has allowed you to build the foundation you need to really build a life upon. If morals, interests, goals, attention, and time are equally shared and exchanged, neither conversation nor fellowship will feel forced or manipulated. Both people should be fully engaged, and though effort and investment will be required, both people will feel that the satisfaction and enjoyment they have gained was worth the time and energy used to build relationship.

If you are not at the point of marriage, minor adjustments are to be expected, but if you find that you have nothing to talk about, nothing in common, and are headed in different directions, this may not be the person you are supposed to spend your life with. God created a tailored mate for you, and you do not have to settle, "make something fit or work," or change who you are and what you like in order to maintain a relationship. If you don't like the person you are dating and cannot see loving and committing to that person just as he or she is, keep moving. Be grateful for a friendship and continue to walk toward God—expecting Him to unite you with the person He is preparing for you. If you are married and struggling to build intimacy, you will need to revisit these stages in the relationship with your mate and create a connection based on your covenant. Failure is not an option, and God's desire is for you to find pleasure in the love you committed to.

Now…let's head toward the moment you've been waiting for (or running from!). Let's go beyond the veil…

Endnotes

1. Studies on the psychological effects of isolation and solitary confinement have been performed by justice programs, non-profit organizations like Amnesty International, and many others. An online sourcebook, compiled by Sharon Shalev, can be accessed at http://solitaryconfinement.org/sourcebook.

2. Strong, *Strong's Exhaustive Concordance of the Bible*, #H7453.

3. Ibid., #H1695.

4. Ibid., #H1695.

5. Hershberger, *Seeing Christ in the Tabernacle*.

6. "Dialogue." Wikipedia.com. http://en.wikipedia.org/wiki/Dialogue (accessed 17 February 2010).

7. Martin Buber, *I and Thee* (Continuum International Publishers, 2004). "I and Thee," originally published as "Ich and Du" in Germany in 1923, was translated to English in 1937 and is considered a classic theological text.

8. Messianic Rabbi Gennady Livshits provides an excellent analysis of almond trees in the article "The Almond Tree" on the teachings page of the House of David Messianic Jewish Television Program, http://www.houseofdavidministry.org/teachings/view.php?id=56.

9. Strong, *Strong's Exhaustive Concordance of the Bible*, #G2842; "Communion." The Online Oxford English Dictionary; T.F. HOAD. "Communion." *The Concise Oxford Dictionary of English Etymology*. 1996. Encyclopedia.com. 17 March 2010 http://www.encyclopedia.com.

10. "Date." *American Heritage Dictionary Online.* www.thefreedictionary.com/date.

11. "Dating." *American Heritage Dictionary Online.* www.thefreedictionary.com/date.

12. Strong, *Strong's Exhaustive Concordance of the Bible*, #H6440.13.

13. "Break Bread." Urban Dictionary.com. http://www.urbandictionary.com/define.php?term=break percent20bread (accessed 13 April 2010).

Chapter 7

BEYOND THE VEIL: COMMUNION, COVENANT, AND GOD'S PLAN FOR SEXUALITY

"Marriage is not just spiritual communion, it is also remembering to take out the trash." —Joyce Brothers

I grew up reading the stories of Sleeping Beauty and Cinderella, of Snow White and the Princess and the Frog. All of these stories carry the same basic premise—two young people, destined to be together, are separated by time, trouble, and circumstance. The forces of fate intervene, and at the end of the story, the prince and the princess live blissfully ever after. As a child, these stories were the stuff that marriage was made of. And as an adult, I can't say that I have completely let the idea of my own fairy tale go.

As I began writing this chapter, I had several conversations with married individuals who told me that marriage was "hard work," filled with struggle and compromise, that the first and the seventh years are the hardest, and that they had no idea how difficult marriage would be when they said "I do." If I listened to those people, I may have allowed their experience to color my own, rather than looking to the Word of God to establish my vision, my goal, and my pattern. God's relationship with the human race has been tenuous, strained, inconsistent, and downright hard since the Garden of Eden.

It has been overwhelmingly filled with disappointment, anger, misunderstanding, reconciliation, ups and downs, good days, bad days, failures, and breakthroughs. But there will come a time—no man knows the day or the hour—when all of the struggles will come to an end, and we will be eternally reunited with God. The struggle, the trial, the confusion, the temptation, and the frustration will all be worth the wait in the rapture. The Bible calls the celebration of that day the "Wedding of the Lamb," and that wedding celebrates the triumphant union of humanity and God in spite of all the forces of evil that were stacked against it.

 The Bible is the original fairy tale.

The Bible is the original fairy tale—the beautiful truth on which the fictions are patterned. The journeys of Cinderella and Prince Charming, Shrek and Princess Fiona, and of the Church's reconciliation with Christ are filled with twists and turns, with challenges and threats, but the stories all end with a wedding and a "happily ever after." I am just crazy enough to believe that our marriages should follow the same pattern—with two young people destined to be together, separated by time, trouble, and circumstance, until the Holy Spirit intervenes and brings them together to unite at an altar and live happily (not angrily, bitterly, or stressfully) ever after. I believe in my heart that marriages do not emerge as fairy tales because people do not understand the purpose, process, and principles of courtship.

As a result, couples live their unions in reverse order, experiencing joy, satisfaction, and blind euphoria during their dating and engagement, but failing to ask the difficult questions and to negotiate the terms of their union that could lead to a successful marriage. Couples get caught in their infatuation, sexual immorality, or a super-spiritual "word from the Lord." Some may be running from their pasts, are motivated by unplanned pregnancy or financial ease, are focused in their determination to please other people or want to have the "wedding of the year." Couples skip the most necessary parts of their process and fail to build and properly evaluate the foundation of their marriage. As a result, they may spend years of their marriage trying to patch up or build upon an unstable beginning. The problem with most failed marriages has nothing to do with issues that began within the marriages—the problems were initiated and instigated by failures and faults that were not revealed, acknowledged, or addressed within the couple's courtship (in their singleness, dating, or engagement).

At their best, the periods of dating and engagement give a couple opportunities to learn about and to test their compatibility and commitment. In order to have a "happily ever after" marriage, a couple's love and devotion must be sustainable beyond the initial attraction and/or infatuation. It takes time, talking, and, yes, trouble to produce the type of bond that leads to a happy marriage.

Consider it pure joy, my brothers, whenever you face trials of many kinds, because you know that the testing of your faith develops perseverance. Perseverance must finish its work so that you may be mature and complete... (James 1:2-4).

The text provides a spiritual truth: trial and testing develops endurance, and endurance must be allowed to work through an individual's life and a couple's relationship in order for it to be *"perfectly and fully developed [with no defects], lacking in nothing"* (James 1:4 AMP). A couple's time and progression through the steps in the outer and inner courts should give them a chance to figure out if they are a true "fit" for one another. Not only will this process give a couple the opportunity to learn about one another, but it also will include periods of external and internal conflict and challenge, as the couple learns to negotiate their expectations and to practice the strategies that they will need to be successful as one. Successful courtship is difficult and straining, but the consummation of the process, the joy, satisfaction, and gratification of the wedding and the "happily ever after" marriage are worth the investment and the wait.

 Successful courtship is difficult and straining, but the consummation of the process, the joy, satisfaction, and gratification of the wedding and the "happily ever after" marriage are worth the investment and the wait.

In this final chapter, we will explore the sacred inner chamber of the tabernacle, the holy of holies, as the third stage in courtship: holy matrimony. I enter my discussion of marriage with my own idealistic, biblically based assumptions: that any failure that a couple faces in marriage can be attributed to a mistaken step in courtship and that those failures can be restored and repaired by revisiting the outer court and inner court and walking back through the process. For the rest of this chapter, I will treat marriage as the final and lasting result of a Spirit-led, holy, sacred, complete, and thorough trouble-tested courtship. The Bible does not say that marriage is hard work, or a struggle, or that it is difficult—what makes it seem that way is that our flesh often refuses to submit to the Word and the will of the Lord, which results in our conflicts with one another.

In contrast, God's Word describes the union of two believers as a wonderful thing. Proverbs 18:22 states, *"He who finds a wife finds what is good and receives favor from the Lord."* Solomon instructed men to *"enjoy life with your wife, whom you love..."* (Eccles. 9:9). Not only does marriage benefit its partakers, but it also provides a witness of God's love to the world. The writer of Hebrews admonishes us that *"marriage should be honored by all..."* (13:4). In this text, the word *honorable* is taken from the Greek word *timios*, which translates as "valuable, costly, beloved, dear, precious, esteemed."[1] Our marriages, built upon our love for God and our desire to reflect His love and His glory in the earth, will prove genuine, rare, and costly, and as a result they will be valuable and highly esteemed. While worldly couples cheat, complain, and criticize, a couple who lives by the principles of courtship will reflect and release the love, glory, and presence of God as they pursue Kingdom purposes.

Cleared for Covenant: Entering Marriage Within the Holy of Holies

Prior to obtaining and accepting any position within the United States federal government, an individual must obtain a security clearance. A security clearance is a status granted to potential employees that gives them access to classified information, secret intelligence, and restricted areas and places. The degree to which information and places are kept secret is known as "sensitivity," and the assigned level of sensitivity is based upon the amount of damage that could be caused if trust and relationship were to be broken and the data was to be released. The U.S. has three levels of classification: confidential, secret, and top secret. When an individual without the proper clearance accesses information or areas that he or she should not enter, the punishments are swift and serious.

The tabernacle not only was a secret place; it also was a sacred place, and access to its courts was highly restricted. Entrance required security clearance. Only the Israelites could enter the "confidential" outer court and only one family, the Levites—the priests—could enter the "secret" inner court. The holy of holies, the third dimension of the tabernacle, was absolutely "top secret." Only one person in the entire nation, in the entire world, was granted access, and the high priest could only enter the holy of holies through the process that God Himself had predetermined. Access to the tabernacle generally, and the holy of holies specifically, was restricted because it was God's dwelling place, the abode of His glorious presence and His favor. Anyone who entered this sacred dimension without God's permission, the official position, or while violating the process, subjected himself to the penalties of leprosy or death.

When a person applies for or is considered for a classified position in the government, he or she must participate in a process known as "vetting." Vetting is designed to gather information, examine, and evaluate a person's credibility, assets, and personal conduct. A candidate gains clearance, or is chosen for a position, based on what is uncovered during this process.[2] If a detailed process of application and examination is required for obtaining security clearances, driver's licenses, and employment, how much more seriously should a person take the process in which he or she is permanently joined with and attached to another person?

The Bible says that we are now the tabernacle, the temple, and the dwelling place of the Holy Spirit. When we come into the Kingdom, accepting Christ as Lord and Savior, we are regenerated, born from above as vessels and vehicles of His glory, and filled by the Holy Spirit. Our lives and our bodies become the sacred places where Christ dwells, and consequently should be restricted in terms of who we allow clearance to certain dimensions of our lives. Courtship is a vetting process, a season of examination and evaluation through which information is gathered about yourself and a potential mate to determine whether or not that person should have access to the most private and the most sacred parts of your life and your body (and vice versa).

Top-secret classification should only be awarded in covenant.

Just as only the high priest could enter the holy of holies, only one person—your spouse—is supposed to gain top-secret classification in your life and have access to your deepest emotions, to your hopes and dreams, and to your marriage bed. Top-secret classification should only be awarded in covenant, after two individuals are completely "vetted" and are ready to unite and become one. Allowing an individual who is not your spouse into the holiest places in your life can result in detrimental results—mentally, emotionally, spiritually, financially, and, possibly, generationally.

Revisiting Roles in Marriage

The high priest entered the holy of holies once per year for the purpose of atonement and redemption. It was his role to cover and stand in the gap for the nation of Israel and to offer the sacrifices that would please God and that would invite His presence and ignite His glory.

> *When everything had been arranged...the priests entered regularly into the outer room to carry on their ministry. But only the high priest entered the inner room, and that only once a year, and never without blood, which he offered for himself and for the sins the people had committed in ignorance* (Hebrews 9:6-7).

The external sacrifices and the cleansing offered by the high priest on the Day of Atonement were only an illustration for the time to come. They were based on regulations and laws that were temporary, and the atonement was not enough to produce God's abiding presence.

The writer of Hebrews draws the connection between the natural tabernacle and the spiritual one:

> *When Christ came as high priest of the good things that are already here, He went through the greater and more perfect tabernacle that is not man-made, that is to say, not a part of this creation. He did not enter by means of the blood of goats and calves, but He entered the Most Holy Place once for all by His own blood...* (Hebrews 9:11-12).

What the high priest and the law symbolized in Exodus, Christ fulfilled in the Gospels. What the high priest and the animal sacrifice provided temporarily, Christ provided permanently. While the high priest operated out of obedience, Christ's sacrifice was motivated by love. Not only did Christ gain access to the most holy place, but His indwelling also gives us the power to walk in the most holy place and to fulfill our roles in advancing the Kingdom as kings and priests.

 His indwelling also gives us the power to walk in the most holy place and to fulfill our roles in advancing the Kingdom as kings and priests.

At this point, you are probably asking, "What does the high priest and all of this stuff have to do with relationships and marriage?" Excellent question! What the high priest fulfilled in the tabernacle, Christ fulfilled within the Kingdom, and a husband is supposed to fulfill within marriage. Just as Hebrews 9 tells us that Christ came as the "high priest," John the Baptist proclaimed that Jesus had arrived as the "bridegroom" (see John 3:28-29), and John the Revelator proclaims Him King of kings and Lord of lords (see Rev. 17:14; 19:16). Within the courtship, the roles of high priest, king, and bridegroom are one and the same.

Paul established the analogy of marriage as the relationship between Christ and the Church, and through this analogy God establishes the roles that a husband and wife subscribe to as they enter their marriage (see Eph. 5:21-23). The Bible challenges each spouse to submit to one another, but it specifies individual roles for both the bridegroom and the bride, as *"each one of you* [husbands] *also must love his wife as he loves himself, and the wife must respect her husband"* (Eph. 5:33). Just as Christ operated as High Priest, Lord, King, and as the Bridegroom, a husband should be vetted to ensure that he understands and is ready to walk as a priest (in integrity and intercession), as a king and lord (for headship, protection, and provision), and as a bridegroom (with sacrifice, love, and patience). Because of her analogous relationship to the Church, the position of wife is comparative to the tabernacle, the Kingdom, and the bride. As such, a wife should be vetted to ensure that she is walking in sanctification, honor, respect, loyalty, and preparation to receive, serve, and support her husband emotionally, spiritually, and, yes, sexually.

When the high priest advanced beyond the altar of burnt incense, leaving the other priests in his approach toward the holy of holies, he found himself separated from the next dimension by a veil (see Exod. 26:31; 36:35). The veil in the tabernacle was a curtain made of *"blue, purple and scarlet yarn and finely twisted linen."* The priest's attire, as we learned in Chapter 6, was made of the same materials and colors and spoke of divine right, royalty, sacrifice, and righteousness. When a man and a woman meet at the altar for the purpose of entering a marriage, they should be equally attired in these characteristics. The veil was the door covering for the most sacred place in the tabernacle, and a bride also symbolically covers herself with a veil.

In Genesis 24, Rebekah veiled herself upon her first encounter with Isaac in preparation for their wedding and marriage. She didn't remove her veil until he had made a formal commitment to her by bringing her inside of his tent. Her veil represented modesty and mystery, two things that a bride should wear in preparation for union with her husband. To this day, a bride continues to wear white linen (her wedding dress) and a veil as a demonstration of chastity, purity, loyalty, and modesty when she is presented before her bridegroom. A bridegroom should be intrigued by what lies beyond the veil and willing to sanctify himself in order to access the glory and favor that lies in communing and consummating a marriage with the bride he loves.

 A bridegroom should be intrigued by what lies beyond the veil and willing to sanctify himself in order to access the glory and favor that lies in communing and consummating a marriage with the bride he loves.

Crossing the Threshold

When the high priest was ready to advance through the veil into the holy of holies, he had already covered two-thirds of the ground that he needed to walk through in the tabernacle. The tabernacle proper, the tent within the courtyard of the tabernacle, measured 300 square cubits. The inner court was 200 square feet, or two-thirds of the tabernacle, and the holy of holies measured 100 square feet, or one-third of the tabernacle proper. He had encountered and rendered service at five of the seven pieces of tabernacle furniture for an entire year prior to the day he entered the most holy place. The high priest had to walk through an exact process before going beyond the veil, and faithful, daily service at every piece of furniture within the outer court and the inner court was significant and necessary for the high priest's advancement into the next dimension.

When a groom meets a bride at the altar, a significant portion of what he will offer within the marriage should have already been obtained and developed. He must carry the lessons and disciplines developed during his periods of singleness and dating/engagement into the dimension of marriage, and the same is true for the bride. When two people meet at the altar, they must truly be ready to become one flesh and to build upon a foundation of spiritual and emotional maturity and proven love. Entering the dimension of marriage too quickly would have produced disastrous results for the high priest and for Israel, as it will for you and for your spouse.

Leviticus 16 provides a description of the Day of Atonement, which for the purposes of courtship, represents the wedding day. God instructed Moses to tell Aaron the high priest *"not to come whenever he chooses into the Most Holy Place behind the curtain* [veil] *in front of the atonement cover on the ark, or else he will die..."* (Lev. 16:2). God made it very clear from the beginning that the dimension beyond the veil was sacred, and that the high priest could not enter it whenever and however he wanted to. As the high priest crossed the threshold into the most holy place, he was bathed and clothed in sacred garments, and his path was lit by the light from the golden lampstand. As he entered the holy of holies, he carried burning coals and handfuls of incense, along with two types of sacrifice (one for himself and one for the people he was connected to) to the place of covenant. Upon that place, he burned the ground incense and sprinkled the blood from the sacrifices. This process not only prevented his death and covered the sins of Israel, but it also produced the visible, manifested glory of God.

 The foundation of our marriages is laid through sacrifice and sanctification, through being clothed in the correct attire, and through communion with God and with one another in open dialogue, fellowship, and prayer.

Once the foundation for the high priest was laid in the outer and inner court, all he had to do was walk uprightly and carry the right things into the next dimension. The same is true for our marriages. The foundation of our marriages is laid through sacrifice and sanctification, through being clothed in the correct attire, and through communion with God and with one another in open dialogue, fellowship, and prayer. Once these things are established, building upon them will be an exciting adventure that is designed to usher us into the very presence and glory of God. Once the priest entered the holy of holies, he could not neglect the disciplines he developed in the other two dimensions of the tabernacle. Once we enter marriage, we cannot forsake the habits and practices that produced the intimacy that led us to the altar. The Day of Atonement was to be a "lasting ordinance" to the Israelites, continuing year after year in order to maintain the relationship between God and His people. Likewise, the progression through the courtship should be a lasting ordinance within your marriage, as you continually seek to grow in your relationship with the Lord and with one another, and as you move and adjust as God leads you together into His Kingdom purposes.

Passage Through the Veil: Sanctified Sexuality as a Seal of Covenant

A rite of passage is a ritual or event that marks growth, transition, and/or membership. Celebrations and ceremonial events—like earning a driver's license, graduation, obtaining a job, and baptism—all represent the shift from one phase in a person's life to another. A wedding ceremony, and entrance into the marriage that the wedding initiates and establishes, is the rite of passage that contains elements of all of the others listed above. The couple obtains and signs a license, which represents the permanent permission and acceptance of a governing authority for the union. A couple is responsible to submit to the governing boundaries and expectations in order to enjoy the privileges extended by them. It is the end of one's journey as an individual and the commencement of a new life to be shared with another person. It is an agreement to fulfill one's role and responsibilities in exchange for adequate satisfaction and compensation. It is a transition of body, soul, and spirit, as all of you is immersed into all of another person, and vice versa. A wedding is a transition into covenant relationship that should be joyous, memorable, and symbolic of the life and the future that two people are committed to building together.

In Israel, the Day of Atonement, when the high priest entered the tabernacle's sacred dimension, was the holiest day of the year. This holiday was truly a rite of passage, marking the end of one year and the start of the next, and marking the visitation of the glory of God. This day of new beginnings carried deep significance for the nation of Israel as a period of rest, repentance, prayer, and fasting. When the high priest entered the holy of holies, he carried the fate of the nation on his shoulders. The Day of Atonement was a day of covenant, as the high priest offered sacrifice and prayer to elicit the presence of God and the outpouring of His glory before the people. The blood and prayers offered by the high priest would either appease God or anger Him—his life was on the line, and so were the lives of every family and every tribe of Israel (see Lev. 16:16-17). If a high priest entered the sacred place of covenant in defiled garments or with an inadequate sacrifice, he died as soon as he crossed the threshold of the veil.

In Chapter 4, we defined covenant as a legally binding contract or agreement, made and kept under the promise of a seal. We discussed God's use of the blood of sacrifice as the seal of His covenants with Adam, Noah, and Abraham. When Israel was delivered from Egypt, the sacrifice of the Passover lamb and the placement of the blood over their doorposts marked a transition into a new beginning and liberty from bondage through covenant relationship with God. We see the use of the blood for redemption and reconciliation within the courtship of the tabernacle, just as we see it when the covenant between Christ and the Church is sealed through His sacrifice on the cross at Calvary. Not only does blood seal the covenants of God with man, but God designed our bodies in such a way that it also seals the covenant of man and woman.

Not only does blood seal the covenants of God with man, but God designed our bodies in such a way that it also seals the covenant of man and woman.

Within a woman's body, the hymen is a thin layer of tissue that surrounds and/or covers the external vaginal opening.[3] Like the tabernacle's veil, this membrane is a protective shield designed to control access to the intimate parts of covenant relationship, blocking or allowing the flow of fluids into and from within a woman's body. In sexual penetration, the hymen separates and is stretched in order to allow a man access to the vagina. In this act, the two bodies join to become one. It was a cultural expectation in Israel and for other ancient peoples (and, some argue, a biological fact today) that the first time a woman was penetrated, the stretching of the hymen would produce bleeding, marking and sealing their covenant. In addition, a man's erection is produced when the blood sinuses and vessels within the tissue of a man's penis become filled with blood. Any sexual act is a blood seal.

It is a spiritual and a legal truth: sex is the seal of covenant relationship. Just as it was a lasting ordinance for the high priest to go beyond the veil and enter the most holy place on the Day of Atonement to solidify the relationship of God and Israel, the husband enters his wife through the hymen to solidify their covenant and their bond of love. In the United States, consummation is the first act of sexual intercourse between two people following their marriage. A wedding ceremony alone is inadequate to create a state of matrimony, and until a marriage is sealed by sexual intercourse, it is not considered a binding contract. Sex does not form a bond, but it seals a bond and a connection already built through the non-sexual intimacy as practiced in the process of courtship. Each time that a husband and wife engage in sexual intercourse, they reconnect to the covenant they have made with one another.

When the high priest entered the holy of holies, God considered his acts of service as worship. Sex is always worship, and it is important for the success and enjoyment and life of a covenant relationship that two people are able to consummate their sacred union as God intended—without distortion, disillusionment, or defilement. When two people enter a sexual relationship in covenant, their marriage bed is undefiled, pure, and unrestricted (see Heb. 13:4). God considers the physical union worship to Him, and He blesses it to produce life and to strengthen bonds (remember the three-strand cord?). Sex outside of covenant is immorality, a counterfeit and corrupted imitation of covenant love and sacred union. God considers the physical act idolatry, and false worship invites curses and consequences. In the life and ministry of a believer, an undefiled marriage bed invites blessing, but sexual immorality in thought or deed will always produce disagreement and deleterious effects.

The Anatomy of Sexuality and Marriage

For proof of the sovereignly ordained connection between sex and the sanctity of marriage, you need only revisit your biology and anatomy classes. A man's anatomy is designed to stretch in order to give, to fill, and to plant, and a woman's anatomy is designed to stretch in order to receive, to hold, and to nurture. The sexual act of giving and receiving, of reciprocal love and pleasure, is designed solely for covenant, and even science itself describes the sexual act in terms connected to marriage! For those of you who don't believe that sex is only supposed to exist within marriage, ask a biology or anatomy teacher or your family physician. It is impossible to even talk about a human being's reproductive or sexual organs without referring to concepts of covenant and matrimony.[4]

1. The genitals are the visible parts of the male and female reproductive system. The term *genitalia* is derived from the Greek word meaning "pertaining to generations or birth." The term *penis* is derived from the Latin word *pene*, which means inside (also the root word for penetration). The term *vagina* is derived from a Latin word meaning "sheath" or "scabbard," as in the protective covering for a sword. The external organs are designed to stretch to fit one another, with the vagina encircling, protecting, and cleaving to the penis that enters it.

2. In male anatomy, the term assigned for every sex organ is connected to a husband's role as high priest, king, bridegroom, and father. Externally, the scrotum covers a man's testicles. The term *scrotum* is derived from a Greek word meaning "garment" or "robe" (a priest's attire), and the word *testes* is derived from the Greek *testis*, meaning "witness" (as in testament). The term *erection* is derived from a Greek root meaning "to raise or stand up" or to "direct, keep straight, or to guide." During an erection, the internal sex organs produce sperm and semen released during ejaculation. The Greek root for the term *prostate* (which secretes the semen) is *prostates*, which means "one who stands before" as a "guardian" or "protector." The roots for the terms *sperm* and *semen* mean "seed" and "to sow" (as in the Word).

3. In female anatomy, the term *hymen* is a biological word for the veil that covers a woman's vaginal opening. It

is derived from the Greek word *Hymenaios*, the name for the Greek god of marriage and of membranes. A *hymenaios* is also a genre of Greek song performed during the procession of a bride to the groom's home, as she crossed the threshold of marriage. The clitoris is the most sensitive zone of pleasure on a woman's body. The term *clitoris* is derived from the Greek *kleitoris*, meaning "lock or key," or "little hill" as in a closed-off dimension or territory under protection from outsiders. The uterus is the largest organ in the female system, which though originally only the size of a fist, stretches to hold the seed she will carry, nurture, and deliver. The term *uterus* is derived from the Greek word for "womb" or "ground."

4. The *gametes* are the reproductive sex cells that join together during intercourse to form a *zygote* that develops into a new human being. The Greek root of *gametes* is *gamos*, which means "marriage." The term for the female sex cell literally translates "wife," and the term for the male sex cell translates "husband." The term *zygote* is derived from the Greek word *zugotos* meaning "to join or to yoke."

 Every act of arousal and climax is designed to be a divine experience connected to God's purposes in the earth.

All of the sexual organs are designed to produce the type of pleasure and gratification that can only be found and maintained in covenant relationship. Even the sexual act is reflective of Christ and the Church, as new life is produced in a believer once the Word and the Spirit of God has penetrated a person's soul and spirit. Every act of arousal and climax is designed to be a divine experience connected to God's purposes in the earth. A single sperm cell received by an egg and planted into a healthy womb emerges as a new human life, and God considers sex—the act of intimacy of a husband and wife—worship because it testifies to the new life produced through intimacy with Christ through the planting and nurturing of the Word and Holy Spirit.

The Chemistry of Sexuality and Marriage

Sex is not just a spiritual or biological act, but it is also mental and emotional. It is designed to impact every dimension of a human being's existence, to enact and establish a physical, psychological, and supernatural bond. No matter what people say and agree to or see on movies, it is impossible to separate sex from its mental, emotional, and spiritual consequences. God designed our bodies to release hormones and chemicals during sex and orgasm that are purposed to produce feelings of connection and pleasure. Sex was purposed for pleasure, productivity, and permanent bonding, and God designed it to be shared with the one person to whom we have already been joined by God as "one flesh."

Oxytocin is a hormone produced in the pleasure center of the brain that is released during childbirth, breastfeeding, and sexual orgasm in both men and women. Scientific research has shown that oxytocin plays a significant role in recognition, bonding, and the formation of trust. Oxytocin, which is only released in mammals, is the hormone responsible for "pair-bonding," the selection of a mate in a species that choose lifetime mates.[5] When a couple initiates sexual activities that lead to orgasm and the release of oxytocin, they form a psychological and neurological connection and develop affectionate intimacy. In covenant, this bonding is not only positive, but also is absolutely critical. Outside of covenant, it is downright dangerous.

The first time that a human being experiences oxytocin, it is through the relationship of parent and child. The parental relationship often establishes the norm in regard to a person's future relationships. If the parental attachment was unstable or unhealthy, psychology says that he or she may face challenges in establishing the intimate bonds of relationship, marriage, and sexuality later in life. If a son or daughter is too attached he or she may find it difficult to grow up or to leave mom/dad in order to connect completely to a mate; if someone was not attached enough to a parent, he or she may engage in promiscuous behavior or rush into sexual relationship or intense infatuation in search of the attachment, approval, love, and safety that was missing in childhood.

Whether a person's parental experience was healthy or unhealthy, the Word of God gives clear instructions for individuals who cross the threshold of marriage. When God unites two individuals in matrimony, they leave their childhood and their pasts and commit to serving one another. Real love requires maturity.

But when perfection comes, the imperfect disappears. When I was a child, I talked like a child, I thought like a child, I reasoned like a child. When I became a man, I put childish ways behind me (1 Corinthians 13:10-11).

Immaturity in love, in sex, and in the building and maintenance of marriage is manifested in selfish motives—a person who is still throwing tantrums with God or who continually seeks his or her own satisfaction and timing in love, sex, or in marriage is ill-equipped to be a responsible lover or partner.

A man is to *"leave his father and mother and be united to his wife, and the two will become one flesh"* (Matt. 19:5; see also Gen. 2:24). *Cleave* is the word used for that physiological and psychological union, and the original Hebrew and Greek words carry two meanings that on the surface appear to be opposites: "to split" and "to join."[6] When a husband, who is a high priest, splits the veil of his wife's hymen, he is joining himself to her physically, emotionally, and spiritually. They are one flesh—naked and without shame—and the Word of the Lord declares that what He has joined together, *"let man not separate"* (Matt. 19:6; see Gen. 2:25).

In First Corinthians 7, Paul describes sex within a marriage, not only in terms of pleasure and selfishness, but also as a duty and a responsibility to your spouse.

> *The husband should fulfill his marital duty to his wife, and likewise the wife to her husband. The wife's body does not belong to her alone but also to her husband. In the same way, the husband's body does not belong to him alone but also to his wife* (1 Corinthians 7:3-4).

 When a couple enters covenant, they agree to share ownership of their bodies.

When a couple enters covenant, they agree to share ownership of their bodies. You give yourself away, forsaking all others, and committing to the pleasure of your spouse. Paul says that you should not deprive one another except in mutual periods of consecration and prayer, and to come back together quickly in order to prevent the temptation and division that the enemy will introduce if you are separated. Your bodies are built to please and satisfy one another.

In Deuteronomy 23–24, God reviews the miscellaneous laws and customs in Israel, and among His many instructions regarding covenant, He instructed,

If a man has recently married, he must not be sent to war or have any other duty laid on him. For one year he is to be free to stay at home and bring happiness to the wife he has married (Deuteronomy 24:5).

God must have known how difficult women can be to please! (Just kidding!) God instructed Israel's leadership to remove from a bridegroom any other responsibility other than learning how to be a good husband and how to bring happiness and pleasure to his wife—to give her his attention in conversation, in compliment, and in climax. From the beginning, God's plan and design was for a husband and wife to *know* each other—to learn each other's bodies, minds, hearts, and spirits in such an intimate way that each spouse's gratification is unlocked in the pleasing of his or her partner. Husbands should come home and bring happiness to their wives, and in return, wives should bring happiness to their husbands by satisfying their appetites.

Not only does sexual activity release the bonding agent oxytocin, but it also releases endorphins into the brain. Endorphins like adrenaline, serotonin, and dopamine are natural pain relievers, known to decrease stress, boost confidence, and actually stimulate feelings of overall well-being, excitement, and pleasure. The chemicals released in intercourse and through orgasm naturally regulate your moods, altering your brain and your physiological functions. What a gift to offer in your marriage! Orgasm is considered a miracle, even by scientists, as it involves a simultaneous convergence of three different systems in your body: your brain and nerves, your hormones and emotions, and the vessels involved in movement and release of your blood and the other bodily fluids.[7] Science can't explain how all of those nerves and emotions and fluids converge without your entire body shutting down because the process is supernatural. It could only be created by God, and it should only be used within the covenants He establishes.

Solomon and the Secrets to Sacred Sensuality

The Song of Solomon is an Old Testament book understood within Jewish and Christian tradition as an allegorical representation of the relationship of God and Israel and of Christ and the Church. It is a poem about love and bonding in all of its dimensions: *eros* (eroticism or sexuality), *filios* (friendship), and *agape* (unconditional acceptance). The alternate name for this book in the Bible is the Song of Songs, which comes from the first verse. "Song of songs" is a Hebrew grammatical construction used to express the superlative or the highest form of something. (In the same way that English grammar adds most or -est to a word to indicate the highest form of something. For example, most powerful or most wonderful, greatest or richest). It is the same construction used for "the King of kings," "the Lord of lords," and the "holy of holies." The construction, reserved for the attributes of God, connects the highest and deepest dimension of the tabernacle (the abode of God) to sexuality and the consummation of marriage, which is the highest and deepest dimension of human relationship. As a result, this book demonstrates that the marriage bed is a sacred dwelling place for God's presence.

 The Song of Songs demonstrates that the marriage bed is a sacred dwelling place for God's presence.

The setting for the consummation of the relationship is the king's garden, indicative of the Garden of Eden or Heaven, and of the marriage bed. The poem is filled with sensual garden imagery, representing the restoration of sexuality and marital bliss to its undefiled and unrestricted state prior to the Fall of mankind. The characters describe their love, their bodies, and their sexual union in terms of vineyards and trees, fruit and rivers, and Song of Songs is a book of sensuality without shame. The Lover and the Beloved are completely open, comfortable, and unlimited in their attraction for one another, experiencing and describing one another in ways that made me blush as I studied their union.

The most basic definition of sensuality is "relating to or consisting in the gratification of the senses or the indulgence of appetite."[8] The consummate couple in Song of Solomon describe their attraction to one another in terms of sight, sound, taste, smell, and touch. They were engaged on all five levels. He notices and compliments her cheeks, her earrings, her eyes, her hair, her smile, her lips, her neck, her breasts, the sweetness of her voice, and the enticement of her scent. He calls her flawless and tells her that she has stolen his heart. The Lover expresses his desire for her, saying,

> *...How much more pleasing is your love than wine, and the fragrance of your perfume than any spice! Your lips drop sweetness as the honeycomb, my bride; milk and honey are under your tongue.... You are a garden locked up...a spring enclosed, a sealed fountain* (Song of Solomon 4:10-12).

She has been diligent to prepare for intimacy and to keep her "garden," "spring," and "fountain" locked away for him. He also prepared for intimacy with her, and she craves and calls for him, speaking of his kiss, his name and reputation, his scent, his provision for her, his courage in battle, his work ethic, and his wealth. She brags about him to her friends, noting,

> *My lover is radiant and ruddy, outstanding among ten thousand. His head is purest gold....His eyes are like doves....His lips are like lilies dripping with myrrh. His arms are rods of gold....His mouth is sweetness itself; he is altogether lovely. This is my lover, this is my friend...* (Song of Solomon 5:10-16).

The secrets of sacred sensuality and divine intimacy are contained in Song of Solomon. Not only do they maintain their desire for only one another, but they also are careful to exhibit the qualities that will draw their mate and to privately and publicly compliment the qualities that they appreciate in one another. There are three keys to sacred sensuality and commitment found in Song of Solomon.

1. Affirmation and Ownership

Throughout the poem, both the Lover and the Beloved use pronouns that indicate ownership. They claim one another through covenant language, speaking words of belonging and possession. The Lover affirms his choice of her, saying that there were many maidens and virgins to choose from, but *"my dove, my perfect one, is unique"* (Song of Sol. 6:9). The Beloved affirms that she has given herself only to him, stating, *"I belong to my lover, and his desire is for me"* (Song of Sol. 7:10). God wants to hear of and see our devotion to Him, and He continually speaks of and demonstrates His love and devotion to us. Your marriage must be filled with public and private expressions of commitment, appreciation, and affirmation.

2. Anticipation and Timing

Throughout the poem, the Lover and the Beloved's greatest and most intense desire is to be in one another's presence. She begs for him to take her away, searches for him in the city, and when she cannot find him, she waits for him, eagerly anticipating his arrival (see Song of Sol. 3:1-4). He calls for her to come to him, he hunts for her and chases after her, he goes to claim her, and even though his efforts are thwarted and the timing seems off, he continues his pursuit (see Song of Sol. 5:5-8). Distance should only make your hearts grow fonder, and anticipation should build your desire for one another.

3. Appeasement and Increased Desire

As much as I have read and studied Song of Solomon, I cannot pinpoint the single act of consummation. Instead, the poem builds a rhythm of mounting desire and climax, followed by another period of mounting desire and climax. At the end of the poem, the couple appears to have as much passion for one another as they did in the poem's opening stanza, if not more. In the last verse of chapter 4, the Beloved invites the Lover into *"his garden* [to] *taste its choice fruits"* and in the first verse of chapter 5, the Lover brags, *"I have come into my garden, my sister, my bride...."* Immediately afterwards, they begin their pursuit of one another again, progressing through the stages of affirmation, compliments, anticipation, and pursuit all over again. Satisfaction of our intimate desires should always produce in us increased pursuit of the same experience. Once we experience the glory of God, we should do whatever it takes to remain there, and the same is true about reaching climax (mentally, spiritually, emotionally, and sexually) with our spouses.

 God designed intimacy in worship and in marriage to be driven by desire.

Relationship was never intended to be dry, distant, or based solely on duty. God designed intimacy in worship and in marriage to be driven by desire. With lovingkindness God draws us, and with lovingkindness we respond. The same should be true for our relationships. Our sex lives in marriage should follow the pattern of our worship experiences, filled with love and affirmation, building anticipation and passion, and increasing levels of satisfaction that leave us wanting and waiting on more.

King Solomon, the attributed author of Song of Solomon, was like the Bible's Wilt Chamberlain. With 700 wives and 300 concubines, Solomon was no stranger to sexuality, sensuality, or seduction—the problem is that he refused to enjoy them within the context and confines that God gave him. Solomon was also a worshiper who had the type of intimate relationship with God that allowed him to complete the building of the temple, yet he allowed himself to be seduced by foreign women and their foreign gods. Though Solomon could marry and enjoy sex with any woman in Israel, he was uncontrollably drawn to women outside of the covenant he walked in with God. Solomon thought that he could separate his personal life from his spiritual life, and that his household and kingdom would not be affected. He couldn't have been more wrong. Illicit pleasure was far more attractive to him than using his wisdom and talents for the pleasure of sex enjoyed as God intended and instructed. As discussed in Chapter 2, Solomon, and the generations he produced, paid the consequences.

Seduction is an art, and I think that it is downright sad that the enemy has stolen and perverted the anticipation, creativity, and passion of sensuality that God created for marriage. God's plan was for our passion to reflect His passion, within covenant, but our cultural understanding and practices of sexuality and relationship have produced relationship patterns that are completely out of order. Individuals devote so much of their time, energy, and creativity to seduction and sex during their singleness and within their dating seasons that they have completely used up their reserves before they even get to their marriage bed. People who were "superfreaks" prior to their salvation and their marriages turn into "supersaints" once in covenant, depriving themselves and their partners of the pleasures and benefits of sex as God intended. Once willing to do anything in pursuit of the object of their affection, they forget to maintain their relationship by being diligent to the things that drew them together as a couple in the first place.

Christ, speaking in parables, equated the Kingdom of God and spiritual treasure to pearls.

The kingdom of heaven is like treasure hidden in a field. When a man found it, he hid it again, and them in his joy went and sold all he had and bought that field. Again, the kingdom of heaven is like a merchant looking for fine pearls. When he found one of great value, he went away and sold everything he had and bought it (Matthew 13:44-46).

Christ, as High Priest, King of kings, Lord of lords, and the Bridegroom, set out to establish His Kingdom in the earth. He saw so much value in the Church, His bride, that He was willing to give up everything that He had—His place and position, His comfort, His ego and pride, His will, and His last breath—in order to demonstrate His love for us and to draw us toward Him. His passion for us didn't stop at the cross; to this day, He continues interceding for us and making sure we are provided for, and He sent the Holy Spirit as a comforter so that we would never feel like we're alone.

In marriage, you must make a conscious decision and concerted effort toward gratifying the senses and satisfying the appetite of your mate. You should be comfortable and love one another with morning breath, in hair rollers, and in holey (not holy) underwear, but every now and then, you should spice things up and remind your mate of the treasure he or she found in you. Get your hair and nails done, put on your high heels, and your lingerie. Spend the money to take your wife out to a great dinner and wear the expensive cologne. Hug, hold hands, and kiss often. Send sweet text messages and whisper "sweet nothings" in each other's ears. Send the kids away, light some candles, turn up the music, and give one another a massage. Indulge one another—take pleasure in your covenant and refuse to take your marriage and your intimacy for granted. It'll be worth the investment of your time and your attention.

A marriage and a spouse are pearls—gifts from God, valuable treasures—and no matter what, you should treat them accordingly.

When you find divine love, true commitment, and the blessing of covenant, you should be willing to do whatever it takes to maintain them. In the first story, a man found a treasure in a field, sold all that he had to have access to that treasure, purchased the field, and then he buried the treasure all over again. Why did he rebury the treasure instead of placing it into a setting or in a display case? I believe that Christ is teaching us that there is a joy in continuing to seek out and find the things that are valuable to us. Even when you purchase your field, whether through your investment in your marriage or even a career or a ministry, you should hide the pearl again for the challenge and joy of rediscovering it. Even when the joy or the pleasure in your marriage is seemingly lost or covered in dirt, you must keep in mind that you purchased and own the field. If you are patient and persistent in your pursuit, you can experience the joy of seduction and marital bliss over and over again.

 When you open yourself up too soon, you make yourself common.

If you are not married, sexuality and seduction in covenant is something to wait upon and look forward to, to seek after and desire, and to save yourself for. I challenge you to commit your body and the most sacred parts of yourself to your future spouse, and to reserve for that person all that you have to offer psychologically and physically. The merchant in Matthew 13 searched for the pearl and sacrificed all he had to obtain it, which meant that it was hidden, rare, and expensive. When you open yourself up too soon, you make yourself common (just like other men or women within the world) and, consequently, you diminish your own value. In Matthew 7:6, Jesus, speaking directly to the disciples, said, *"Do not give dogs what is sacred; do no throw your pearls to pigs. If you do, they may trample them under their feet, and then turn and tear you to pieces."* I could not have said it any better myself...

Un(veiling) the Dangers of Sexual Immorality—Masturbation, Fornication, and Adultery

On an April 2009 episode of *The Oprah Winfrey Show*, Dr. Laura Berman was invited to discuss the topic of parents talking to teens about sexuality. I just happened to be flipping through the channels, and I stopped to watch the show when I heard Dr. Berman making the argument that the way to raise sexually empowered youth is to help them familiarize themselves with and learn to stimulate their own genitals. When Amy, a parent on the show, expressed to Dr. Berman that she would have no idea how to talk to her daughter about masturbation, the psychologist replied, "We're going to show her a picture of her vulva and [say], 'This is your clitoris and it has lots of sensations, so some girls find that it feels good to touch themselves there, and that's totally *normal.*'" Dr. Berman argued that sex was about pleasure, and that mothers should buy their daughters vibrators and teach them how to reach orgasm alone.[9] After the episode ended, I sat on my couch and cried, incensed and frustrated by the methods the enemy uses in disguising and distorting sin, but determined to make sure that the young adults in our ministry, and the readers of this book, experience freedom from the cycles of guilt and shame and dissatisfaction that sexual immorality produces.

Orgasm is always designed to produce or to strengthen a bond. In masturbation, an individual bonds with himself or herself, or with electronic gadgets, or visual images. When you masturbate, you condition your body for orgasm that only you can produce, and it immediately produces embarrassment, guilt, and even increased loneliness. When a person conditions his or her orgasms through masturbation, it becomes increasingly difficult to achieve the same level of pleasure through relationship and intimacy with another person, forcing that person to compete with the way you stimulate yourself, with a battery-operated machine, or with the images on your screens or in your mind that you can no longer control, get rid of, or do without. Just because you're alone when you're having sex, doesn't mean that it isn't fornication.

> **Just because you're alone when you're having sex, doesn't mean that it isn't fornication.**

Scientists and researchers for the Centers for Disease Control argue that when an individual has sex with another person, he or she also joins him or herself to the last ten people that person had sex with, and the last ten people that those people slept with. In other words, the acts of fornication and adultery introduce your body and your spirit to bonds with individuals you may have never met. You are exposed to whatever they have been exposed to, and you expose that person and your (future) spouse to whatever you are exposed to. Within marriage, sex is the bond that seals a covenant, and your courtship process cleanses the marriage bed that you will share. In the absence of (or when stepping outside of) covenant, you are defiling your temple and your marriage bed. You are physically, spiritually, and psychologically unprotected, and so is the person you have sex with.

The Danger of Sexual Chemistry Without Covenant[10]

Celebrities and public figures including Michael Douglas, Russell Brand, David Duchovny, Eric Benet, Kanye West, and most recently, Tiger Woods, have found themselves under media scrutiny and sought treatment for being unable to control their sexual urges. Living promiscuous lifestyles and committing adultery caused these individuals to risk their reputations, their careers, their marriages and families, their health, and their livelihood, all while damaging the trust of their constituents and fans, the people who believed in and supported them. Their public scandal has caused a stir in medical circles and in America's living rooms about the existence of "sexual addiction." In a recent ABC News report:

> Sexuality expert Dr. David Greenfield, clinical director of The Healing Center, LLC in West Hartford, Conn., claimed that the celebrity cases could open up awareness and dialogue about the addictive nature of sex. "I think that what [the public has] been sensitized to is that sex can be used as a drug," he said. "The concept that sex can be a drug and therefore can be addictive is a new thing for the public to sink its teeth into."[11]

Sex is always an addictive substance, both physically and psychologically, as well as spiritually and mentally/emotionally. Within covenant marriage, it creates a passionate drive and desire toward one another; outside of covenant, it is a drug that poses the potential to cause damage to your heart, your mind, your health, your children, your career, your finances, and the future of your relationships. A controversial study conducted in 2001 by Dr. Eric James Keroack, a former deputy assistant secretary for Health and Human Services, proved that premature and/or promiscuous sexual activity thwarts the brain's ability to develop bonds with another person. Comparing sex to drug use, he argues that extensive release of oxytocin, especially with multiple partners, will eventually diminish a person's ability to form emotional attachments. Premarital (or extramarital) sex can lead to overproduction of oxytocin, and its effects are tantamount to substance abuse. Because it is not being used for the purpose originally intended, the chemical becomes less and less effective, and greater amounts and wilder types of stimulation are necessary to produce similar levels of orgasm. Dr. Keroack's 2001 paper for the Abstinence Medical Council concluded:

> People who have misused their sexual faculty and become bonded to multiple persons will diminish the power

of oxytocin to maintain a permanent bond with an individual….Just as in heroin addiction….the person involved will experience 'sex withdrawal' and will need to move on to a….new sex playmate.[12]

Like heroin and other drugs, orgasm produces a surge of euphoria, a rush of hormones and emotions, or a "high" when introduced to the body, which is immediately followed by relaxation and drowsiness. The danger in substance abuse is that the drive to achieve or experience that momentary sense of pleasure thwarts an individual's ability to recognize and make appropriate decisions regarding the risks and inevitabilities of the long-term consequences. They have an escape from pain, a release of pressure, a goal to achieve. It only takes one time to trigger addiction, but it can take years to break it. Chronic heroin users risk heart failure and blood clots in their brain and lungs. So do individuals who engage in fornication and adultery, inviting infection and damage to their emotions, their minds, and their relationships with God as they grieve the Holy Spirit (their breath). With regular heroin use, tolerance and physical dependence develop. This means the abuser must use more heroin to achieve the same intensity or effect. Over time, individuals who engage in sexual immorality find themselves driven to more partners and to increasingly hardcore activity in order to produce orgasm. The concept of sex with a single partner becomes less and less satisfying.

 Over time, individuals who engage in sexual immorality find themselves driven to more partners and to increasingly hardcore activity in order to produce orgasm.

The development of addiction is thought to involve a simultaneous process of 1) increased focus on and engagement in a particular behavior and 2) the attenuation or "shutting down" of other behaviors. As people focus more and more on achieving orgasm through any combination of masturbation, fornication, or adultery, they decrease more and more in their engagement and participation in activities that would promote increase in areas of their own life and increase in their connection to God, and consequently they forfeit His favor and anointing upon their life. The physical effects of any addiction are far less damaging than the social, emotional, spiritual, and psychological ones, and the consequences of sexual sin and of any other addiction include: broken trust and intimacy, guilt, shame, fear, hopelessness, failure, rejection, anxiety, humiliation, depression, infection, and, ultimately, death.

With physical dependence, the body has adapted to the presence of the drug and withdrawal symptoms may occur if use is reduced or stopped. Withdrawal, which in regular substance abusers is most intense in the hours and days after last use and can last up to two years, produces insatiable craving, anxiety, restlessness, and a range of other physical and psychological issues. The chemicals released by the drugs, and by orgasm, literally rewire your brain over time. Often the feelings of "love," the pain of a breakup, the crazy "chemistry" two people may feel, the blatant "horniness" or desire that suddenly comes upon a person is very simply a symptom of withdrawal from the addiction to orgasm produced by sexual immorality. Withdrawal feels like a "roller coaster of emotions," and can produce mood swings, feelings of depression, lack of motivation and enthusiasm, and the inability to rest or concentrate. The inability to deal with the symptoms of withdrawal draws people into cycles of financial debt and struggle, abusive and unhealthy relationships, and a real lack of productivity and effectiveness in other areas of their life.

 Sex is designed as the union of two bodies already made one in spirit.

"Safe sex" may prevent disease or pregnancy, but there is no protection that will prevent the inevitable suffering and damage caused by forming and breaking the chemical bonds people characterize as love when they cross the thresholds of sexual relationship outside of the safety of covenant. Sexual activity creates an addiction, a permanent attachment, a "soul tie." Because the bond and benefits of orgasm are designed to be shared between two people who have made a lifetime commitment, the breaking of that tie causes unnatural, painful, traumatic, and, eventually, numbing separation, a "broken" heart. Sex is designed as the union of two bodies already made one in spirit—not a body to itself or a body to a machine or a visual image. When two people unite in a sexual bond but the hearts, minds, goals, of those two people remain separate and go in opposite directions, there will be consequences.

Refusing Defilement and Recovery From Sexual Immorality

Contrary to the rules of cultural engagement, sex is not a way to boost your ego, a way to satisfy your hormonal cravings, a strategy to get or keep a man, or a way to escape boredom or pain. Sex is a seal and an agent of psychological bonding designed to produce life and joy as two individuals metaphorically and physically become "one flesh" in marriage. Any sexual act carried out for any other purpose, through any other process, is considered fornication and adultery and produces addiction. The problem with any addiction, especially sexual immorality, is that it feels good! If it didn't feel good, it wouldn't be so hard to stop. The only way for an individual to avoid an addiction is to abstain from the behavior, and the only way for an individual to break the power of an addiction is to abstain from the behavior (see Acts 15:29).

When the high priest crossed the threshold into the most holy place, he had sanctified himself, and he relied on the atoning sacrifice to cover his sin. He protected his white linen and his anointing, refusing to allow it to come into contact with anything that would defile him, and washing away anything unclean that tried to attach itself to him. The high priest knew that he could not take anything dirty into the holy of holies, and God is trying to get us to adopt the same attitude and to take pride and honor in our priesthood and in our sonship.

God, in His infinite wisdom, recognizing the addictive nature of His sexual creation, gives us the following instructions for handling masturbation, fornication, and adultery: Run! In his first letter to the Corinthians, Paul wrote, *"Flee from sexual immorality. All other sins a man commits are outside his body, but he who sins sexually sins against his own body"* (6:18). In other words, a murderer hurts the person he kills, and a thief hurts the person he steals from, but a person who engages in continual sexual sin invites death into his or her own body. Sexual sin is spiritual suicide. Paul continued,

> *Do you not know that your body is a temple of the Holy Spirit, who is in you, whom you have received from God? You are not your own; you were bought at a price. Therefore honor God with your body* (1 Corinthians 6:19-20).

To the Ephesians Paul wrote,

> *Be imitators of God…and live a life of love, just as Christ loved us and gave Himself up for us as a fragrant offering and sacrifice to God. But among you* **there must not be even a hint of sexual immorality.**…*For of this you can be sure: No immoral, impure, or greedy person—such man is an idolator—has any inheritance in the kingdom of Christ and of God* (Ephesians 5:1-5).

 In telling us to abstain from sexual immorality, God is not trying to keep us from its pleasures.

People only break addictions when they recognize what they have to lose, and you should know that abstinence is a key to your inheritance. Preparation for covenant relationship requires abstinence (see Exod. 19:14-15). The word *abstain* is translated *apechomai* in the Greek, which means "to hold oneself."[13] In telling us to abstain from sexual immorality, God is not trying to keep us from its pleasures; He is trying to keep us from its pains. Delayed gratification is the best gratification, and if you can "hold yourself" and control your desires, you'll reap the rewards in covenant relationship and walk in the benefits of priesthood and the inheritance connected to our sonship. When we pursue God and fill ourselves with the Holy Spirit, the fruits of love, joy, peace, patience, kindness, gentleness, and self-control are produced in our lives. It is easier to fall prey to temptation when you are running on empty spiritually, but it is impossible to gratify our sinful natures when we live and walk after the Spirit. Every time we say no to something our bodies and our hormones want, and say yes to something connected to building intimate relationship with Him or that extends or builds the Kingdom, we honor God with our bodies, our time, and our finances.

One of my favorite characters in the Bible is Joseph. Joseph was a dreamer who knew that he had the love and favor of his father and didn't mind standing out from his brothers. He wore a garment of righteousness and Kingdom confidence, and he knew that he was destined for greatness even though he was surrounded by haters and people who were supposed to love him but were setting traps for him. No matter what trial or tribulation or test he faced, Joseph maintained his relationship with the Lord. Joseph was so blessed that everyone who became connected to him got blessed, too. He was trustworthy, handsome, strong, courageous, and the favor of God was upon his life. He was attractive and powerful, and he had "charisma," but he refused to use the position and favor God had blessed him with to participate in sexual sin.

In Genesis 39, the wife of Joseph's boss took notice of him and tried to seduce him, and Joseph recognized her advances as evil. Recognizing all that he stood to lose—his position, his reputation, his wealth, his dreams, and the favor of the Lord— Joseph refused to give in to temptation. When the woman grabbed him and tried to bring him to her bed, the Bible says that Joseph *"left his cloak in her hand and **ran** out of the house"* (Gen. 39:12). When it comes to sexual sin, you don't have time to consider it, to think about it, to argue about it, or to see how close you can get to it without being burned. Trust God to provide you a way of escape, and when you find it, run toward it.

As you take the steps to establish or to maintain purity, there are things you can do to assist you in handling the symptoms of withdrawal.

1. Eliminate temptation—stay away from sexually immoral people and from any influence that will cause you to think about or to act upon your sexual desires.

2. Learn your body and your turn-on cycles—know your emotional and hormonal triggers. Both men and women have periods during the day or month when their hormones are elevated and this can produce sexual desire. Protect yourself and avoid intimate contact with a person of the opposite sex during those times. Know what triggers desire for you, and use the power of prayer to build yourself up against temptation.

3. Practice patience—don't pray for your sexual desires to go away! One day you'll need them! Dedicate those desires to your future spouse and speak in terms of anticipation. Be patient with yourself. If you are tempted, reject satan's guilt trap when he tries to get you to repeat your mistake. Pick yourself up, dust yourself off, repent, and refuse to look back.

4. Eliminate stress from your life and use this season to pamper and invest in yourself. Keep your mind and your heart from idleness, pursue the things that bring you joy and peace, and seek fulfillment and satisfaction in your intimate relationship with God, in hobbies and interests, and in time with friends and family. Use all that energy for something productive!

Establishing Sexual Boundaries: Keeping Intimacy Sacred

The Word of God teaches us that there is now no condemnation for those of us who are in Christ Jesus, so no matter what you have experienced prior to reading this book, there is no reason for you to walk in guilt, embarrassment, or fear. The enemy's strategy is to keep us in bondage to sin, even though Christ has freed us from it. He wants to make us slaves to cultural influence and to our own hormones and habits, but when we hold to Christ's teachings and gain understanding, we shall know the truth, and the truth has [already] made us free (see John 8:32). All too often, we enter relationships and marriage with an improper sexual education. We hear about condoms and STDs, but no one teaches us God's plan for sexuality and marriage and the psychological and spiritual consequences of operating outside of that plan. Though we hear and know that sexual immorality is wrong, parents, educators, and pastors often fail to articulate why. We know that marriage makes sex "okay," but most people do not understand why or how.

 We hear about condoms and STDs, but no one teaches us God's plan for sexuality and marriage and the psychological and spiritual consequences of operating outside of that plan.

After studying the revelation contained in this chapter, I have begun to understand just how perfect God's law and will are. God's desire is for all men to be saved and to know the truth—to walk in the liberty and peace that accompanies trusting God's Word and doing things His way. God has continually reminded me of the charge that He gave me when I started writing this book: to seek out the truth and to discover His plan and pattern. I have learned so much in this process that I did not know before; and as you are reading, the anointing of God upon His Word is destroying strongholds and yokes of bondage that the enemy has placed in your life through ignorance to your calling to sexual purity and commitment to your spouse.

God tells us that *"My people are destroyed from lack of knowledge. 'Because you have rejected knowledge, I also reject you as My priests; because you have ignored the law of your God, I also will ignore your children'"* (Hos. 4:6). The last sentence of that verse is one of the scariest verses to me in the whole Bible. Any rejection of knowledge that we receive, any failure to subscribe to the truth that is revealed to us can open us to losing the rights and privileges of our priesthood, and will ultimately produce generational curses in our bloodline (see Heb. 10:26-29).

If fact, studies show that children of addicts are eight times more likely to develop their own addictions. Even now, you should bind the root of any generational curse that has been in operation in your own life and make a decision that it will not fall upon your children. God is willing and ready to purge your past and prepare you in the present. Thus the question becomes, what decision are you going to make about your future?

 Any action that is intended to lead to sexual pleasure, gratification, orgasm, or a bond outside of covenant relationship and marriage is too far.

The most common question that I am asked about dating and sexuality by individuals who truly love God and want to enjoy intimacy without violating God's command is "how far is too far?" I've heard different responses from different people, and I have often struggled with the answer to that question for myself. The easiest way for me to answer that is to define a boundary based on the definition of sexuality we've built in this chapter. Any action that is *intended* to lead to sexual pleasure, gratification, orgasm, or a bond outside of covenant relationship and marriage is too far. If you want to express your love for someone, if you want to please and satisfy someone, if you want to demonstrate what type of spouse you will be, the greatest gift you can give that person is an undefiled marriage bed.

True sexual empowerment is not the pleasure that one can give to him or herself, or the physical feeling produced by bumping and grinding without any emotional or spiritual connection. The ultimate, and the only truly gratifying, sexual relationship is the one produced in marital covenant between two people who understand and maximize their opportunities for intimacy. The "private parts" and pleasure produced by their use and stimulation have been sovereignly ordained for covenant. Any misuse of those parts carries significant consequences: disease, sexual addiction, unplanned pregnancy, guilt and shame, forfeiting of ministry and anointing, and the transport of negative residue into future relationships. Our society tends toward encouraging individuals to experience the momentary pleasure, while ignoring or covering up the penalties. There are consequences for trying to bypass God's process and achieve the type of gratification that the Holy Spirit and science so clearly and convincingly testify should be reserved for marriage. The easiest way to avoid those consequences is to keep your private parts private.

 Premarital sex does not bond a couple—in fact, it kills the bonds of intimacy that should be developing and eventually leads to argument and division.

You can always tell when a couple is not aligned with God's plan for sexuality based on whether or not one or both of the partners has initiated psychological and spiritual withdrawal. Premarital sex does not bond a couple—in fact, it kills the bonds of intimacy that should be developing and eventually leads to argument and division, a purely sexual relationship, or the inevitable breakup. Abstaining from sex in marriage wears down the bond of a couple—in fact, the lack of physical intimacy and affection can lead to breakdowns in communication, diminished effectiveness in career, child-rearing, and ministry, and eventually the temptation toward adultery or divorce. God's glory and favor cannot abide in a relationship that does not operate based on the principles He provides in courtship. Why settle for an empty relationship when you can experience the love and manifested glory of God upon your union? Abstaining from sexual activity outside of marital covenant—and participating in sexual intercourse within marital covenant—are counted as acts of obedience and worship within your relationship with God, and are investments of trust, loyalty, devotion, and respect in the most important human relationship you will ever have: the one with your husband or wife.

Happily Ever After: Fulfilled Promise and Testimony at the Ark of the Covenant

Once the high priest passed through the veil and entered the holy of holies, he stood face to face with the sixth piece of furniture within the tabernacle, called the ark of the covenant (see Exod. 25:10-16; 37:1-5). The ark was made of acacia, or shittim, wood, which was so hard and strong that it resisted heat and decay to the point that it was described as indestructible.[14] It was covered by pure gold on both the inside and outside, and its borders had a gold crown molding. There were four rings attached to the four feet that the ark stood upon, and poles made of wood overlaid by gold were inserted into the rings to carry it. The ark was so holy that no man could touch it. In fact, only the Levites were allowed to carry it on poles, and the high priest was the only person who could even look upon it. The ark of the covenant and its sanctuary were considered the splendor or the beauty of Israel, representing the promise, presence, provision, and protection of the Lord toward His people.

The word *ark* from the Hebrew *aron* means a "chest" or a container for storage.[15] An ark is a place of safety and covenant, a vessel designed to hold and carry precious cargo. In the story of Noah in Genesis 6–9, Noah is told to build an ark according to the exact instructions that God provided. Noah was a righteous man in a corrupt, wicked, and sexually immoral generation, and God sovereignly chose Noah to produce a new standard of righteousness and dominion in the world. God warned Noah that he was about to destroy all of the life on earth, but that He would *"establish My covenant with you, and you will enter the ark—you and your sons and your wife and your sons' wives with you"* (Gen. 6:18).

Noah brought his entire family into the ark and into covenant with God, and the ark protected them from the corruption of the world, from God's wrath, from the storm, and from the floodwaters. He and his family were the only survivors in that storm, and when they escaped, they rested upon the mountains and built an altar there to offer a sacrifice that sealed the covenant that Noah had entered into with God. Our covenant with God, and in marriage, protects us from storms and from the flood, as God lifts us up and establishes a new standard for the world in our relationships. God *extended* the covenant to Noah in Genesis 6, and after Noah proved faithful through surviving the tempests and the tests, God *established* His covenant in Genesis 9. Noah's covenant resulted in the divine blessing offered to Adam prior to the Fall: fruitfulness, productivity, increase, dominion, authority, supernatural presence, and provision (see Gen. 1:28; 9:1).

Like everything else in the tabernacle, the ark was designed as a foreshadowing of the redemptive and reconciliatory work of Christ and was a picture of His marriage and covenant with the Church. The acacia wood and gold symbolizes God Himself being poured into a flesh suit, producing a perfect and complete balance of humanity and divinity (see John 1:1-2,14). It also symbolizes Christ as the bridegroom and the "head," being joined to the bride and His "body." The indestructible wood represents the incorruptible glorified Church, and the overlay and crown of pure gold symbolized Christ's headship, kingship, and deity (see Eph. 1:22-23; 5:23).

 The Church was betrothed, or engaged, to Christ in the heavens before time began.

The Bible proclaims that Jesus was the lamb, the ultimate sacrifice, slain before the foundations of the world (see Rev. 13:8). He was the bridegroom, the high priest who offered Himself as a sacrifice to establish covenant with the Church, before the earth existed. The Church was betrothed, or engaged, to Christ in the heavens before time began. Ephesians 1:3-4 says that we have already been blessed in the heavenly realms in Christ, chosen in Him *"before the creation of the world to be holy and blameless in His sight."* God works out everything in conformity with the purpose of His will so that Christ and the Church, the bridegroom and the bride, are reunited in salvation and live together in the Kingdom.

He is Alpha and Omega, the Beginning and the End, and He always sees and declares the end of a thing even prior to the beginning. In His eternal salvific plan, God wrote the entire love story by starting with the final scene; then He went back to the beginning and started time so that the audience could enjoy watching the story unfold. He is the "author and finisher" of our faith, and He gets glory, a standing ovation, every time the plan develops and ends just as He wrote it. He seals us with the Holy Spirit, and we get the reward of inheritance for trusting God enough to walk out the process. The joining of wood and gold—of sacrifice, sanctification, divine process, and timing—always produces the manifested glory that will rest and abide upon our lives (see John 1:14).

The tabernacle was patterned to produce a shadow, a visual representation and copy, of the sovereign plan for salvation. The ark, representing God's presence and sovereign plan, was the very first piece of furniture described and built for the tabernacle, and it was the last thing that the high priest encountered in his process of courtship. The entire tabernacle was set up to walk the high priest and the nation of Israel through the step-by-step process to get them back into covenant relationship and intimacy with God. Moses was given a pattern for the ark of the covenant on the mountain, and he watched as it was built and placed behind the veil, but the high priest had to completely change his life and his identity, then serve, and wait, and walk with God for an entire year before he could gaze upon the ark of the covenant again. Though God promised the nation of Israel that He would come down and dwell with them, they had to walk through a process and maintain their end of the covenant in order to receive the promise. God, in His sovereign love, gave Israel the exact directions and instructions that they needed to ensure that He would be able to join with them in the holy of holies.

Just like the tabernacle, the institution of marriage was purposed and designed to reflect God's salvific plan. Woman is chosen out of man prior to either's recognition and knowledge. When man and woman emerge from bondage to sin and to the world and have a transformational mountaintop experience with Christ, God begins to reveal to them vision, purpose, and destination. As the man and woman develop their individual identities and spiritual journeys with God, their paths join, and they recognize through prayer, fellowship, service, and conversation that God created them to walk together. They are reunited in covenant through their vows in the presence of God, and their marriage covenant is sealed in the marriage bed. Their love, demonstrated in their commitment and unconditional acceptance of another, and manifested in their intimate union, is a reflection of Christ's love and commitment to us.

Our marriages become arks, vessels, and vehicles designed to hold and to carry the presence and glory of God. Consequently, our courtship-built marriages emerge as places of safety, designed to keep and protect the most sacred parts of our lives: our dreams, our goals, our hearts, our intimate secrets, our wealth, and our children.

The entire tabernacle was built and designed to house the ark of the covenant and to provide a dwelling place for the presence and glory of God. Priests walked through the courts with the ark of the covenant in mind, just as we must walk through the process of courtship focused on the presence, glory, and favor of God as our ultimate goal for entering and maintaining covenant. Our faithfulness to walk in faith and the Spirit through the courtship, and to trust God with the sanctity and sacredness of our relationships, will always produce the blessings of covenant upon our lives. The Bible says that He watches over His Word to make sure that it is fulfilled. He cannot lie, and we can trust Him to fulfill whatever vision and promise He extends to us during our worship on the mountain. Just as God keeps and maintains His covenant with His people, it is critical for us to extend and establish vows and promises that we are diligent to keep and to fulfill in marriage.

 Just as God keeps and maintains His covenant with His people, it is critical for us to extend and establish vows and promises that we are diligent to keep and to fulfill in marriage.

Within the courtship, the ark represents the fulfillment of covenant vision and promise in marriage. The ark within the holy of holies was a reminder of God's faithfulness to His vows and to Israel's obedience and submission to God's will. Ultimately, marriages produced through courtship present the same witness. While the veil represents sexuality as the seal of covenant, the ark represents marriage itself, and the contents symbolize the substance through which covenant is built and maintained. The ark of the covenant, also called the ark of the testimony, held three sacred items: the tablets of the covenant, the golden jar of manna that fell from Heaven, and Aaron's budding rod (see Heb. 9:4). All three of these items represented aspects of God's love and commitment to Israel and, consequently, reveal the three keys to extending, establishing, and maintaining your covenant in marriage. These were all given to Israel in the wilderness, and housed in the tabernacle, as a witness of their journey and of God's love and commitment to His children. Everything that you need to be successful in covenant relationship is developed in the process of the tabernacle, and when two people join themselves through the vows of marriage, all they need to do is remember their journeys together and allow the testimony of their love and commitment to one another produce glory unto the Lord and a witness to the world.

Tablets of Covenant: Order and Boundaries in Covenant Relationship

In Exodus 19, God promised Moses that He was going to establish His covenant with Israel. He sent the nation into a period of preparation, obedience, abstinence, testing, and consecration, promising them that He would fulfill His vow and dwell among them at the end of the period of engagement. He called Moses and Aaron to the top of Mount Sinai where He had descended and began to reveal to them His laws and commandments. In addition to laws concerning servants, injuries, arguments, property, justice, mercy, and annual festivals, God gave Moses ten principal rules called the Ten Commandments, regulations that would govern their relationship with God first, and then with one another.

On the day that Israel was joined to God through covenant ceremony, Moses read from the Book of the Covenant, from these regulations, and the people responded with one voice, *"We will do everything the Lord has said; we will obey"* (Exod. 24:7b). Immediately afterward, they were sprinkled with blood and sealed in their relationship. The stone tablets on which the commandments were written were placed within the ark of the covenant and served as a permanent reminder of their commitment to God.

 Before God could enjoy relationship with Israel, He had to create order, and before a couple can walk in the benefits of covenant, they must establish order and boundaries within their household.

Before God could enjoy relationship with Israel, He had to create order, and before a couple can walk in the benefits of covenant, they must establish order and boundaries within their household. God had ten basic regulations for the people to follow in relationships; those commandments were written in stone, not once, but twice, and they were non-negotiable. A couple in covenant should base their vows, and their promises to one another, on their commitment to following God's regulations first.

A covenant couple should place nothing in their lives above their relationship with God. They should honor the name and the reputation of the Lord, which they walk under when they enter covenant. They should keep the Sabbath, a period of rest dedicated to God and to one another. They should honor their parents and require honor from their children. They should refuse to invite death into any area of their lives through their thoughts, speech, or deeds.

They should keep the marriage bed pure. They should not take from one another, but give. They should not lie or act deceptively or falsely. They should not walk in jealousy or envy. How many problems in marriages could be avoided if individuals and couples would simply obey the commandments God has established for relationship?

In addition to submitting to these regulations, a couple should discuss and decide on their roles, the regulations, and the boundaries that will exist to establish and maintain order within households. The foundational principles of marriage are already written in stone (within the Word of God) and should be written upon your hearts (see Ps. 119:9-11). A couple's vows are promises to the Lord and to one another and should be woven into the fabric of your heart in such a way that the love you have for God and for your spouse keeps you from sinning against either of them.

In addition to the foundational principles of their vows, a couple will need to negotiate and determine roles, responsibilities, and regulations to govern their daily lives. This may include scheduling, approaches to raising children and discipline or education, budgeting, balancing work/ministry/family, and so on. The clearer a couple's roles and expectations are, the easier it is for them to walk together in agreement without confusion or misunderstanding. A couple must build and maintain order within their household in order to see productivity and increase. True love and true divine witness require keeping God first and honoring one another by the continual fulfillment of one's vows.

Manna From Heaven: Divine Provision and Satisfaction in Covenant Relationship

Shortly after the children of Israel were delivered from bondage in Egypt and began their journey though the wilderness, they reached the Desert of Sin and began to complain about their hunger (see Exod. 16). The people were seeking satisfaction through natural means—grumbling, complaining, and wanting to return to their bondage—but God offered to satisfy their hunger through the supernatural instead. He promised to *"rain down bread"* for them each morning, and the manna represented the type of satisfaction that only God and His love can provide. The bread was always fresh—it was replenished every morning so that it would not spoil, and the Israelites could consume until they were full each day, expecting the bread to fall again with each new morning.

God told Moses to put away a day's worth of manna and *"keep it for the generations to come, so they can see the bread I gave you to eat in the desert when I brought you out of Egypt"* (Exod. 16:32). Moses kept the manna alongside the testimony, as proof of God's supernatural provision, and placed them together within the ark of the covenant as a constant reminder to the nation.

Whenever an individual or a couple reaches a dry place, it is easy to fall into the temptation to grumble against God and to think about going back into bondage to the world or back to the "days before you got married." Whenever there is hunger or a desire in your life, you must reject any temptation to satisfy your emptiness with anything that is not connected to covenant. Jesus Himself declared, *"I am the bread of life. He who comes to Me will never go hungry, and he who believes in Me will never go thirsty"* (John 6:35).

In a single chapter in Scripture, Jesus calls Himself the manna, the living bread, eight different times! He is adamant in letting us know that all of our needs, all of our desires, all of our passions will and should be satisfied within our covenant relationship with Him! Whatever you may need—love, housing, food, clothing, transportation, protection, opportunity—you can expect God to provide. He is a good Father who takes pleasure and pride in caring for His children. Before we stress out or complain or talk about walking away from God, we should pray, believe Him at His Word, and truly trust Him to work things out.

Everything that you desire, and that your spouse desires, should be offered within the confines of your covenant and marriage.

God's covenant with His sons and daughters obligates Him to provide our basic physical and spiritual needs, and when we enter covenant relationship with one another, we are obligated to share the psychological and sexual needs of our partners. Everything that you desire, and that your spouse desires, should be offered within the confines of your covenant and marriage. You should offer one another quality time and enjoyment, affection and attention, support and encouragement, laughter and joy, comfort and pain, friendship and understanding, appreciation and trust. Even when you or your spouse feels as though a need is not being met in the relationship, your hunger or lack of satisfaction is not an excuse for grumbling, complaint, or a decision to meet your needs with something or someone outside of your relationship. Your covenant should force you to talk to each other—to express your desires and to figure out how to best meet each other's needs.

Budding Rod: Authority and Productivity in Covenant Relationship

As Moses and the nation of Israel prepared to advance into Canaan, the land of promise, the people began to rebel against God, Moses, and the leadership he instituted. Within His covenant, God made a vow that He would give the children of Israel this land as their home, but they allowed the size of their obstacles to dwarf their faith in His Word. God was so tired of Israel's disbelief and complaints that He promised Moses that none of the people who have participated in the culture of rebellion and complaint would be able to walk into the Promised Land. God struck down spies with a plague, He refused to go with them into battle and allowed them to suffer losses, and He opened up the earth to swallow up the rebellious leaders and their entire households. God was tired of being challenged and questioned and doubted, and He was only going to allow those who walked in faith, trust, and submission to authority have access to His promise and to a land of fruitfulness, productivity, and increase.

In Numbers 17, God told Moses to request the staff (or the rod) from the leader of each tribe or household and to place the staffs of those leaders before the ark of the covenant in the tabernacle. God said, *"The staff belonging to the man I choose will sprout, and I will rid Myself of this constant grumbling against you by the Israelites"* (Num. 17:5). Moses placed the staffs before the Lord in the tabernacle, and when he returned to the holy of holies the next morning, he saw that Aaron's staff had *"budded, blossomed and produced **almonds**"* (Num. 17:8). The word for rod in Hebrew is *matteh*, which means a "rod, a staff, or a branch," and rods and staffs were symbolic of authority and responsibility carried by leaders, rulers, and shepherds.[16]

In Psalm 23, David acknowledged God's supreme authority as his "Lord" and his "shepherd," leading him to rest in green pastures, causing him to drink in still waters, and restoring his very soul to paths of righteousness. In the hands of his Shepherd, David fears no evil for his *"rod and...staff, they comfort* [him]*"* (Ps. 23:4). A shepherd's only concern was the care of his sheep, and the sheep would find comfort, rest, food, safety, water, goodness, and mercy if they would learn to trust in and follow the shepherd.

God wanted to be trusted, and He wanted the people to follow the authority He instituted so that they could be led into His promises.

The rod and staff speaks of protection, correction, instruction, provision, and the supernatural rest that accompanies submission to divine authority and leadership. Aaron's rod was made of a dead branch of an almond tree, and we learned in Chapter 6 that almond trees spoke of truth and trust, as God used the almond tree to symbolize His faithfulness to keeping His Word. More than anything else, God wanted to be trusted, and He wanted the people to follow the authority He instituted so that they could be led into His promises. When God caused the rod to blossom *overnight*, He was trying to show the people how blessed, beautiful, and fruitful their own lives would be *as soon as* they decided to trust and believe in Him and in the authority He established. In a single night, His word brought life back to a dead branch and brought out fruit that should have taken an entire year to produce. He wanted them to see that if they would stop complaining and rebelling and simply submit to His Word, they could walk as He led them—straight into the land of promise that He had already prepared for them.

In Ephesians chapters 5–6, God set up and established a chain of divine authority for a household, calling husbands and wives to submit to one another and children to submit to their parents. The call to leadership is a call to chief servanthood, as those in authority take on the responsibility for provision and protection in exchange for respect and submission. A wife is to submit to the authority of her husband, who is charged with loving her as he loves himself— washing her with the Word, feeding her, and caring for her.

When you and your spouse submit to the Word and authority of God, when you begin to serve one another, and when you line up with and walk in your God-given roles, God removes any curse of rebellion and commands a blessing upon your household. In a single moment, God can activate productivity and promise, and the areas of a couple's life that were dead can begin to blossom and produce lasting fruit. Trust in the Lord with all your heart—no matter how things seem, for He knows what is best and He wants to order your steps. He has established a land flowing with milk and honey for your household, a dimension of rest, divine order, and divine provision.

Husbands, allow God to lead you to that place, and, wives, believe in and follow your husbands.

Preparing for Glory: Mercy and Agreement in Theocentric Marriage

The ark of the covenant was a symbol to Israel of God's presence and of covenant blessing. A plate of pure gold called the mercy seat covered and sealed the ark. The mercy seat was the seventh and final piece of furniture within the tabernacle, and it was the throne where God's glory fell and rested among the people (see Exod. 25:17-22; 37:6-9). God told the craftsman who built the ark and the mercy seat to

> ...*make two cherubim out of hammered gold at the ends of the cover. Make one cherub on one end and the second cherub on the other; make cherubim of* **one piece** *with the cover, at the two ends* (Exodus 25:18-19).

A cherub is an angel, a heavenly being sent to guard sacred places and to serve in worship. God specifically said that the two angels were to be made of one piece of gold, and placed at each end of the gold plate. When the high priest approached the ark, he burned incense and placed the blood of sacrifice on this seventh piece of furniture seven times, symbolizing perfection and completion. God's glory rested on this place, the throne between the two joined cherubim.

 Love and faithfulness meet in covenant, and when the lips and hearts of a couple united by God meet, so do righteousness and peace.

The final, and perhaps most important, ingredient needed for a successful covenant relationship is the mercy seat, which is the throne of God. In Psalm 85, King David described the tabernacle, and the mercy seat in particular, as the place of unfailing love and of salvation and restoration. It is the place where *"love and faithfulness meet together; righteousness and peace kiss each other"* (Ps. 85:10). Marriages built according to the courtship are centered on grace and mercy, as two people who have received the love and the grace of God extend that love and grace to one another. Love and faithfulness meet in covenant, and when the lips and hearts of a couple united by God meet, so do righteousness and peace. God's glory falls in the midst of two people sharing His love as they become patient and kind, humble and unselfish, forgiving and honest, hopeful and enduring (see 1 Cor. 13). The mercy seat is a place of rest, a sanctuary from work and worry, from fear and anxiety, and a place of peace and prosperity.

God gives specific instructions regarding the cherubim, and through analogy, to a covenant couple. *"The cherubim are to have their wings spread **upward**, overshadowing the cover with them. The cherubim are to **face each other, looking** toward the cover"* (Exod. 25:20). A couple should always keep their hands lifted before God and their focus turned toward seeing God's presence and glory upon their lives and their household. God must remain at the center of the relationship, and whenever the two reach for one another— physically, emotionally, or spiritually—God moves between them and on their behalf.

If both people keep their focus on God and the Kingdom, they will always find themselves in agreement and looking toward one another. Agreement is the place where God speaks, where He answers prayers, where He intervenes, where He opens doors, where He commands blessings, and where His glory falls (see Matt. 18: 19-20). God's desire is to rest and to remain on the earth and to establish the Kingdom and His blessings here. Whenever two believers walk in true unity and worship, the courtship is complete, and God finds a home where He can dwell.

Endnotes

1. Strong, *Strong's Exhaustive Concordance of the Bible*, #G5093.

2. The analogy of a security clearance/vetting process has been included in other studies, including, "Into the holy of holies." *Walk with the Word.* http://www.walkwiththeword .org/Studies/01_OT/03_Lev/03_Leviticus_16-02.34.html. Additional information regarding security clearances and the vetting process was obtained at "Security Clearance" and "Classified Information in the United States" on Wikipedia.com. http://en.wikipedia.org/wiki/Security_clearance; http://en .wikipedia.org/wiki/Classified_information_in_the_United_ States.

3. "Women's Sexual Health: Virginity and the Hymen." *Discovery Health.* http://health.discovery.com/centers/sex/ sexpedia/hymen.html.

4. Each of the terms discussed in this section were researched individually through searches on Wikipedia.com, Biology Online, and the Brittanica Online Encyclopedia at www .biology-online.org and www.britannica.com.

5. The research on the neurological effects of sexual intercourse is extensive. The studies cited here are online articles published by the Crisis Pregnancy Centers' "Facts on Human Brain Development" found at www.choicesaz.orgresources/ brain_development/ and "What Is the Purpose of Sex and What Forms of Sex Can Lead to STDs" at www.choicesaz .org/sexual_health/sex/.

6. Strong, *Strong's Exhaustive Concordance of the Bible*, #G2641; #G4347.

7. This information was contained in an article written by a sex education correspondent for a men's dating website. Though the scientific information provided was accurate, I took particular note of the advice offered by the author that men should experience orgasm as often as possible without any mention of doing so within the confines of marriage, which seems to be the advice given to men within the greater American culture. Oskar McHendry. "Chemicals That Fuel Your Sex Life." AskMe.com. http://www.askmen.com/dating/love_tip_250/271b_love_tip.html.

8. "Sensuality." *Merriam-Webster Online Dictionary.* http://www.merriam-webster.com/dictionary/sensuality.

9. The content of this episode is summarized in an article written by the guest posted on *The Oprah Winfrey Show*'s website. Dr. Laura Berman. "Having the Sex Talk With Your Kids." http://www.oprah.com/relationships/Talking-to-Your-Kids-About-Sex/15.

10. Unless otherwise noted, the descriptions of addiction in this section are appropriated from the definition and description provided by *The Diagnostic and Statistical Manual of Mental Disorders (DSM-IV)*, published by the American Psychiatric Association. Additional information on addiction and heroin use was found in the following articles: "The Definition of Addiction." http://www.addictionsandrecovery.org/definition-of-addiction.htm.

    "Heroin" The Partnership for a Drug Free America. http://www.drugfree.org/portal/drug_guide/heroin; and within the entries for "Addiction" and "Heroin" on Wikipedia.com. The assertions made connecting the patterns of addiction to sexual immorality are my own.

11. Quoted in online article. Dr. Timothy Johnson. "Tiger Woods May Be Role Model for Battling Sex Addiction."

ABCNews On-Call+ Wellness Center. http://abcnews.go
.com/Health/Wellness/tiger-woods-sex-addict/story?id=
9649709andpage=2.

12. As quoted in the Crisis Pregnancy Centers' article, "What
Is the Purpose of Sex and What Forms of Sex Can Lead to
STDs" at www.choicesaz.org/sexual_health/sex/.

13. Strong, *Strong's Exhaustive Concordance of the Bible*, #G567.

14. Hershberger, *Seeing Christ in the Tabernacle*, 17.

15. Strong, *Strong's Exhaustive Concordance of the Bible*, #H727.

16. Ibid., #H4294.

ABOUT CHRYSTAL ARMSTRONG

Chrystal Armstrong has served as Associate Minister and Youth Pastor at Overcoming Believers Church in Knoxville, Tennessee, and is the founder of Rising Reign, Inc., which inspires and empowers the next generation of Kingdom thinkers and leaders in calling, career, and connection. Chrystal truly believes that God is establishing a chosen generation who will manifest His glory in every aspect of their lives. She is humbled to be part of that priesthood, and the Word that she decrees is evident in her personal testimony of God's grace and her sincere desire that every believer fully accept God's love, understand His purposes, live in His will, and experience the abundant life and inheritance promised to the children of God. Chrystal is available for speaking engagements and ministry opportunities; to learn more about her or Rising Reign, visit www.chrystalarmstrong.com or www.rising-reign.com.

In the right hands, This Book will Change Lives!

Most of the people who need this message will not be looking for this book. To change their lives, you need to put a copy of this book in their hands.

> But others (seeds) fell into good ground, and brought forth fruit, some a hundred-fold, some sixty-fold, some thirty-fold (Matthew 13:8).

Our ministry is constantly seeking methods to find the good ground, the people who need this anointed message to change their lives. Will you help us reach these people?

> Remember this—a farmer who plants only a few seeds will get a small crop. But the one who plants generously will get a generous crop (2 Corinthians 9:6).

EXTEND THIS MINISTRY BY SOWING
3 BOOKS, 5 BOOKS, 10 BOOKS, OR MORE TODAY,
AND BECOME A LIFE CHANGER!

Thank you,

Don Nori Sr., Publisher
Destiny Image
Since 1982

DESTINY IMAGE PUBLISHERS, INC.

"Promoting Inspired Lives."

VISIT OUR NEW SITE HOME AT
WWW.DESTINYIMAGE.COM

FREE SUBSCRIPTION TO DI NEWSLETTER

Receive free unpublished articles by top DI authors, exclusive discounts, and free downloads from our best and newest books.

Visit www.destinyimage.com to subscribe.

Write to: Destiny Image
                P.O. Box 310
                Shippensburg, PA 17257-0310

Call: 1-800-722-6774

Email: orders@destinyimage.com

For a complete list of our titles or to place an order
online, visit www.destinyimage.com.

FIND US ON FACEBOOK OR FOLLOW US ON TWITTER.

www.facebook.com/destinyimage   **facebook**
www.twitter.com/destinyimage   **twitter**